TRUTH AT LAST

TRUTH AT LAST

The Untold Story Behind James Earl Ray and the
Assassination of Martin Luther King Jr.

John Larry Ray and Lyndon Barsten

Alameda Free Library
1550 Oak Street
Alameda, CA 94501

THE LYONS PRESS
Guilford, Connecticut
AN IMPRINT OF THE GLOBE PEQUOT PRESS

The Lyons Press is an imprint of The Globe Pequot Press.

Designed by Kim Burdick

Library of Congress Cataloging-in-Publication Data is available on file.

ISBN 978-1-59921-284-5

Printed in the United States of America

10 9 8 7 6 5 4 3 2 1

I dedicate this book to the family of an unknown young African-American soldier named Washington, wounded and confined to a wheelchair while in service to his country. May his living family finally know the truth about why their loved one was so horribly wounded and received a dishonorable discharge from the United States Military.

And, to the late Coretta Scott King and the four King children; one of the very few prominent families in this nation to speak the truth about the injustices of absolute power.

Contents

Preface

As recently as the year 2000, I have been threatened with imprisonment by the Justice Department if I ever revealed what I know about the murder of Dr. Martin Luther King Jr. I have paid dearly for being the brother of the patsy, James Earl Ray, and a patsy is exactly what the family of Dr. King believes him to be. Truth be told, I believe I was nearly the first patsy myself, in the murder of America's greatest civil rights leader. Just as my brother was asked by the Mob to be a getaway driver in Memphis, I was also asked to do the same in San Francisco when Dr. King was there. My name is John Larry Ray, and I believe my brother was maneuvered into a false confession after being framed by a terrifying mix of government and criminal forces. This book is an exposé of a series of history-changing revelations and incidents of criminal abuses of power that have been—and are still being—practiced at the national level by those sworn to serve this country.

This is the story of two brothers whose lives were destroyed by powerful and corrupt men. I am now an old man, and it is time to tell all of the things that I couldn't say while my brother James was alive. For me, it's all about the how and why behind my brother's gradual and thorough transformation into the FBI's mole, and eventually, one of the most reviled men in American history.

TRUTH AT LAST

one

The Mole and the Mule

"The family had it pretty poor," remembers
a local resident. "I've seen times when they
had a sack of potatoes to eat—that's all, just a
sack of potatoes."

—"The Revealing Story of a Mean Kid,"
LIFE magazine, May 3, 1968

Please let me put the Ray family into perspective for you. It will greatly
help in understanding why our family was a natural breeding ground
for a man who could be made into a black-ops victim without a hue
and cry from the public.

My brother and I spent our formative years in the Mississippi River Valley, the land of Mark Twain. As we grew from children to young adults, our
hometowns were river towns. For the most part we lived in Ewing, Missouri;
Quincy, Illinois; and Alton, Illinois, which has since been absorbed into the
suburbs of St. Louis. Alton is where my oldest brother, James Earl, was born,
five years before me, on March 10, 1928.

Our father's side of the family, the Rays and the Mathews, have lived in
Quincy since before the Civil War. The old man's family, like much of Quincy,
was Irish-American. During the Civil War, many citizens of Quincy were
strong abolitionists, and Quincy was a vital part of the Underground Railroad, which aided the escape of Southern slaves.

Alton became home to our mother's side of the family, who are also of
Irish descent. Many of their people fled to the United States to escape the Irish
potato famine of the 1840s, and settled in that area, along the river. Very few

members on either side of the family voted, as we never really trusted many of the candidates. We were not social in an outward way. Although we were Catholics, we were generally not religious, but we tried to be ethical.

My maternal grandparents were John Maher and Mary Fitzsimmons. They had two children: my mother Lucille, who was often called Ceale, and my uncle, Willie. My grandfather, John Maher, blew glass for a living, while my grandmother had a rooming house in Alton. John's family also came from Ireland, and he married an Irish-American girl. Although she was our grandmother, we always referred to her as "Mom. "

The Mahers were left-wing liberal Democrats; Mother thought the Roosevelts were gods. My mother would stand up for her rights against anyone—this from a woman who was afraid of the dark.

On the Ray side, in Quincy, my grandparents James and Louise had three children: my uncle Earl, my aunt Mabel, and my father George, who would sometimes sarcastically be called "Speedy," because he was anything but quick on his feet.

My eldest brother was named after my paternal grandfather, James Ray. Both my grandfather James and father George had been in trouble with federal agents during the U.S. involvement in World War I. They avoided the draft—they weren't going to go over to Europe and kill people just because the government told them to. Fortunately, U.S. involvement in the European conflict only lasted a little over a year, and since the war ended before action could be taken against the Rays, their resistance was soon forgotten and the charges were dismissed.

My grandfather, James Ray, who had a bar in Quincy on Fifth Street, started organized crime in that area. When I use the term *organized crime*, I mean he answered to the Chicago rackets bosses. This only lasted so long, but at one time he made so much money that it was stored all over the house in fruit jars and the like. My grandmother Louise was able to take frequent vacations all across the United States because of these funds. My grandparents lived at 413 Vermont Street, and Ted Crowley, who lived across the street from them, was what you would call then the local rackets boss, or, in my adulthood, "the godfather." Sometimes, when I close my eyes at night, I can almost hear the metallic ring of the brass spittoons knocking against my grandfather's hardwood bar, or the beer glasses slammed on his bar, louder and louder still as the night progressed.

Many of the Rays came from out West. My grandmother Louise was married twice, which was unusual in our family, as divorce still doesn't occur much to this day, and her prior family was out in California. Her father had been a West Virginia preacher and religious leader.

I want you to know these things, these trivial details, of an unusual yet unremarkable family of independent Americans. Certain authors who support the official story of the death of Dr. King—authors such as Gerold Frank in the 1960s, to the more contemporary author, Gerald Posner—have put a negative spin on the Ray family, painting us as a loose group of convicts and thieves. While there is some truth to that, the same thing could be said about many of the families living up and down the Mississippi at that time. Although it may surprise most Americans, at least one of the authors putting a negative spin on our family, Gerold Frank, has documented ties to the FBI leadership in 1969, and indeed, he was chosen by the FBI to write the James Earl Ray story. If you wanted to put another spin on the Rays, you could say that I'm a relative, through my Irish family, of the respectable film star of *How Green Was My Valley*, Maureen O'Hara. Her real name was Maureen Fitzsimmons, spelled FitzSimons in Ireland.

The feds and their contacts in the press might choose to make up a few things, but we were never sexual predators; we were never stool pigeons or informants; and we never testified against anyone. We certainly never put anyone behind bars. We never went along with the all-too-often corrupt criminal justice system. With only one or two exceptions, if anyone in the Ray family went behind bars, it was for a nonviolent act. Inside of the criminal justice system, none of us ever informed on a codefendant to receive leniency. Nobody in the family ever served in the military, except for our indelible black sheep, James Earl Ray. And in doing so, I say that he proved the rest of us right about placing blind trust in the federal government. He would later repeat to me, "The army put me on the road to ruin."

In the spring of 1921, my old man was arrested while sitting on the banks of the Mississippi in Keokuk, Iowa, cooking up a mulligan stew. At this time my father George was essentially living the life of a hobo, sometimes being paid for work with food or vegetables, which was the case when he was arrested. The police officer who came upon him didn't believe he had worked for all the ingredients. The arresting officers claimed that some of the ingredients in his stew were taken without a farmer's permission, and on May 19, 1921, Dad was sentenced to ten years in the Iowa State Prison at Fort Madison, for burglary.

My old man never worked much on the outside of prison, and he wasn't going to work on the inside. However, the warden had other ideas about my father's lack of desire to work. First, my father George was put in solitary confinement on bread and water. This didn't do the trick. The next step was to have my father hung from his thumbs as he stood on his tiptoes. This torture went on for fifty minutes of every hour, twenty-four hours a day. The other ten minutes of each hour he was allowed to rest, sustaining himself on a diet of bread and water. Dad's body required ten minutes of sleep more than it required nourishment, even if it was just resting on a concrete floor. A few times he was even able to fall asleep while dangling from his thumbs, although the intense pain would always bring him back to consciousness. The prison knew this would break a man before too long.

When a Fort Madison inmate was taken to the gallows and hanged, the entire prison population was brought out to experience the spectacle. My father knew firsthand what death looked like from watching these prison hangings. In fact, while my twenty-three-year-old father hung in his cell by his thumbs, he often thought of trying to kill a guard himself, thus hurrying his own death at the end of a rope. During one of these public Fort Madison hangings, the death-row felon's neck didn't snap. My father witnessed the man dangling from the noose, in agony. An overweight guard ran over to the man and wrapped his own body around the inmate's body until his neck snapped.

My father told me how one day, shortly after the botched hanging, he daydreamed about killing that overweight guard and just taking the hanging that he would get for the guard's death. No matter what he might have fantasized about under torture, he was basically a nonviolent man who was only pipe-dreaming himself out of a painful and unfair situation.

George Ray would not be the only member of the Ray family to be falsely accused or to wrongly suffer in prison. He claimed that while he dangled by his thumbs, he had a vision of a ghostly man dressed all in white, wrapping his hands around George's neck. This vision brought to mind the biblical teachings of his youth, our old man hung from his thumbs in a similar fashion to how Jesus hung from his hands. After several days of this torture, the

4

guards took him down as usual for his ten minutes of rest, but this time he was dragged to the visiting room. Within minutes he was mumbling his story to his mother, my grandmother, Louise. He was in a state of semiconsciousness when he told my alarmed grandmother about the thumb-hangings.

Dad was surprised by my grandmother's reaction. As a matter of fact, he said it brought him "back to life." She was screaming at the top of her lungs, using cusswords he thought she had never heard, let alone used. Her tirade was directed at the warden and the guards. At this time my grandmother had money and political connections through the Chicago outfit, which the Chicago mob or mafia was generally known as, and she was not going to have her favorite son "treated the way the heathens treated the Lord Jesus Christ," as she described in the language of her world.

After just one discussion between the warden and my grandmother, my father was paroled to a work farm; in 1920s Iowa, this was the equivalent of being paroled to a halfway house today. At that time, the big farmers would put sheriffs in office with the understanding that the sheriffs would supply them with free labor during the summer. This was often done by dragging homeless men or "hobos" off of freight trains and charging them with vagrancy, then paroling them out to the farmers.

According to my father, in June of 1923 he was released to the outside walls to a prison farm where he ended up getting into a verbal altercation with the guard in charge of the inmate detail, about his lack of desire to work. The guard picked up a club, at which time my old man picked up a pitchfork. The guard stormed off in the direction of the warden's office, and my dad took off in the direction of the freight train yards, where he became a fugitive from justice for the next sixty years, often changing his name, right up until his death in 1986.

According to the Iowa State Penitentiary at Fort Madison, my dad was paroled to the farm on June 21, 1923, and absconded from parole on July 10 of the same year, at which time a warrant was issued for his arrest. In the 1920s, a parole violation was considered an escape. Today some states call parole violations from a halfway house "escapes," and some don't. The feds see it this way: If you are under their custody and you take off, you are an escaped prisoner, whether you were paroled to a farm or not.

Growing up, my brother James knew about our father being an escaped prisoner, just as I did. James mentioned it in interviews and wrote about it in his 1987 autobiography, *Tennessee Waltz*, which was reworked by his publishers and put out five years later as *Who Killed Martin Luther King Jr.?*

In his book, *Killing the Dream*, author Gerald Posner accuses James of fabricating our old man's escape story, writing, ". . . in fact, he was paroled." However, James didn't fabricate anything about that.

After his escape, our father rode the rails for a while, playing the banjo for money. As a young man in his twenties out on the road, my father went downriver to Alton, where he met my mother, Lucille. The old man played her his banjo and told her his stories. He was about twenty-seven when they met, and she was ten or eleven years his junior. They fell in love and were married shortly thereafter.

In his young adulthood, my dad resembled the classic and very handsome actor George Raft. My mother had a bit of a complex about her looks, believing she was less than attractive. Because of this, she developed an admiration for strong women who were not generally considered attractive, such as Kate Smith and Eleanor Roosevelt. Later, as my mother slipped into middle age, I think she began to resemble film star Hedy Lamarr.

My parents went down to Florida on their honeymoon in 1926. There was no concern about finding a place to stay, since my grandfather was involved in bootlegging and organized crime. He had land all over the country, including Florida, so they'd gone down to check out his real estate. Unfortunately, most of it bordered the Florida swamps and was the next thing to worthless. They pitched a tent there but left abruptly when Mother found that water moccasin snakes had invaded their temporary home.

Grandfather Jim had given the newlyweds an expensive brand-new automobile, a Hubmobile. When the newlyweds left Florida, they drove up to Atlanta where my father, who wasn't working, traded in his expensive new car for a less-expensive model. They kept the difference in cash. When they left Atlanta, they drove to Chicago to meet up with my dad's sister, Mabel. They decided to stay there for a while, and moved into a place on South Michigan Avenue, between the Stevens Hotel (now the Hilton) and Al Capone's Hotel, the since-demolished Lexington.

My mother was employed by Bell Telephone in Chicago at this time—a dangerous job of sorts, because lightning could travel through the telephone wires and electrocute you. This was the Roaring Twenties, before the depression of 1929. Mother was only eighteen, and while her friends were busy having fun, heading down to South Chicago to the black jazz clubs "on the QT," my mother had made the decision to settle down.

My father didn't believe much in regular employment, or in going out partying, either. He spent much of his time in bed. In those days, when he was up, he made a modest living trading diamonds with Jewish jewelers on Van Buren Street in the Loop. My father also believed that you shouldn't stray too far from home, so by 1928, they had moved back to Alton, after a short stay in St. Louis.

I was born in Alton on Valentine's Day, 1933. The name on my birth certificate should have read John Larry Ray, but the attending physician was drunk, and my legal name became James Ray. This would make me my parents' second James Ray, as James Earl had been born in 1928. The drunken doc left a thumb indentation on the inside of my mouth that caused a speech impediment—the mark of Satan if there ever was one.

While the family was in Alton, our uncle Earl came along. Earl had been in the Illinois State Prison because he had shot a man in the arm, causing him to lose his limb. This affair happened over a woman, and was Uncle Earl's regular modus operandi; he had a problem with women throughout his life.

At this time, Uncle Earl used our home address in some type of failed check-forgery scheme. The police mistakenly arrested my dad, who was still a fugitive from justice because of that prison farm break years earlier. The family wanted Dad out of Alton before the authorities actually found out who he was, so we left town after bail was made. The property used to secure Dad's release was the worthless swampland in Florida that my grandfather had purchased. We managed to get out of Alton before the police figured out who Dad was or how worthless the land deeds that secured his bond actually were. This false arrest of my father is twisted by authors such as Gerald Posner in his book, *Killing the Dream*:

```
In January 1935, Speedy was arrested
in Alton for forgery. When he was free on
bond, he decided to move, even though it
meant pulling James [Earl] out of the first
grade at St. Mary's Elementary School.
```

First we moved to Missouri, where Dad worked for approximately five years with the Stark Brothers' Nursery, which was famous for its apple production. The Stark Brothers were known for producing the Golden Delicious apple. This is where my father's habit of changing the Ray family name to Raines, Ryan, and other variations began. Even today, my younger brother Jerry's driver's license says "Jerry Ryan."

As I remember, it was 1936 when we moved to a fifty-six-acre farm in Ewing, Missouri, a community settled mostly by German and a few Dutch immigrants. Ewing was twenty miles west of Quincy. Our grandmother, Mom Maher, had bought the farm, known as the old Adams place, three miles out of town. Ewing was very small; it had only one hotel, which was mostly a rooming house, and one tavern. I recall just one filling station and one drugstore, and I believe there were two grocery stores. The barbershop had a pool table in the back room. The train did actually stop in Ewing, though our schoolhouse was a one-building facility, kindergarten through high school, typical of the smallest towns in the United States at that time. There was no industry in Ewing, so men had to drive twenty miles to Hannibal or Quincy to work.

We were becoming a large family, with four children by this time. The boys were Jimmy, Jerry, and myself, and we had a sister, Marjorie, who years later would be killed in a horrific accident. My parents would go on to have five more children before our family was complete.

The old Adams place had no electricity. During the summer when my father was away, my rather nervous mother would nail the windows shut, which would make the place uncomfortably warm, just like an oven. The old man used to read *True Crime* magazine, and my mother would pick them up just often enough to become skittish about being left alone.

Our house had a large stone fireplace and a big porch in the back. The house was framed by lilac bushes. The porch is where my sister, Marjorie, was severely burned at about the age of six while playing with matches. Margie must have feared getting in trouble for banging on the door (as she normally would have), even though her dress was on fire. She died about three weeks later of infections in St. Mary's Hospital in Quincy. This is the kind of pain a parent can never heal from. The death of our sister Margie also had a big impact on our neighbors, the Lochers, who still live by the old Adams place.

Mrs. Johnny Locher put flowers on Margie's grave for almost sixty years, until her own death, and her daughter has since followed suit.

The logs that formed the walls of our home tended to settle, so you had to fill the cracks between them with rags in the wintertime. The big fireplace wasn't much good at heating the house. You'd feel burning hot near the fireplace and freezing cold away from it. We had old-fashioned fireplace irons that our mother would put in the fireplace and then wrap in towels before putting them in the bottom of the bed to keep away frostbite.

Though the land on the farm was not very fertile, the government would pay people to raise tomatoes. In those more Socialist days, we would receive gallon cans of beef from the government during the last years of the Depression. I can still taste that beef—to me, better than any you can get today.

At one point in 1939, just after the birth of our sister, Melba, my folks spent our Christmas money from our aunt on an old schoolhouse that we relocated to the site of our log house. It cost more to move the schoolhouse than the structure itself cost. Since we didn't need the log house anymore, we used it for firewood. But some authors who have written about our family made it sound like we were burning pieces of our own house to stay warm, and that we essentially had no place to live. Here is an example from Posner's *Killing the Dream*:

> In 1940, when James was twelve, the Rays began slowly cannibalizing their decrepit house, pulling it apart plank by plank in order to use it as firewood. It gradually disintegrated until they needed a new home.

The obvious question is, Why would you burn your own house when you had fifty-six acres of potential firewood? Yet this ridiculous story had played for thirty years by the time Posner repeated it. We were not the poorest family in the neighborhood; in fact, we were better off than most. As children we regularly took vacations to see Mom Maher and other relatives, which was very rare for families during the Depression. Our neighbors, the Peacocks, had only cornbread and beans to eat. My mother always used to comment on this when she went to see them. Other authors have claimed that my mother never left our land. This silly assertion is not the case. Mother regularly visited the Peacocks and other neighbors, and behaved like any other woman of the day.

When President Franklin Delano Roosevelt created the Works Progress Administration (WPA), everybody was glad to get a $30-per-month job—except for my old man. Speedy worked five or six months and then quit. Aside from his laziness, my dad also had a tendency to involve his family members in crime, as my brother James did later. This was without a doubt a trait James inherited from our dad. Our father never did anything illegal without a family member working with him (although he drew the line at involving his children). When our father would go out and burglarize some neighborhood store, it was usually for food. If he'd go out and steal a cow, he'd wait until his uncle or brother-in-law could help him. Our aunt Mabel remained part of organized crime for years; she'd send food over to us, and I can tell you, this contributed to our family being better off than most around us at the time.

Some authors who support the official story of the King assassination have claimed that my father and mother were alcoholics. Although in her later years this would be true of my mother, it was not the case for much of her life, including our formative years, and it was never true of our old man. I lived on the farm from 1936 to 1945, and during this time I never witnessed my mother having a drink.

For anyone who may have a tendency to believe the official myth of James Earl Ray's cruelty, there is a story from our childhood that reveals the type of person he truly was—a decent kid. One Thanksgiving Day, James and I were at the farm with our mother, Ceale. Somehow we got it into our heads that we'd like duck for dinner. Our mother agreed that if we'd kill the duck, she'd cook it for us. First, I held it down and Jimmy would try to take an ax to its neck, but he couldn't do it. Then we reversed roles, which didn't work any better.

So I ran down the road to get Charlie Peacock to kill the duck, which he did without a second thought. When Charlie came to the house, Jimmy hid because he didn't want anybody to know he didn't have the nerve to kill a bird. At this time in rural America, there might have been a fight over something like that. Anyway, my mother gagged every time she opened the oven to check on the bird, which by now none of us could stomach eating. Our German shepherd, Patsy, had a great Thanksgiving dinner that year.

This story reveals what Jimmy was really like: a kind child, who in many ways was the opposite of what he was later made out to be. The intelligence community calls it a "legend" when they create a false personality for someone they wish to set up or "sheep-dip." The false legend of James Earl Ray taints even the memories of our childhood.

An article appeared in the May 13, 1968, issue of the *St. Louis Post-Dispatch* (about three weeks after the murder of Dr. King), claiming that a young Jimmy had once stabbed me in the ear over a piece of meat. The article stated: "Jimmy displayed a mean streak also while he lived in Ewing. He was known to run with a group of bullies and once ran a knife through his brother's ear in the school lunchroom in a dispute over a piece of meat." Reporters came around my tavern in St. Louis, the Grapevine, after this story hit *LIFE* magazine, asking to see the scar from my childhood attack over twenty years earlier. There wasn't any scar to show. St. Louis–based reporter John Auble finally printed that fact in the now-defunct *St. Louis Globe-Democrat*. The story of the sliced ear was developed somewhere in Washington to make the Rays, especially Jimmy, look violent.

Although my family was supposedly solidly criminal, in reality, we represent the full spectrum of American lifestyles. My great-aunt Rosemary Maher was a very high official within the U.S. Navy. She received a big pension and had little to spend it on due to the fact that she was bedridden from arthritis, spending her last years at Walter Reed Army Medical Center. She would send money or gifts surprisingly often. At one point she gave her nephew, William, a $1,500 diamond ring (this was a tremendous amount of money in the 1930s), and I remember she once sent my mother $500. Many men would have had to work for two years to accumulate $500 at this time. Each year Aunt Rose sent us checks for Christmas, and when she died in the late 1950s, our family inherited about $10,000. Unfortunately, this money was stolen when the wrong people heard about the inheritance. Two men who knew about the money from gossip at the corner bar broke into our home and put knives to the throats of my mother and Mom Maher. (Fortunately, they didn't get all of it, since the money was hidden in different spots.)

On the other end of the spectrum was our uncle Earl, a good-looking man, and a smooth talker. Like the Rays, he wasn't one for hard work, but he was always able to get a beautiful woman and keep her, until he drank too much whiskey and did something foolish. Often, I'm sorry to say, he would beat these women when he was drunk. One time he had a nice girlfriend named Fanny Robinson and, as usual, he drank and abused her. Her brother, Junior Robinson, came to Quincy with a gun to kill Uncle Earl. This time it was Uncle Earl who was in the crosshairs, but he hid out until everybody had cooled off. Later on in life, Uncle Earl also abused an Italian-American girl named Pat—but she took a baseball bat to him. A Quincy doctor spent months saving his arm, and Uncle Earl decided that this was his kind of woman. Pat had disappeared, so Earl set out to find her. When he finally traced her to Nebraska, he found she had been burned to death; there was nothing left but her grave.

Uncle Earl was behind bars three times, as I remember, and it always had something to do with a woman. It is unfortunately true, as it has been reported, that years later, Uncle Earl threw acid in the face of his teenage wife (although she was not disfigured, or even seriously hurt, as was also reported). Nonetheless, Earl was sentenced to ten years for this regrettable incident, served partly with me in Illinois State Prison.

As James and I grew, our grandfather, James Ray, was pushed out of organized crime in Quincy by the Monckton brothers, Charlie and Leo. Grandfather Jim was becoming a rather henpecked, weak-minded person. He would have to go outside to smoke his pipe, which was very rare at this time. Grandmother Louise wouldn't even let him smoke his pipe outside in peace; she'd accuse him of sending smoke signals to another woman across the street. I got to feeling sorry for my grandpa, who was more or less kicked to the curb by the Monckton brothers and the Chicago syndicate. My grandfather had also been financially reckless, losing two houses and a tavern in a single poker game.

Our aunt Mabel and her husband, Frank Fuller, continued working in organized crime with Charlie and Leo Monckton and other local elements that answered to Chicago. As of 1935, with Al Capone in prison, a new generation had taken over as rackets bosses in Chicago: Paul Ricca, Frank "the Enforcer" Nitti, and Antonino "Joe" Accardo. The latter would still be in a leadership position twenty or thirty years later at the time of the King assassination.

Although the base of their power was in Quincy, the Monckton brothers' operations reached all the way to Indiana. Unlike our grandfather, who was much more civilized, anyone who tried to strong-arm the Monckton brothers met up with a contract killer by the name of Johnny Shirts. Because they controlled the sheriff's office, the Monckton brothers had absolute control of Quincy, so Aunt Mabel was able to safely go about her work as a courier with bags of cash, or "bag woman" in FBI terms. Aunt Mabel would go as far as Tampa, and frequently made trips up to Chicago. When she traveled to the Windy City, or St. Louis, she'd occasionally take my brother Jimmy with her. This started before Jimmy was even in his teens. Many Chicago Mafia people met Jimmy and knew our family at this time.

This brings up the first of many similarities between my brother and Lee Harvey Oswald, who the great majority of Americans feel was a patsy, along with James. Both James and Lee were known to organized crime members since childhood. James was well known to the Chicago Mob. Lee Harvey Oswald was known to the Marcello organization in New Orleans, through his uncle, Charles "Dutz" Murret, who, according to Robert J. Groden's book, *The Search for Lee Harvey Oswald*, became a sort of surrogate father to Lee. Dutz Murret was a New Orleans bookmaker. On one occasion, the Chicago Mob took Aunt Mabel and Jimmy to a cave where they'd hidden a bunch of slot machines. They told Jimmy that he could have all the coins in the slot machines, but they wanted to keep the one-armed bandits for themselves. In 1931, even the manufacture of slots had come under the control of the Chicago rackets bosses (they were made in Cicero, Illinois). Young Jimmy and Aunt Mabel spent all day on their score, dumping their coins into a big gunnysack. Aunt Mabel assumed the slot machines were stolen and that the coins might be considered evidence.

In 1944 James was sixteen. He had dropped out of high school in Ewing and moved down the Mississippi River from Quincy, Illinois, to Alton, which is twenty-three miles north of St. Louis. He moved in with Mom Maher, our other grandmother, and her son, our uncle Willie. James got a job at the International Shoe Company, where he worked until the end of World War II.

Six months later our father decided he wanted to move the family away from the farm and away from Ewing. Our neighbors, the Lochers, purchased the farm from our folks. Jimmy's leaving probably had something to do with our parents' decision to leave the farm, which, in retrospect, was probably the worst thing they ever did. The family would split up after this move. Since the old man knew he would never work steadily, I can't imagine why he'd want to leave the old Adams place. But he sold it, and ended up working in Galesburg, Illinois, as a switchman for the C., B. & Q. Railroad—the Chicago, Burlington and Quincy. Like Quincy and Alton, Galesburg had hosted one of the Lincoln-Douglas debates during the election season of 1858.

My mother never drank a drop while we were in Ewing. In fact, she never drank a drop until my father left to start working on the railroad. My parents were not separated—just living separately—but this was hard on her. I would go and get her a jug of beer (they'd give it to kids for their folks in those days), and I'd usually take a few swigs on the way home. My mother didn't like to be alone, and I'm sure that's what started her drinking. If she drank before going to bed, she could get to sleep without nailing the windows shut. The disease ran in Mother's family; her father, the glassblower, had died an alcoholic.

My parents' alcoholism has been exaggerated by some authors. If my father had been an alcoholic, I don't believe he would have lived as long as he did; alcoholics rarely live to be nearly ninety years of age. My father wasn't a big drinker; if you asked him to go out for a beer, he usually wanted to go to bed after consuming just one.

Eventually, the old man found a place for all of us in Galesburg. He bought a car that cost $500, a 1938 streamlined Hudson. He drove us down to 936 South Broad Street, where he had rented our new house near the railroad yard where he worked. The yardmaster was a man by the name of Joe McCarthy. Joe's son Larry was a friend of mine, a clean-cut kid admired by the whole town. My dad liked his boss, so at first it was a cozy situation.

About this time I got a job delivering the *Galesburg Register-Mail* newspaper. I made $2 a week with the possibility of a 50-cent bonus if nobody called in saying I'd missed their house. Once I got my $2.50, I'd go buy War Bond Stamps. If you bought $18.75 in War Bond Stamps, you could fill a book and turn it in for a $25 War Bond. The War Bond would mature in ten years, and you'd get $25.

One of my good customers was a neighbor who also worked on the railroad, a hardworking, older black gentleman who worked every day of the week. His backyard nearly bumped into ours. He always gave me half a dollar, though the paper was only a quarter. You would see him crossing the sandpit every afternoon at the same time, around 4:30.

As soon as I started delivering the Galesburg paper, I got my social security card. When my father had moved us to Galesburg, he had added "ns" onto Ray, transforming our last name to "Rayns," sometimes spelled "Raynes." So, my first social security card was issued to me as John Larry Raynes. This would be the social security number and the name variation that I would give to Jimmy years later when he escaped from the Missouri State Pen at Jefferson City.

As we all predicted, our father didn't work on the railroad very long, but it was partly for a good reason. It was dangerous working around those trains, especially at night. I worked around them myself years later and nearly had accidents that could have been severe. When I was working on the trains in Milwaukee, I witnessed an eighteen-year-old coworker of mine get cut to pieces when a train backed up unexpectedly.

Our father's nickname—Speedy—was a favorite joke, as he never moved very quickly. This made him dangerous to himself and others. There was a guy working with our old man on the railroad who was afraid that Dad's slow pace was going to get him (the other guy) killed. He may have been right. Dad's slowness to react was responsible for his tumbling from a train. He spent quite a bit of time recuperating in bed after this mishap, being paid by the union. Railroad officials came around the house to check to see if Dad really was in bed recuperating; since he actually enjoyed spending time in bed, this is how they always found him.

Because my brother Jimmy had money by this time, and he was in Alton, we eventually picked up and moved near Alton, too. My mom asked her mother to buy us a place there, but none was available. Instead, Mom Maher rented a house twenty miles away on old Route 66. We kids used to have to walk about two or three miles to go to school at this time. Susan and Max, who are the youngest children in the family, were not yet born at this time.

Since there was not much work to be found near our rented farmhouse, Mother got a job right in Alton, in the kitchen of a Coney Island restaurant. During the week when she was working, she generally stayed with her mother, in Mom Maher's rooming house. When the weekend came, she'd ride the bus on dusty country roads through the cornfields and silos to see us. She always arrived carrying bags of food to last us for the coming week.

Later on, my brother James would join the army, removing our dad's reason for being in the Alton area, so the old man decided to move back around

Quincy to Adams, which is approximately thirty miles east of Quincy, farther from the Mississippi. He decided that he needed a bit of cash to help us move from the farm, so he went down to shuck and sell some of his neighbor's corn—only he didn't tell the neighbor. He thought that he'd be gone by the time the county sheriff discovered what he was doing.

He wasn't. A warrant was issued for his arrest. The sheriff and his deputy showed up at our place, pounding on the door. When they were let in, they grabbed our old man, forcing our mother to think fast. She told the sheriff that the old man was her "brother William" and that her husband was actually "up at the elevator, selling corn." Our father was in a serious situation. He wasn't just a fugitive from justice in Iowa; he had also jumped bond a few years earlier because of Uncle Earl's check-forgery scheme in Madison County. Luckily, the sheriff believed my mother's story. He ran out the front door with his deputy, heading for the grain elevator and hoping to catch Dad in the act.

The old man had to run off across the cornfields to escape, and wound up in Quincy. So, my mother, who had never driven a car, had to learn how to drive with an old '33 Ford that James had. With us kids in the back, we drove to Quincy to meet the old man, who was still in hiding from the sheriff. On the way, we ended up in the ditch a couple of times and caused some damage to a few gas pumps at filling stations, but somehow, we made it to Quincy, where the Ray (or Rayns or Raynes) family would settle down for the time being.

I am now on the sunny side of seventy. After many years of travels, released from a quarter-century of false imprisonment as a political prisoner, I have found myself once again on the banks of the Mississippi River in Quincy, a place where I shall eventually find eternal rest next to the many generations of Quincy Rays.

two

The Trail of Private Ray's Bootprints

By April of 1948, he was transferred from
the more prestigious Military Police to the regular
infantry, Company B in Frankfurt, which he disliked.
"Everybody kicks you around there," he later said.
Ray was unhappy and "asked to get out."

—*Killing the Dream*, Gerald Posner

Shortly after World War II ended, James lost his job when the shoe factory where he had worked for two years closed down. International Shoe had been part of the war economy, producing military footwear. In the last days of his life, James would say that he'd "probably still be working there if they hadn't shut down the plant." It's worth noting that in less than two years of factory work, James had saved $7,000 in cash and war bonds; today, this would be worth more than $40,000. This thriftiness was part of his personality before the army got a hold of him. At this point in time, James didn't drink, he never smoked, and his only car was his old '33 Ford.

No matter what others may believe, our older brother James was always a positive role model to my brother Jerry and I. James would often lecture us, saying, "Don't get into trouble," and "Honesty is the best way to make a living." Before he went into the army, these were strong beliefs of his. Later in life, James would frequently say that when he joined the army, it put him "on the road to ruin." From the time he left the service in 1948 until his death in 1998, James Earl Ray spent forty-three of those fifty years in prison.

The mainstream media and the government have tried to portray James as a racist. In 1968 when James was arrested for the murder of Martin Luther King Jr., I was shocked to see how he was portrayed by the mainstream media as a longtime racist and anti-Semite. The press even claimed he asked the U.S. Army to send him to Germany because of his Nazi beliefs. This surprised me, because most of the ballplayers and boxers Jimmy admired as a teen were Jewish; his favorites were Buddy Baer, Max Baer, Hank Greenberg, Ralph Kiner, and Maxie Rosenbloom—all Jewish. I strained my memory, trying to recall whether James ever once made a racist comment. I couldn't remember anything then, and I can't now. In fact, when the Jewish boxer Bummy Davis was killed in a holdup in New York City, James was very upset about it.

When James joined the U.S. Army, he wanted to go to Ireland, where our ancestors are from. The military wouldn't let him pick the country, but he could pick the continent, so he picked Europe. Like most postwar soldiers, he ended up in Occupied Germany. Contrary to what other authors would later claim, James didn't want to go to the bombed-out nation.

When James joined the army in 1946, it made him a bit of a black sheep in our family—we never believed in military service. The family distrust of governmental authority extends to the armed services. When Jimmy went off to the service, he told our family, "I should be an officer before too long." He hoped to do well so he could come back and buy a filling station where our dad could work.

After arriving in Europe, James heard stories of Soviet soldiers raping German girls during their occupation. This strengthened in him strong anti-Communist beliefs that he would hold for years.

Initially, James was a gopher in the army—a "bullet and bean hauler," which involved working on refrigerated trucks. At a certain point James was told "the only way to get ahead during peacetime is to join law-and-order–type groups." Always one to try to advance himself, James became a military policeman (MP) for a year and a half in the 382nd MP Battalion. Later, he joined a new organization largely formed out of the old OSS, the Office of Strategic Services, which had been the army's wartime intelligence service. Although James would call this new organization by its old name for several years, after 1947, the outfit was generally known as the CIA.

When James joined the Central Intelligence Agency, he was given a new U.S. Army serial number that contained a code. The code, he told me, included the numbers 16 and 24. Servicemen at this time would reenlist years after their initial stint and often keep the same serial number, but James's serial number was switched during a two-year stint. The government apparently tried to cover up this serial number issue but botched the job. A lay historian loyal to Dr. King named Lyndon Barsten found evidence of the second serial number. Lyndon first sent an associate to the National Archives in Maryland to examine the histories of the army units James had served in. The one that stood out as unusual to the military experts was the 7892nd Infantry Regiment, where Jimmy transferred during early April of 1948. The unit had only a two-month duration, and the 7892nd had four digits when all U.S. Army Infantry Regiment Units limit that to three digits. From all indications someone insisted that all the i's got dotted regarding the initiation and discontinuance paperwork to an unusual degree. To the experts that was an indication that someone did not like the idea of this unit's formation in the first place.

Lyndon then reviewed the morning reports (or daily records) of the 7892nd at the National Archives depository in St. Louis. In the morning report file of the 7892nd Infantry Regiment in St. Louis are nearly chronologically identical documents that list Jimmy by his "official" serial number—16163129—and by the one he was told was an encoded one: 16242515. Here, in official government documents, was powerful evidence that the story James had told me was true; his serial number had been changed. And, according to Lyndon, it happened about the time Jimmy was in a unit labeled "unusual" by the military experts at the National Archives.

Lyndon asked the military experts in St. Louis, "Did these military serial numbers ever change?" Lyndon was told, "No; they wouldn't change them, as it would only cause confusion."

But confusion, it appears, is exactly what somebody in the army wanted to create. When Lyndon recently asked a former army covert operative why the army would change an enlisted man's serial number, he was told instantly, "He was doing something the army didn't want attributed to him." This is not the way the serial number change was explained to Jimmy, but it makes sense, since later morning reports from the fall and winter of '48 have returned his serial number to the older, official one: 16163129. Additionally the "Barsten" document has James's company listed as Company C, when he was officially in Company B, and his Military Occupational Specialty in this document is Rifleman (745), when he was really an MP. We know that Jimmy was not in Company C because the army later published a troop list for this unit, and he was not on it. This troop list is available in the back of the book *Redesignation Day*, copies of which can be ordered through the New York Public Library.

And additionally this same document lists the unit Jimmy was transferred from, into the 7892nd as the 7838th Reserve Vehicle Detachment, a four digit outfit that had been formed the previous October. His assignment to this unit, if true, is totally contrary to his Official Statement of Military Service, which places him in the 382nd MP outfit from December of 1946 right up until his transfer to the 7892nd in April of 1948.

James would later tell me, "When you join the OSS, it's like joining the Mafia: you never leave." I suppose today the CIA is the closest thing to a worldwide Mafia that has ever existed.

Lyndon Barsten has been studying the MLK assassination since the early 1990s. Years ago Lyndon became horrified when speaking to Dr. King's friend, Rev. Hosea Williams, when he realized that Hosea believed the government was likely behind the murder of Dr. King. Since that time Lyndon has issued literally thousands of Freedom of Information Act (FOIA) requests to government agencies. Lyndon became a tireless pain in the neck to the government, demanding explanations from the FBI about their filing system, pressuring the FBI to put the King murder file on a CD-ROM so the public could have it at an affordable price, and releasing hundreds of files the public had never seen before.

When he learned what James had told me, Lyndon started checking into the 7892nd unit, and has since been told by an intelligence officer that "the four-digit army units, like the 7892nd Infantry Regiment, were often used for cover." The man who told him this reportedly spent his life doing military intelligence work; like James, he was in the 7892nd Infantry Regiment in the spring of '48, during its short two-month life. This makes at least two spooks from this unit, the other being James. The 7892nd Infantry Regiment was partially based in Frankfurt am Main. The European headquarters of the CIA was also located in Frankfurt, housed in the old I. G. Farben building, which had been spared during Allied bombing attacks.

An interesting omission of Gerald Posner's can be found on page 94 of *Killing the Dream*. He says about Jimmy, "By April 1948 he was transferred from the more prestigious Military Police to the regular infantry, Company B in Frankfurt which he disliked…"

"Company B in Frankfurt" is not how a unit's name would normally be described. Posner appears to know that the four digit Army unit number would raise some eyebrows among those familiar with unit names.

While on duty as an MP in Occupied Germany, Jimmy spent much of his time arresting AWOL soldiers. In so doing, James was involved in several shootings, but there was one particular shooting of a soldier that had a major impact on James, haunting him for the rest of his life. In this incident, James wounded an African-American soldier named Washington, from Tennessee. Another MP named Walker—a white man, also originally from Tennessee—was also somehow involved in the Washington shooting. James felt horrible about shooting this soldier—horrible in a life-altering way. For the rest of his life, James appeared to be plagued with guilt and always grasping for a deeper understanding of the shooting. Later, when speaking about the King case, he'd say, "It all goes back to the shooting of [that] soldier, Washington."

Washington had reportedly been arrested earlier by my brother and the other MP Walker for beating up Jews on the German streets and had not taken kindly to the arrest. He started spreading the rumor that if he caught the two arresting MPs, he'd send the men stateside in boxes. James had also been told that Washington had raped an officer's female family member—or even the officer's girlfriend (although he later found out this wasn't the truth). Another officer, someone much higher up, convinced James and Walker to shoot Washington. The details as James told them to me were a bit murky, though the importance of the incident to James cannot be questioned.

The shooting transpired during their duties as MPs, possibly just prior to James's transfer to the 7892nd Infantry. However, military experts claim that James could have still performed his functions as an MP in the 7892nd, so it could have been later. The shooting severed Washington's spinal cord, and the young man never walked again. He appears to have suffered from the medical conditions associated with spinal cord injuries, spending a great deal of time in the hospital later in life.

Although the shooting was deliberate, James had not wanted to do it.

I—and later, Lyndon Barsten—did everything we could to identify Washington, placing ads in African-American papers and the like, but it has been sixty years. James went through court-martial proceedings, because Washington claimed my brother didn't holler "halt" the required number of times prior to James shooting him, as per regulations. However, at the trial, James insisted he did yell "halt" and, consequently, Washington lost his military pension. Washington would end up back in the States by the early 1950s, destitute and in a wheelchair, spending much of his time at the old VA hospital in Nashville. I know he existed because years later I held letters he'd written to James in my own hands.

Lyndon Barsten discovered through an FOIA request to the army that all official records of courts-martial from this era have been destroyed due to their age. In addition, Jimmy's army file has been (1) "lost" by the FBI; (2) taken out of his Illinois prison file, where a copy once was filed; and (3) incinerated at the epicenter of a massive fire at the National Personnel Records Center shortly after CIA director Richard Helms left the agency.

I would later discover from James's writings that after the Washington shooting, my brother tried unsuccessfully to get out of the army. James also went AWOL four times according to documents in his army file, quoted by the FBI in the investigation following the assassination of Dr King. Oddly enough, his going AWOL this many times was not recorded on the morning reports that are the daily record of his company.

After Washington's shooting, my brother was transferred into the 16th Infantry Regiment with most of the personnel of the 7892nd. Lyndon has shown me records that clearly list James's "official" serial number when he was in the 16th Infantry Regiment. It was during this period that James was court-martialed a second time. Near Nuremberg, in late October of 1948, he maintained that he became sick, causing him to miss his shift. He was accused by the army of being drunk in quarters, a charge James strongly denied.

While awaiting his second court-martial for being drunk in quarters, James was ordered to be confined to quarters. Instead, he and several other soldiers took off into Nuremberg, where they were picked up by MPs. My brother was court-martialed for both being drunk in quarters and breaking arrest and sentenced to three months in the prison at the Palace of Justice, where the Germans had been held for war crimes trials. James must have been a model prisoner, for he was released quite early from the Palace of Justice prison compound.

According to George McMillan's book, *The Making of an Assassin*, U.S. Army records (no longer in existence) show that the army gave James two lumbar punctures (spinal taps)—one in the spring, on March 25, shortly before or around the time his army serial number changed, and the second at about the time James claimed he was sick and missed his shift. Remember the government has lost or destroyed these original army records. Lumbar punctures can be used to administer drugs. Why did the army claim James was "drunk" when he had just had a spinal tap? Did the first spinal procedure have anything to do with the Washington shooting?

Lyndon Barsten suggested to me for the first time that the meaning of the Washington shooting might have been an early mind control experiment—that this is what haunted James. I have seen FBI documents that show Jimmy later saw two hypnotists in LA, one of whom had been an army intelligence officer during the war. It wouldn't be like James to tell me he saw these "bug" doctors. But he did tell me that he thought the feds were messing with his mind. It makes perfect sense, this idea that the Washington shooting was a federal experiment. Jimmy was in the land of captured, unethical Nazi psychiatrists, hoping to promote their services to the Americans.

Documents clearly indicate that the CIA was busy trying to reprogram people, and it was doing it in '48. Several thousand mostly financial documents on mind control, drugs, and many other subjects the public would consider crazy survived a document-destruction project ordered by the director of Central Intelligence, Richard Helms, and Sidney Gottlieb, head of mind control studies, as they left the CIA in '73. Today you can get the surviving several thousand pages of CIA mind control documents on three CDs that detail the bizarre experiments done in the name of "national security." The army had their own programs that paralleled the CIA's; tens of thousands of surviving government documents detail, among other subjects, how they endeavored to create human robots to be used as killing machines. The CIA's own documents say it best. This document, "Hypnosis and Covert Operations" (written May 5, 1955), is released through the Freedom of Information Act by the CIA as MORI 428311.

Narco-Hypnosis

Barbiturates acting as cortical depressants can be made to produce hypnotic sleep
even if all other methods fail. Chloroform
and ether were the first narcotics used for
this purpose. Now various derivatives and
modifications of the phenobarbital family
are used. Sodium amytal and sodium pen-
tathol are the most commonly used brief-
acting barbiturates, though others of quite
different derivation show great promise and
may be adaptable to clandestine use.

Can a subject be hypnotized against
his will? Excepting the use of drugs, the
answer must be "no" if he understands what
is going on. However, if the question can
be rewritten to read, "Can a subject be
hypnotized without his knowledge?" the
answer appears to be "yes" under favorable
circumstances: disguised induction and a
good subject.

Lyndon Barsten would say, "This would mean a good subject was a valuable tool, important to keep around for clandestine operations."

Lyndon has found at least one surviving 7892nd Infantry Regiment medical file from a twenty-two-year-old man named Neal Thompson, who was given the hypnotic drug Phenobarbital "in the line of duty." Thompson was in Company F of the 7892nd Infantry Regiment. Although Thompson had strep throat, tonsillitis, and a sore eye, he was given a typical MK-Ultra era drug classified as a hypnotic, which is most commonly prescribed as therapy as an anticonvulsant. Three years earlier the Nazi's had used Phenobarbital in horrific atrocities by deliberately overdosing children considered inferior by the Reich.

The question is this: Was the shooting of the soldier Washington part of a drugging operation; and was James's psychological makeup the reason he was chosen to be the patsy years later, in the murder of Martin Luther King? Was my brother a "good subject," as the document describes?

Lyndon Barsten attempted to contact some of the men who were in the 7892nd Infantry Regiment with James, to see what he could find out about the Washington shooting. He was told that the unit was composed of the army's greenest—and worst—recruits. He also discovered that some of the men whose names were listed in the unit records were not really there. Although they did exist, according to Lyndon's VA records, they just were not part of the unit. A former member of army intelligence told Lyndon that "if it was a spook unit, the ranks would probably be at least partly falsified."

A soldier who was in the service with James told Lyndon an interesting story. When Lyndon asked him if "anything strange happened" while he was in the 7892nd, he said he knew a soldier he called "Candy Ass" Walker (possibly the Walker from Tennessee who had been involved in the shooting?) who became involved in an altercation similar to the Washington story. In this case, he said, a purse was stolen by a "black German." One can imagine that prior to twelve years of Nazi politics, there may have been Afro-Germans in Germany, but what are the chances of this happening in 1948, just three years after the end of the war? Were these incidents experiments?

Robert J. Groden, who has spent most of his life examining the murder of President Kennedy, writes extensively in *The Search for Lee Harvey Oswald* about the CIA's MK-Ultra brainwashing program and related aspects of Oswald's U.S. Marines service at Atsugi Naval Air Station, ". . . where the Agency regularly fed mescaline, sodium pentothal, depressants, amphetamines, and LSD to off-duty U.S. Marines both on base and at the local bars." Groden also tells an eerily familiar tale possibly involving Oswald from ten years after the Washington shooting. On January 15, 1958, marine private Martin Schrand was shot to death while he (along with Oswald) was on temporary duty serving in the Philippines. Schrand was shot under his right arm by his own firearm. It was not suicide, as the firearm was too long for the trigger to have been pulled by Schrand and create that wound. The Warren Commission verifies that there were rumors Oswald shot Schrand and, according to Groden, the Office of Naval Intelligence reportedly investigated Oswald for possible involvement in the shooting.

Were these shootings actually tests involving the use of drugs?

In 1970 Rep. Mendel Rivers wrote Army Maj. General Kenneth Wickham in an attempt to get James's entire army file for official-line author George McMillan. General Wickham wrote that the file could not be released, and "This is particularly true since there are medical aspects that cannot be disassociated from any discussion of Mr. Ray's military background."

James's army enlistment was up on Christmas Day of 1948. After he had nearly served his full stint, my brother was double-crossed by someone in power in the army, who gave him a general discharge just forty-eight hours before his enlistment was up on December 23. A general discharge is much less desirable than the standard honorable discharge. This general discharge would later hinder his employment options. The feds have been known to hang diminished labels on their own people to discredit them, just in case they talk. This was certainly true in the case of men like James Cooper Green, a federal asset who plays into this case, who was arrested on the flimsiest of charges when he became unreliable in the eyes of the feds.

James is not the only patsy or "asset" plucked from the military. There are also irregularities in the service records of Lee Harvey Oswald and Timothy McVeigh. McVeigh was able to leave the service early, also for the flimsiest of reasons. According to Groden's book, *The Search for Lee Harvey Oswald*, in November of 1963, Oswald was identified by New Orleans district attorney Edward Gillen as having inquired about legal issues relating to the importation and sale of LSD. If you put two and two together, it's obvious that the same type of drug experimentation also went on with James. He believed so and told me that something of the kind had been done to him.

James was shipped back to the States from Bremerhaven after his general discharge to New York, and then on to Camp Kilmer in New Jersey. On the ship returning to the States, my brother saw something that would shock him. Many of the black guys had married German girls to take them back home. All married couples were allowed to ride in first class on the ship. This angered many of the white guys on the ship, and reportedly, many black American soldiers were thrown overboard by white soldiers, although some of the soldiers did fight back. Many of the soldiers went overboard during the riot. They either swam back to shore or drown. The ship did not stop but went full speed ahead for the United States. When the ship reached New York harbor, James expected a general lockdown of the ship and a major investigation, but there was none. It was business as usual.

James stayed for a couple of days in New York City, where his army buddies were placed in hotels. While he was there, out on the town, someone rifled through the belongings in his trunk. James believed that the government was behind this invasion. There is no other proof but his word; however, his suspicions become more meaningful when you look at them in context with the rest of the strangeness hovering around him throughout his military career.

James left Camp Kilmer in uniform and traveled by train back home to Quincy for the Christmas holiday season of 1948. Mom Maher had bought us a rooming house at 214 Spring Street in Quincy. At this same time our aunt Mabel arranged for James to buy a canary yellow 1947 Mercury convertible. Despite the family support, James was very upset by the whole army experience. He feared for his future in terms of earning a living because he had received a general discharge, rather than an honorable one.

My brother was a changed man when he returned from Germany. To be frank, he seemed drugged, even though I never saw him take anything. My dad and other family members commented that "he must be on goof-balls." Also, he seemed easily persuaded to do things he never would have done before. This was never truer than his involvement in criminal activities. The young man who had carefully saved every nickel prior to his going into the service now seemed more than a bit reckless.

In the spring of 1949, James moved up to Chicago and began hanging around with many of his old army buddies there. Many of the men who had been in James's army unit were maneuvered into employment with the FBI and other federal organizations in the Chicago metro area. A few found themselves on the other side of the law in organized crime, as part of the Chicago Mob.

Although he wanted to work for the FBI as a special agent, James couldn't be employed by the Bureau in that capacity due to his general discharge from the army. His buddies who now worked for the FBI used James, but in an undercover position. Because of this, James decided to go to private investigator school in Chicago, but the negative army discharge also interfered with these plans. During this time, James worked in Chicago in factory jobs and also received payments under the GI Bill in Chicago from May 2, 1949, to January 31, 1952.

James also received several monetary payments from the CIA at this time, according to my uncle, for whom James was briefly working.

My uncle said that if he needed money, James would disappear for a while, and when he returned, he'd always have the money he needed. This is one of the most suspicious and confusing aspects of his life at that time. I heard this story about James from my uncle and did not see it myself, as I went to prison in Indiana. In December of 1949 a teenager named Gene Mills and I decided to go to Canada to join the merchant marines. They were looking for people to go to sea at the time, and the ship lines were paying good money. On the way to Montreal, the law in Indiana accused us of committing a burglary, and within twenty-three days we were waived out of juvenile court into adult court, and without a parent, guardian, or a lawyer present in the courtroom, the judge sentenced us to serve five years behind thirty-three-foot concrete walls in Pendleton, Indiana.

James would later tell me that between 1949 and early 1952, James's federal buddies used him as an undercover operative on several Chicago cases. The FBI gave him the code name "the Mole" for these operations. When his supposed prison nickname, "the Mole," appeared in magazine articles much later, it was nothing less than a nasty private joke from the feds at James's expense.

Between 1949 and 1952, the feds were using the Communist scare to justify practically anything that they wanted to do. No matter what the official position on James Earl Ray may have been at that time, James was performing undercover operations for the federal government to investigate supposed Communists. One of the cases concerned a Christian church set up near a USO center where American troops were entertained. The FBI believed the church was set up this way so the Communists could pump more information out of the recruits.

Another case that my brother James helped to investigate concerned a supposed Communist plot involving prizefighter Max Marek. Marek was famous for having fought Joe Louis, and he used his fame to open a tavern. In his tavern, there was a cast iron mold of Adolf Hitler's upturned face in the urinal. The FBI special agent investigating the tavern questioned

Marek, saying "Hitler wasn't alone in starting the war. Churchill, Stalin, and Roosevelt were all involved. Would you have any objection to putting their pictures in the urinal too?" Marek replied, "You can put all of them in there but Stalin." The Marek Tavern came under investigation after that. These are examples of the sort of work that James was doing at the time.

When the FBI's file on Dr. King's death was recently moved from FBI control to the National Archives in College Park, Maryland, researcher Lyndon Barsten issued an FOIA request for it. He was then able to examine the original FBI files. Lyndon was amazed when he came across an index from July 31, 1967, for documents on James Earl Ray. Two of the eleven files seem to be mistakes, oddly relating to a Rev. James E. Ray with Martin Luther King's Southern Christian Leadership Conference. The remaining nine appear to deal with James's work with the feds as a mole. When he issued FOIA requests for the files, he was told many of the files were "lost," as one would imagine. The ones that have been released are heavily redacted (blacked out). But they are all from Chicago and all from the 1949–1952 period—except for one that was re-serialized (meaning, the file numbers were altered) that is from slightly earlier yet, from Chicago. Four of the nine files described in the index are file classification 100 files—meaning they relate to domestic security issues, usually involving Communists. So how does a small-time crook have four files from a short period in history with a national security classification?

In the fall of 1949 my brother traveled to Los Angeles, and this is where James was arrested for the first time. He claimed in his cover story that he'd jumped trains heading toward the coast from the Midwest and ended up in Southern California. With that kind of luck, he should have bought more lottery tickets. The truth is that if he needed money to take a passenger train, he could have easily gotten it from the government. I have no idea why he should need such a cover story; personally, it did him no good. I can only conclude that its purpose was to cover up his true purpose there.

In early October of 1949, James was staying in a room on lower Broadway in Los Angeles, hanging out in his usual tavern. One night, while drinking, he felt like he was blacking out, as if he had drunk much more than he'd thought, or like someone had slipped him a drug without his knowing it. Today we hear about drugs like Rohypnol (often called "roofies") all the time, usually in connection with cases of sexual assault in bars, but the government has long known about the fast-acting effects of certain tranquilizing drugs and has studied their use for years.

When James regained consciousness, he was no longer in the honky-tonk. He was in a hallway of a building adjacent to a cafeteria called the Forum, a place where he had never been before. He was barely coherent, but he later recalled that a man was talking to him, making sure he came into the side hallway that led upstairs to the cafeteria's office. Still slipping in and out of consciousness, Jimmy was then shaken by this man, whom he had never met, but who was accusing him of trying to steal a typewriter from the upstairs business office of the Forum. The man's name was Lee Strayhorn, and he was an assistant manager of the Forum cafeteria. When Strayhorn began to mention the police, James hightailed it out of there in spite of his condition. Strayhorn later claimed that James had moved a typewriter in the process of stealing it, and that James threw a chair at him, but James vehemently denied this.

Supposedly, James lost his army discharge papers at the scene, along with a bank passbook, when a parking attendant grabbed him as he ran. Days later, while walking down the street, James was simultaneously accosted by Strayhorn from the Forum, the parking lot attendant, and a police officer familiar with the case. In a city the size of Los Angeles, it could barely be considered a coincidence. James was handcuffed and brought in to the station. It was his first arrest.

On December 9, 1949, James pleaded guilty to burglary to minimize his prison time. He already knew that his own testimony would never be believed in this situation. He got three months in prison and two years' probation. There are reports that Jimmy had to ride boxcars home after his release, but in fact, he was given a one-way bus ticket to Chicago through his probation, as Illinois was a court-ordered destination.

Evidently, while riding the boxcars home, James was arrested by a deputy sheriff on vagrancy charges in Cedar Rapids, Iowa. But there seems to be more to this story, too, because if he had been arrested in Iowa with probation papers from California, the police would have sent him back to California. This is especially true since James would not have reached his court-ordered destination. At this time, while supposedly riding boxcars across the country, he called our uncle William. When asked if he needed money, Jimmy told our uncle, "No." But he was riding as a vagabond on boxcars. He knew that Uncle William would have sent him money if he needed it. It seems to me that he may have been performing some function for the feds, although there are records of the vagrancy charge in Cedar Rapids. It seems highly irregular, although I can't prove the truth behind the lie.

Documents verify that the CIA has worked with criminals in the past. In fact, domestically, they have worked mostly with criminals, partly because the word of those with a criminal record is discredited in the eyes of the public. Proof of our government's willingness to work with known arrestees and convicts is that the LA arrest didn't hinder James's work with the FBI in Chicago in the slightest.

As the years went by, nothing much would change for the two brothers from the wrong side of the tracks. Neither James nor I experienced the luck of the Irish. We both had our run-ins with the law; as I've said, we were from a family that didn't hold much respect for authority. I only became aware of Jimmy's 1949 arrest when my uncle William Maher told me about it during a visit to see me in prison in Indiana. James explained more about the California trip to me later.

On March 21, 1952, the Indiana State Prison hauled me out of solitary, dressed me in a gunnysack suit, gave me a bus ticket and five dollars, and led me to the front gates of the prison I had entered twenty-six months earlier. I wanted to become a seaman, and planned to go to California. First, however, I needed to go to Illinois to visit my family and work to save money. I planned to work for my uncle Willie in Alton before heading to California.

My brother was living back in Chicago, and by this time, he was communicating with the soldier, Washington, the one he had shot years before. How James found out where Washington was, I don't know. But if James had asked his army or FBI buddies to look up Washington, it would have possibly red-flagged him and brought surveillance down upon him, including such things as opening his mail. James began to claim random acts of government interference after contacting the soldier, Washington.

Meanwhile, Washington had lost his army pension. It was related to my brother's claim at his court-martial that James had indeed hollered "halt" according to regulations before the shooting—which he had not. Now Jimmy planned to execute an affidavit saying that he had lied at the court-martial nearly four years earlier; this would effectively reinstate Washington's army pension. James felt that the U.S. Army had screwed both of them, and he wanted to relieve his conscience about Washington's shooting. The government had saddled my brother with a general discharge and taken away Washington's pension, so James felt that if he wrote up an affidavit that refuted his earlier testimony, at least Washington would be ahead.

This affidavit would never be executed, because shortly after James agreed to help Washington, he was arrested on a second criminal charge. There are several variations to the arrest story, but most go something like this: Early in the morning on May 6, 1952, James caught a Red Top Taxi and asked the driver to take him to 67 Cedar in Chicago. At that point, James pulled a gun on the driver and demanded the keys. The taxi was supposedly to be used as a getaway car in the robbery of a bookie. The taxi driver, a man named Knox, disposed of the keys and ran away from the cab, but was followed seconds later by my brother. As James chased the cabbie, a man named Robert Everhart began to chase after James. Everhart supposedly happened upon an unmarked police car and told the cops what he had seen. James disappeared into a dead-end alley chased by the police, who then blocked James in the alley. James jumped a fence, ran into a backyard, and dove through a closed window into the basement of a house. When the police caught up with James, they shot him in the arm.

There is evidence that there was more to this case. The indictment gives a slightly different story of the arrest. It reads, "The defendant then drove off in the cab," and claims James was apprehended later while flashing a gun in the taxi.

A peculiar hypnotic take on the crime is found in James's July 13, 1952, "Inmate's Statement," found in his Illinois prison file. It quotes my brother as saying, "I just got arrested for robbery. I was to have stopped the taxi driver, taken $11.00, and driven off with the cab." There is no doubt James was following orders, but exactly who gave those orders has never been revealed. And, why risk your freedom to take "$11.00"?

Whatever happened that morning, there is no doubt Jimmy was shot in the arm.

My brother would later claim that a woman who saw all of the blood started screaming, "Police brutality," and that this caused such a commotion, the cops forgot to pat him down for a gun. However, the arrest did not happen that way. James did have a gun in his possession at the time of his arrest. Under normal circumstances, the police would have immediately patted him down in the basement, where they caught him. The lives of police officers depend on their patting down criminals. James did have a gun, and yet he was later tried on a charge of unarmed robbery. It wasn't a woman accusing the cops of brutality who helped make the gun go away. It was the CIA. A deal must have been made.

By this time I had been paroled and was staying in Alton, Illinois, released from prison in Indiana to my uncle Willie. I was going to work for a couple of months to make enough money to get to California. My plans once again hit a bumpy road when I was contacted by James, who had been arrested in Chicago for this cab robbery. As I remember, James called my uncle Willie, who then told me to head up to Chicago to give James assistance in a possible escape from Cook County Jail. His life was spiraling out of control, and the very act of contemplating a jail break indicates that James had lost all faith in his government handlers. They would help him if they needed him; otherwise, they let him twist in the wind.

I didn't want to leave my Alton job to get involved in this crazy plan, but we are a family who does not turn our backs on each other just because we get into trouble. I didn't have enough money saved up to head westward, so if James needed me to stay in Chicago, I was going to have to get a job there.

I headed from Alton to Chicago by bus. James's girlfriend at the time, a young woman named Marlene, picked me up at the Greyhound station in a new white Cadillac, and we drove to the Cook County Jail. Marlene was an African-American woman who dressed like a movie star. She flashed ID at the jail and bypassed signing in, walking in like she owned the place. My arrest in 1949 had left me feeling like I couldn't walk freely around any jail. My heart was beating twice as fast as Marlene's spike heels clicked on the floor, and I must have flinched. Marlene chastised me: "If you act like that, someone is going to stop you. Now act like you're supposed to be here."

Thinking back, it is my impression that the ultrasophisticated Marlene was a member of the CIA; whichever agency controlled her, she was definitely a federal operative of some sort. The mainstream media would later characterize my brother James as a racist, which is unbelievable to anyone

33

who simply takes an informed look at James's life. James had no problem with a black girlfriend, and he was about to lose his freedom for trying to aid a wronged African-American man. Somebody needs to explain that.

Cook County Jail, where James was being held, had been the temporary home of Al Capone and much of the Chicago Mob. A huge Art Deco stone building from the late 1920s, it's still there as of this writing, rough as ever. Marlene seemed to know just where James's visiting area was. Once there, I asked my brother through the glass, "Now what did you get yourself into?"

Looking around, he responded, "It's nothing. I'll tell you later." He did indeed seem to believe that the arrest was nothing, and that he would be out shortly. There was only one thing on his mind, he told me: "Go to my apartment and collect all the letters from a man named Washington in Tennessee. Get those letters out of my apartment."

I went to the nearly bare north-side apartment at 853 Fullerton Avenue, which showed no signs whatsoever that anyone was living there. I got rid of the letters, even though in hindsight, from the goings-on, I believe that someone in a position of authority probably knew their contents.

My California aspirations and poor economic situation were on my mind when I later told James, "If I'm going to stay in Chicago for any length of time, I'm going to need to get a job here." I took it as a joke when Jimmy responded, "Maybe you want to make some money as a getaway driver for someone who is going to take out one of the presidential candidates." I didn't pay much attention to this at the time, but maybe I should have.

While James was still in the Cook County Jail, a federal agent came to see him. He reminded my brother that he had a record from the 1949 conviction in Los Angeles. According to James, the agent said, "You're looking at some serious time here. We don't want you to send this affidavit down to Tennessee. We don't want old wounds opened up as to the real reason the Negro soldier was shot. We feel that we can help you with this situation you've got yourself into."

The feds were true to their word. James was tried for unarmed robbery in 1952 and spent only two years in the Illinois State Prison at Joliet. In turn, the affidavit that would have helped Washington get his army pension reinstated was never sent by James. Simple logic tells me that for anyone coming off of a bad military discharge, with two arrests in three years, a two-year sentence was a break. James told me in Chicago that he was "working on a deal" relating to Washington, the CIA, and the taxi affair. But he wouldn't give me the details until twenty-two years later.

I further doubt that James pulled this taxi heist, because Tony Accardo's Mafia ran Chicago with an iron hand at that time. They had to give permission before anyone committed street crimes, and they always extracted street taxes from them after the heist was pulled. Jimmy didn't have permission to pull the job he was behind bars for, and I doubt very much that he would have risked crossing the Mob. To pull a job like this on your own was considered crossing the rackets bosses, and when you did that, you ended up in the morgue. The unknown person or persons who talked him into this operation had a different goal in mind than stealing eleven dollars.

James's trial was so quickly arranged it left me rather dumbfounded, because I had expected to be in Chicago for quite some time, waiting for it to begin. Because the deal was arranged so quickly, I did not yet have enough money for my California trip. So I went to work in the railroad camps around Chicago saving my money, and living in different Missions for free.

While I was still in Chicago, something happened that would resemble later events. One evening, several weeks after James had gone to Joliet, I was standing on Michigan Avenue across the street from where both of the 1952 presidential candidates were staying.

Dwight Eisenhower and Adlai Stevenson were next to one another at the now-closed Blackstone and Stevens hotels. Ike was staying at the Blackstone, Stevenson at the Stevens, which is now the Hilton. The boys in blue nabbed me and informed me I was "under arrest." These cops put me behind bars at the Central Police Station on South State Street, seemingly for no reason.

Initially I was taken to a large holding room with a lot of jail inmates. One prisoner said to me, "If the cop standing in front of the elevator points down, they take you down to the basement and beat you with wet magazines until you sign a confession to whatever crime they want solved. If he points up, they take you to the seventh floor and hang you out the window by your feet until you confess. Sometimes they drop you anyway, just to send a message out to other criminals; then they claim it was suicide."

I've recently found out that the feds had been using this same procedure going back to the 1930s, when they dangled fringe mobster Jimmy Probasco from the nineteenth floor of an office building.

The cop pointed up for me, and we did go to the seventh floor. On the seventh floor the elevator doors opened to reveal a plainclothesman sitting behind a desk; there were also several cops behind me. The plainclothesman glanced down at my paperwork and asked me, "Which candidate were you going to shoot?"

"I'm not going to shoot anyone," I protested.

"Why did you hide the rifle in the park?"

"Sir, I'm sixteen; I came to Chicago to see my grandmother who was in Cook County Hospital, and I'm not aware of any type of shooting," I responded, stretching the truth about my actual age, which was nineteen, and the reason for my visit. The cop behind the desk nodded. I was put back on the elevator fully expecting it to be wet-magazine time. Instead, I was taken before a judge, a black man named Sam Sloan. I told the judge the same story. He told me where the Greyhound station was and said I had better be on the next bus out of town. The question remains in my mind to this day, over fifty years later: Was this just a coincidence? Did this incident have anything to do with a planned hit on a presidential candidate, which James had referred to in his cell a few weeks before?

After the judge released me, I took the money I had saved and hiked out to the Route 66 entrance, bypassing the Greyhound depot, and rode my thumb to California on that legendary highway, still hoping to pursue my elusive dream of becoming a seaman.

three

Looking for Loot in All the Wrong Places

> The best picture of Ray came from Walter
> Rife, an ex-convict who had known him since
> they were both fourteen. . . . They had played
> together as boys when Jim used to come from
> Ewing to visit his uncle Earl, in Quincy. Jim had
> great respect for his uncle Earl, who was a
> gang leader and tough.
>
> —*An American Death*, Gerold Frank

My brother James was in the joint from 1952 to '54 for the Chicago taxi affair. They first sent James to the Illinois State Pen at Joliet; he was later moved to the medium-security facility at Pontiac. When he appeared in front of the Illinois parole board in 1953 for consideration of parole, his Institutional Progress Report stated: "He has been highly unsettled after leaving the Army, and we would judge that some traumatic experience occurred that he does not care to tell or cannot verbalize." James later told me that the deal he had worked out with the CIA in Chicago specified that he could never talk about his relationship with them or make any reference to the Washington shooting.

Supervising sociologist Stow Symon, who wrote James's progress report in 1953, still worked at Pontiac after the King assassination. Symon was interviewed in September 1968 by author George McMillan. McMillan's notes state that Symon "was here when Ray was here—the FBI almost lived here [at the pen], tried to find people he knew. He was a real loner." Common sense tells anyone who is willing to listen that the feds would never have "almost lived" at the pen in order to watch my brother, if he was just another convict who pulled a cabbie stickup. Would the FBI pay that amount of attention to the perp in a common street robbery? Does the FBI care who a small-time street criminal knows, or who he might have been speaking to? Consider the manpower that it would take for the FBI to track people in that way. We can use the size of our prison population as a general reference point to get an idea of the task.

From the time James was released from Pontiac in March of 1954, to his final 1968 arrest in London for the murder of Dr. King, he was imprisoned for criminal activity twice. In 1955, he went to the joint for passing forged federal money orders, and in 1959 for armed robbery of grocery stores.

Most of what I know about James's activities at this time came from family members, because in 1953 I was accused by the authorities in Quincy of stealing and burning an old $40 Hudson automobile. I was ordered to serve ten years in Menard Prison, in downstate Illinois. During my imprisonment I often found myself breaking rocks in the prison rock quarry with my uncle Earl, who was also an inmate there. Uncle Earl ran the Catholic chaplain's office when the priest wasn't at the prison.

Uncle Earl told me that his "friend," a gang leader named James "Obie" O'Brien, and a few other gang members, wanted me to go to work for them in the inmates' kitchen as an enforcer. I've never been a joiner. That has been a constant thing in my life; I do not "join," whether it is inside or outside of a prison.

I was looking for a way out of the rock quarry, however, and a deal with the devil seemed to be my only shot. I took Obie up on his offer against my own better judgment, and went to work in the kitchen. The gang leaders who ran the prison were too elderly to do any of the heavy, strong-arm type of stuff. These guys kill each other on a regular basis on the outside, but they work together behind bars. They do this knowing that as soon as they are released back to the streets, they will go back to killing each other again. It was the same then as it is now.

But in the joint, they sit around swapping stories. One of the stories a Berger gang member enjoyed telling was about how they were the first to drop bombs out of an airplane on the Shelton gang fortress. *The Guinness Book of Records* backs up his story. Obie O'Brien told a story about how the feds had a contract out on a black boxer named Jack Johnson, who was behind bars for the then often suspicious Mann Act violation of taking a (often white) woman across the states lines for immoral purposes. This Mann Act violation was the same case law the feds used to put rock 'n' roll singer Charles "Chuck" Berry behind bars for a few years from 1960–1963. Chuck reportedly spent his last time in prison at the Federal Medical Center at Springfield, Missouri, a place I would know well twenty years later.

In the '50s the gangs I was in prison with consisted mostly of the remains of the Charley Berger gang, the Shelton gang, the Egan's Rats gang, the Cuckoo gang, and Obie O'Brien. He represented the Buster Wortman outfit, which was under the control of the Chicago Mafia. Here is where the connections become easier to see.

I must have done a pretty good job for them, because Obie told me that when I got released, he would arrange for me to just show up at the Steamfitters Local Union #562 office once in a while. There, I would pick up a paycheck that amounted to about four times more money than the average working stiff would get in those days. They called it "putting you on the payroll," or something to that effect. I had too many challenges to staying alive at that point and didn't really listen. It went into the back of my mind and stayed there.

My brother James would be in prison in the '50s with Larry Callanan, who ran the Steamfitters Local 562. Callanan was the right-hand man of Obie's boss, Buster Wortman. And all of these men eventually became important to the story of Dr. King's murder.

James is oftentimes referred to as the most inept criminal in the history of small-time convicts, but this does not change the fact that there were many successful heists pulled off in the late 1950s by James and his accomplices. James, to the best of my knowledge, almost never pulled these jobs alone. From the mid- to late 1950s, his behavior suffered as close to a 180-degree change as could possibly be imagined from the pre-army brother I had known. It was as if Jimmy went away to the service and never came back.

After his release from prison for the supposed '52 cab heist in Chicago, James got a bus ticket to Quincy. But once he got there, he found that his chance of employment with Uncle Frank in the slot machine rackets had vanished. Pressure had been placed on politicians regarding the one-armed bandits, by a series of articles in *Collier's* and other national magazines. At the same time that James realized there was no work for him, he sadly found that our parents' relationship was falling apart. He was in no shape to deal with the stresses involved.

Just before James's release, our parents took jobs at the Lincoln Douglas Hotel in Quincy. One day our father, George, disappeared. The old man had run off to St. Louis with a married woman named Ruby, who had also worked at the hotel. At first our mother was in a state of denial about the affair. The old man had spent years judging women who left their husbands and children, and now he was off with a woman who had done the very thing he had often complained about. From that day forward I can honestly say that my mother despised him.

She had given birth to nine of George's children, only to see him run off with this other woman. When he tried to come back, months later, she would have nothing to do with him. When she was told at a later point that he had been killed as the result of a contract put out because of Ruby, she actually rejoiced. When she found out this wasn't true, a sense of guilt and anger overtook her and she became severely depressed.

The horrific death of Margie years earlier, and now her husband leaving her in '52—it was all too much. Mother's drinking became worse. The final assault on her soul was when her youngest children were taken from her by the authorities because of her drinking. When my mother and maternal grandmother moved to St. Louis under pressure from the Quincy police, she had taken all a human being could take.

Our uncle William "Hoss" Maher ran a company named Modern Painting and painted advertisements on the sides of barns. He was helped by my brother James, until the late summer of 1954. It was during this period that James was charged with the burglary of a dry cleaner in East Alton. The break-in took place on Saturday, August 27. This robbery has been widely written about, mostly because of the comic picture that is painted of James supposedly running himself right out of his shoes while racing from the scene. (In reality, his shoes got stuck in some thick mud behind the dry cleaners.)

A local Mob-connected nightclub owner named Dominic Tadaro posted James's bail, and also provided a lawyer for James. Jimmy had to repay Tadaro in monthly payments, and Tadaro's lawyer would continue to delay the trial until the fee was paid off. Shortly after that, the police arrested James a second time on the harassment charge of vagrancy, but Tadaro wanted his money from the first arrest, so he bailed James out a second time. This made the cops unhappy, and by this time the Alton Police Department had it out for James. He decided to head upriver to Quincy, which was essentially our other hometown. In Quincy, James was living in inexpensive hotels and conducting small-time criminal operations in order to repay Tadaro. It was at this time that he met Walter Rife.

Walter Rife and his brother, Ronnie Rife, had both been in Menard Prison with me. Neither Walter nor Ronnie ever told the truth about anything in their lives, being the type of people who would rather lie when it was just as easy to tell the truth. Walter's most important lie implicated my brother James in the March 7, 1955, theft of money orders and validation stamps from the decrepit U.S. post office in Kellerville, Illinois, Walter's hometown. In actual fact, James only met Rife for the first time after the money orders were stolen. This is not to say that James was not knowingly in on the scheme of cashing the stolen money orders. He was in on it, and he was imprisoned for it. But when authors such as Gerald Posner in his book *Killing the Dream* write that James was part of the theft, this is fiction. James was never convicted of stealing the money orders, only of later passing them.

Our uncle Earl strongly warned James of any association with Walter Rife. James normally wouldn't have gotten involved with a person like him, but Dominic Tadaro was being rather forceful about James paying him back for the legal assistance. So, in need of money, James ignored our uncle's warnings and took off with Walter to cash the stolen money orders. They would eventually pass twenty-seven of the hot money orders: James would pass twelve, and Walter, fifteen. The deal between James and Walter was that if James agreed to drive his car and take Walter out on the road to cash the money orders, Walter would make it financially beneficial, splitting the proceeds between them, fifty-fifty. This would allow James to repay Tadaro.

They gathered stolen ID papers from "Skid Row" in St. Louis, and passed these money orders all the way to Miami Beach. In Florida, James traded in his old car and purchased a newer (although still used) Lincoln with the money orders. In Jacksonville, they tried to score a new ID from a gay bar. When there was a ruckus there, they left town and drove west through the

South. For two weeks they were able to joyride, passing these money orders left and right; however, they hit a snag when they were nearly back home. In Hannibal, Missouri, they were stopped by the highway patrol. James would later believe that Walter Rife's girlfriend in Quincy was a police informant, because Walter had called her from Hannibal shortly before the arrest. James's car was searched, and the evidence against them was found. Walter and James were held for postal inspectors.

On July 7, 1955, only four months after the money order heist, James and Walter arrived in Leavenworth Prison. James received the harsher sentence, forty-five months, compared to Walter's thirty-six months—in spite of the fact that Walter had a much more extensive criminal record. James would be released in early 1958, to live in freedom for just one short year.

In 1968, after King's murder, Walter would become a gift to the feds and the press, who were busy reinventing James Earl Ray. Walter would tell early authors writing about the King case that he knew James when James was ten or twelve years old, in the early 1940s, which is false. Walter Rife is from Kellerville, Illinois. At the time he claims to have known Jimmy, we lived in Missouri. Rife claims he met James in Quincy when the two just happened to have been visiting relatives there. This type of lying was typical of several people who wanted to see their names in books and magazines, or who were trying to peddle a story about James. Time-Life publications, other major magazines, and authors Clay Blair, Gerold Frank, and George McMillan repeated Walter's story as if it were the gospel truth.

In reality, Walter Rife met James in a tavern when James was twenty-seven, after James's release from Pontiac. When they met, Walter, who didn't have a car, was trying to cash the stolen money orders from Kellerville. Walter later claimed to the press that our uncle Earl Ray would take thirteen- or fourteen-year-old Jimmy to whorehouses, which is untrue. If Uncle Earl had really done this, my father would have just about killed his brother. But Walter knew which side his bread was buttered on, and that it was in his financial interests to make our family look bad. But even Walter stopped short of making James look guilty of Dr. King's murder.

The first reporter to find Rife after James was implicated in Dr. King's murder was Daniel Greene of the *National Observer*. According to Gerold Frank's *An American Death*, Walter told Greene, "Jim Ray was prejudiced.

He was prejudiced to the point that he hated to see a colored person breathe."
This quote was repeated by the press in spite of the fact that by 1968, it was
well known that my brother always chose the most integrated places, such as
the St. Francis Hotel in Los Angeles, to live; in spite of the fact that several of
Dr. King's African-American friends, such as Rev. Hosea Williams and Rev.
James Lawson, would early on do what they could to help James, and that he
gladly accepted their assistance.

James's criminal background is stretched by some authors to make him
appear violent, more like a cold-blooded killer and less like the decent person he really was. In *Killing the Dream*, Posner claims that James stabbed a
man in a bar during this money order trip with Rife. Posner's only source is
Rife. He has no FBI report, no police report—only the word of someone who
claims he knew James fifteen years before he actually did. According to Walter Rife's story, a guy in a Kansas City bar told James to move his glass down,
at which time my brother left by the front door, reentered by the back door,
and stabbed the guy, who immediately dropped off the barstool.

If there was a shred of truth to this Kansas City story that Rife was ped-
dling in 1968, wouldn't the FBI have identified the stabbed man and checked
to see whether or not he had lived? Wouldn't the story have been covered in
the local newspapers? The stabbing would have been big news; it would have
been the only known violent act in my brother's life aside from the top-secret
shooting of the soldier, Washington, which was an official action.

After the King assassination, Walter Rife made all of these false statements, but never said that James was guilty of the murder of Dr. King. The
media didn't like Walter making any positive statements about James, even
if those positive statements were limited to the fact that Rife believed James
was innocent of the King homicide.

In 1968 a case was dummied up against Walter because he refused to say
James killed King. It was claimed that Walter stole copper wire from an electric company somewhere in Adams County. The feds would get involved with
the theft of the copper scrap wire. They would give Walter approximately fifty
years for stealing this wire. The joke was that it was useless for anything but
scrap anyway, laying there to be taken. I assume that Walter made some type
of deal to have those fifty years taken off of his back, because as far as I know,
he never served a day of that sentence.

The older you get, the more you realize the ways of the world. This certainly was never truer than for James and me. I never got involved with the Mafia, but I was on the fringe. In prison, James got to know Larry Callanan; although Callanan would later cloak himself in a thin veil of respectability, he was still the right-hand man of the East St. Louis Mob boss, Buster Wortman. Wortman collected a pension from the steamfitters and answered to the Chicago Mob, which was almost surely involved in the murder of King and the framing of my brother. Later, in 1969, when my incarcerated brother wanted to find out information on the King case, he would send our brother Jerry to have a talk with Callanan. Wortman had died in 1968, just after Dr. King was killed, so Callanan was the best source for information on Wortman.

Callanan used Mob lawyer Morris Shenker, just as I would try to do for James in 1968. The average person, unaware of how tight the Mob can be with the government, might be surprised to learn that during the 1964 election, Callanan contributed a reported sum of at least $25,000—and possibly as high as $52,000—to the "Friends of LBJ" fund, according to reports at that time made by the *St. Louis Globe-Democrat*. Lyndon Baines Johnson was the successful Democratic candidate in 1964. President Johnson gave Callanan a commutation of his earlier court sentence in April of '64 for labor racketeering.

Seven months prior to his release from the pen, James was reportedly offered a transfer to the prison honor farm at Leavenworth. At this time Leavenworth was ethnically segregated, except for the honor farm. James allegedly refused the transfer because the honor farm was integrated—or at least this is what has been reported in the press. In 1993 James would testify under oath that he believed the records as they related to the honor farm had been altered by the feds.

James served his time for the federal money orders affair as a model prisoner, as he always was. He was released on April 15, 1958. He had turned thirty the previous month. When he was released, his parole was transferred from Kansas City to St. Louis, where most of the family had ended up. In 1958 and '59, while James was in the St. Louis area, he was engaged in criminal activities. James's main crime partner for this one year of his freedom in the late 1950s was John "Catman" Gawron.

Gawron was Polish-American, and close to my mother. He was about my father's age and originally from Chicago. Gawron had been wounded in World War I, while he served in France. Because he was gassed during the war, he received a pension from the army. But before I was born, while he was still a very young man, Catman had been convinced to plead guilty to a burglary charge that had been brought against him. At the time, lawyers often promised inmates that if they pleaded guilty, they'd be out in a year; this was a lie. The practice was called the "one-year-to-life" sentence.

As happened with too many of these cases, Catman's court-appointed defense lawyer was working with the judge. In Illinois they also called this old one-year-to-life sentence "the death sentence." In reality, you wouldn't be out for twenty or thirty years.

After more than twenty years in the pen, Catman was finally let out in the early 1950s. After successfully serving all of those years, he just decided to jump parole. Catman objected to the confines of parole after they had held him in the joint for over twenty years on what he believed to be a trumped-up charge. There were a lot of people at that time who felt the same way. So Catman went to the Soldiers' and Sailors' Home in Quincy, where they don't make any information available to the criminal justice system. This is how he got by with jumping parole. Somehow Catman got involved with my brother Jerry and my mother while he was staying at the Soldiers' Home. I was behind bars at the time, so I really don't know how they got connected, but they became very close.

Together, Catman Gawron and my brother Jerry robbed a filling station just over the state line in Missouri. They got caught. Jerry was sentenced to Missouri State Prison at Jefferson City, called "the Walls" by the inmates. Jefferson City is the location of the prison that James would later escape from while he was manipulated by the feds on the road to Memphis. Catman was sent back down to Menard Prison for parole violation. Catman got out of Menard Prison at about the same time James got out of Leavenworth. James and Catman were connected in 1958–59, and together they pulled many nonviolent criminal acts.

One of their burglaries took place at the Hub Furniture Store in Hannibal, Missouri. They went there to crack a safe—as a trained safecracker, this was Catman's specialty. Catman didn't like guns; if you had a gun, he wouldn't even go out with you to commit the crime. The way the Hub Furniture Store robbery went down was this: Catman didn't know that James was armed, and when he found out, he got upset. Somehow, as he got riled up Catman fell off the store's roof and broke his leg, so James had to drag him to the getaway car, which was parked some distance away. Catman was on crutches for quite some time after this aborted burglary.

It was about this same time, in 1958, while I was working in the kitchen at Menard Prison, that I was wrongly accused of trying to blow up the warden's office with nitroglycerine. The warden was Ross Randolph, a former FBI man, generally considered by many inmates to be an unhappily married gay man. Warden Randolph ordered me to spend the rest of my sentence, twenty months, in solitary. In solitary my weight dropped 60 pounds, down to 120 pounds.

Since I was in prison from 1953 to 1960, I didn't know about James's exploits firsthand. But my dad would later tell me that at times James would keep several thousand dollars in a container in the refrigerator. James kept the money in the fridge because he believed it wouldn't burn if the house were to burn. My dad assumed that James was getting money from stealing it, but he didn't know for sure. Shortly after my father discovered James's hidden money, James traveled to Mexico, and then up to Montreal, Canada. Interestingly, my dad said that James never took any of the refrigerator money with him on either of these trips.

In December of 1958, James's conditional release was up. He was free to leave the country, which is something he claimed he wished to do. Supposedly, according to Jimmy's writings, he robbed a crooked bar and pool hall in Madison, Illinois, before taking off to New Orleans to get seaman's papers and a trip to a foreign country. But why would he leave thousands in our father's refrigerator and risk robbing a tavern if he wanted out of the country? He certainly would have been free to get a passport like anyone else, but this would have left an official record of his whereabouts. From New Orleans he traveled to Mexico, where he was unable to find any passage out of North America that wouldn't leave a paper trail. In *Tennessee Waltz* he would later write: "Most inbound/outbound ships were liners hauling tourists, rather than merchant ships or tramp steamers that someone wishing to circumvent official procedures in departing a country might hitch a ride on."

In the late 1950s, it was very unusual for an American to distrust his government so much that he would try to sneak out of the country. But James surely had good reason to distrust them—and good reason for his strong desire to get lost in Ireland, or any of the other places he dreamed about.

By February of 1959, James was back in the St. Louis area, engaging in criminal activities, including bootlegging wine to winos on Sundays when the liquor stores were closed. James had sold his car to one of these wino customers, who then used it in a failed caper. The police traced the car to the only stable address associated with it, our mother's. As if our mother hadn't been through enough with her husband leaving her, the police burst through her front and back door simultaneously early in the morning. This attention from the police supposedly sent James, who wasn't there, on a trip to Montreal to avoid the arrest.

A road trip from St. Louis to Montreal is close to 1,200 miles. James could have avoided the police in a city the size of Chicago; he was familiar with the city, it was out of state, and it was an easy drive from the St. Louis area. Or, if he just wanted out of the United States, he could have made it to Toronto, a major Canadian city less than 800 miles away. He chose Montreal instead, and once there, he got to know the area between the 1000 and 2000 blocks of St. Catherine Street East, not far from Montreal's McGill University. In 1959, I believe James still had ties with the U.S. government, and I believe they were likely directing him to go on this trip.

I've been shown CIA documents by investigator Lyndon Barsten that indicate Montreal in 1959 was the home of Subproject 68 of the CIA's MK-Ultra brainwashing program. It was run by Dr. Ewen Cameron at the Allen Memorial Institute of McGill University. Dr. Cameron was an immigrant from the UK who became a lead CIA mind control expert in Canada. It is in this neighborhood of the Allen Memorial Institute that James decided to hide out back in 1959.

Did the CIA order James to go to the Allen Memorial Institute for experimentation? A case could be made that while James was in Germany, the feds repeatedly drugged him with spinal taps or increasingly sophisticated methods; and here he was, more than ten years after his odd army service in the epicenter of brainwashing in North America. Lyndon Barsten talked with

CIA operative Jules Kimble when he was in prison, in Texas. In a recorded telephone interview, Kimble said that in 1967, he and James were ordered to go to McGill's Allen Memorial Institute by the CIA to undergo hypnosis. Kimble's 1967 association with McGill is verified by interviews with his (Kimble's) girlfriend, which are contained in Royal Canadian Mounted Police documents.

James returned to the St. Louis area in the summer of 1959 after his trip to Montreal. When James was arrested in that year, it was for grocery store robberies. The first heist was pulled with Joseph "Blackie" Austin, who had been in the joint in Menard for more than thirty years for the 1927 murder of a man during an armed robbery. Blackie was dark, perhaps Italian-American or of Mediterranean ancestry, and was nearly sixty, very slim, and a likeable person; it was easy to talk with him. Blackie got connected with James, I believe, through a mission in St. Louis called the St. Louis Rescue Mission. It was located in a beat-up old theater and run by a Reverend Wynineger. The Christian mission house was really just a place where like-minded criminal elements made connections. It was so well known at the time that convicts were actually paroled to the mission.

At this same time, James also met James "Jimmy" Loama Owens, a local small-timer who was of the same criminal ilk as Blackie and James. On the morning of July 11, 1959, James pulled his first armed Kroger grocery store heist, this one with Blackie Austin. A security camera, usually used to identify check cashers, snapped the photos of them while they stuffed $1,200 in their pockets. Perhaps Blackie, who had been in the joint since the 1920s, didn't understand the advancements in technology; he stood right in front of the security camera wearing dark glasses and a snap brim hat. They had an unknown accomplice on this job who crashed the car later, leaving it a wreck. This particular heist was an armed robbery as Blackie brandished his nickel plated pistol for the security cameras. Warrants were issued for both James and Blackie, but they managed to avoid arrest for a while.

About three weeks later, Blackie and James pulled the same type of early-morning job in Alton. This time the heist was at an IGA grocery store. They made it out of the store okay, but were later spotted by the cops. A high-speed chase left the getaway car spinning out of control. It luckily crashed near the woods, and James and Blackie took off into the trees to hide. The Alton police had all the evidence, but no crooks—until Blackie decided to trek out of the woods to escape the extreme heat. He was arrested, but in the tradition of the honorable thief, Blackie never identified his accomplice.

Since Blackie was in the joint, the next grocery store heist was pulled with chubby, baby-faced Jimmy Owens, also "procured" from the St. Louis Rescue Mission. The word on the street was that a certain St. Louis Kroger grocery store kept large sums of money overnight in their safe; the safe could only be opened by key lock and combination together. Separate persons knew the combination and held the key. A switch car, a stolen Ford, would be used for the getaway until they reached Jimmy Owens's green and white Plymouth, parked some distance away.

On the day of the heist, October 10, James supposedly couldn't start up the Ford right away, and he was running late. James and Jimmy Owens had planned on forcing their way into the store the instant the manager opened, but they were running too late for this plan. When they arrived, there were already customers in the store, and Jimmy Owens had to control them at gunpoint. The pair got nervous and fled with a small take, only about $200, since the combination-and-key security system was working a bit too well. The manager was not able to call the assistant manager, who was needed to complete the safe's entry code.

As they fled the store, an irate customer followed them to Jimmy Owens's vehicle and gave the license plate number to the police. Within the hour, the cops made their arrest at James's rooming house, 2023 Park Avenue.

Catman Gawron lived around the corner from James, on Mississippi Street, and was supposed to meet him socially later in the morning, after the heist. Catman came around James's place as he was supposed to, but as he walked toward Park Avenue, he heard all kinds of gunshots coming from the direction of James's rooming house. Even though he didn't know what was going down, he wisely decided to get out of there.

The cops had stormed the house, presumably looking for James. Some guy came out of James's room, apparently a government intelligence guy. The cops started shooting at one of these guys. This one man got down and the police started beating him with a billy club and dragging him out, believing he was James. In the meantime, James was actually in the communal bathroom. As he exited the bathroom James saw that the cops were beating this

Intel guy. James raced to his room where he had a couple of guns—he thought at first that this might be some kind of contract being executed.

It is unclear to me what the intelligence operative was doing at the rooming house, and it may be that James didn't know the real reason either. Lyndon Barsten has suggested that maybe the government wanted James out of the way or further discredited, and that the Intel guy was completing an operation to do just this—that James was put up to these robberies by him. Although it sounds outlandish, Lyndon has suggested an alternative possibility: Maybe the government wanted James warehoused, held in a prison for possible use later, since they obviously knew he was a controllable personality. Although this sounds a bit like The X Files at first, there are aspects to the Missouri State Prison that are disturbing to most normal people, and I've learned that anything is possible when it comes to the intelligence agencies of the United States.

James never got to his guns because his bloodied associate flashed some type of official credentials. The police, having realized their mistake, went back into the rooming house. The other guy, the man they had first thought was James, was told to "get going fast." James's associate (or the Intel guy) who took off was supposed to know something, something important. This man is not described in the trial testimony, as his beating was essentially a mistake on the part of a police patrolman and a detective . This man was the reason that James pleaded innocent to the grocery store robberies, because he felt he was a part of an operation, and that he was honestly innocent. Now, nearly fifty years later, I would be stretching the truth to tell more. But at a certain point the number of incidents that reveal the invisible hand of the cult of intelligence and the brutality of Cold War spymasters have to tip the scale enough to make an open-minded reader believe in conspiracy. These robberies were a move that cost my brother several extra years behind bars. When I first picked him up after his 1967 prison escape, he mentioned this mysterious Intel man to me almost immediately.

Catman confirmed to me that James's associate, this Intel guy, was supposed to know something important. James tried hard to find this guy, and actually expected him to come forward to free him or to cut his time, the way that they had in Chicago. James looked for this man through back channels from prison for almost eight years.

Blackie Austin, Jimmy Owens, and James Earl Ray all ended up in prison. My brother James and Jimmy Owens were tried together before judge John C. Casey. Blackie Austin ended up in the Illinois State Pen at Menard, and my brother was imprisoned with Jimmy Owens on the Missouri side of the river, in Jefferson City. Blackie was down in the Crank Gang, short for cranky, the old men down in Cell House B. These were the older people who were washing and peeling potatoes and carrots and the like in the kitchen.

But up above Blackie and the Crank Gang in Gallery One in Menard, there were two or three segregation tiers. I was up above Blackie on the second tier, locked in segregation for twenty months. Sometimes Blackie would holler up to me when the guards weren't watching. Joseph Burnett, who I believe would later play a minor role relating to the King assassination, was also down there; he was a runner in that cell block, which means he carried things for the Crank Gang and retrieved the meals and mail for those who needed them delivered.

Uncle Earl had been down there for a while, as well. Before he got out of the joint, he was a runner for the prison's Catholic chaplain. Earl talked about how the prison's young Catholic priest would take trips down to New Orleans, where nobody knew he was a priest, to attend wild parties there. My cousin Charley Cain was also in the pen with us at this time, and he had also worked with Uncle Earl as a runner for this chaplain.

During one of the chaplain's trips to a party, a group of officials from the prison went into the Catholic chapel and really shook it down, looking for something. When the priest came back he told Earl and Charley: "I'm going to see who has more power in this institution—Warden Randolph or me." The priest must have won, because after this, you couldn't even drag a prison employee into the chapel.

At one point Uncle Earl had a room in the chapel that he rented out to Jimmy "Obie" O'Brien, who taught classes to the inmates on how to boil dynamite and skim off nitroglycerine. Since the prison chapel was no longer monitored, it could be used for a variety of functions, none of which were particularly religious. Within months of his release, one of O'Brien's slower students came back to Menard in a wheelchair, his body covered with skin grafts.

My cousin Charley Cain also had a room in the chapel that he would rent to inmates who wanted to have sex with other inmates. The prison authorities were probably led to believe they were praying. Charley became a pimp in Quincy when he got out. I remember talking to one of his eighteen-year-old prostitutes a few years later, in Ted Crowley's bar. Charley was like Blackie Austin; he was likeable, and he'd do anything for you.

At one point Charley had close to fifty grand in a safety deposit box in Iowa when one of his jealous girls put the feds on him. The feds took his money and pocketed it. They told Charley that if he squealed, he'd "go back in the slammer for tax evasion." They told him the loss of the fifty grand was just a case of "easy come, easy go."

By this time, remember, I had been in the joint for some years. Blackie Austin told me when he came in that he'd seen my uncle Earl up on Fourth and Hampshire in Quincy. Blackie said that after he was released from prison, Uncle Earl had gone up to 240 or 250 pounds; Blackie predicted that Earl would probably die of a heart attack, gaining that kind of weight. Shortly thereafter, my uncle did die of a heart attack, on a bridge in Rochester, New York.

By the way, Jimmy Owens, my brother's second accomplice, was in Menard with me earlier in the '50s, but I didn't know who he was at that time. On January 31, 1960, I had a choice to make: I was twenty-six years old, and I'd spent all of the '50s behind bars, except for the year of 1952. The choice was to take a job that Obie O'Brien had offered with the union, or to be free and wander the world. I chose the latter, but first I had to visit my brother James in the St. Louis jail about an escape plan he was concocting before he was sent down the river to the Missouri State Prison. My record shows that I would always come to the aid of my brother, unless it involved hooking up with the Mob for some long-term contract or relationship.

The next morning I was given a threadbare suit, $10, and a bus ticket to the state line.

four

The Riddle of the Feds and the Bughouse in Fulton

Besides Ray's dope dealing and abuse, the
last contentious issue about his years at Jeff City
is whether or not he was an avowed bigot.

—*Killing the Dream*, Gerald Posner

T he year was 1962. My brother James had languished in the Missouri
State Prison at Jefferson City (known as "Jeff City") for nearly two
years. Across the globe from East to West Berlin, a Cold War spy
exchange straight out of a James Bond flick is commencing while my brother
James is incarcerated in E Hall, in solitary. American U-2 pilot Francis Gary
Powers is being exchanged for Soviet Col. Rudolph Abel.

It is well known that CIA agent Powers was shot down in May of 1960
as he flew a top-secret spy mission over the Soviet Union. His Soviet coun-
terpart had been arrested the year before while trying to set up a spy network
for the Soviets in New York. Both men stand at the edge of the Glienicke
Bridge on Berlin's Havel River. On a signal, the two men stride across the
bridge, Powers to the side then controlled by the Americans, Abel over to the
Communist side. As both men meet in the middle they slightly nod. This is
important to my brother's story because the man handling the spy exchange
for the Americans is Fred T. Wilkinson.

Wilkinson, who is revealed by that story to be a U.S. intelligence–
cleared operative, would turn up in less than two years as the director of the
Missouri State Prison system. Wounded at Iwo Jima in World War II, and a

53

former deputy director of the Federal Bureau of Prisons, are we to believe Wilkinson took the job in Missouri as a career advancement? Along with Wilkinson as director came two other feds: The deputy director was a man named Ward Kern, and the warden of Jeff City was white-haired Harold Swenson from the Federal Bureau of Prisons. Swenson was a well-known federal prison inspector.

Swenson would replace Warden E. V. (Elbert) Nash, who allegedly died by his own hand. Nash was a local patrol sergeant who made a name for himself at Jeff City in 1954 when the Missouri Highway Patrol helped quell one of the worst riots in the nation's history. The official Nash suicide explanation is that Nash, who was on his second marriage, killed himself due to personal reasons involving his daughter. Also, he was under stress from a committee examination of Jeff City (known to inmates as "the Walls"). False suicides are extensively rumored to be one of the classic ways that the intelligence community kills those who have been deemed expendable.

Nash's grandson verifies that the Nash family has always considered the "suicide" of E. V. Nash to be a murder. The gun that killed Warden Nash after his return from a Christmas party was reportedly found in a separate room in the house, well away from the body. Federal officials were called in to "investigate" Nash's death. At family gatherings some members of the family blamed the murder on U.S. intelligence agencies. Nash's sister, who worked as a secretary for the FBI, begged her employers to reinvestigate the death she considered a murder.

Nash's "suicide" was almost immediately followed by the suicide of Jeff City's chief engineer, a man named Wagner. Two "suicides" by guys who were called "tough as nails" was a lot of suicides for a small area in a short period of time. We are not the only ones to connect the dots. When Lyndon Barsten phoned E. V. Nash's grandson and told him that he didn't believe Nash committed suicide, the grandson replied, "Did the CIA or FBI do it—and does it have anything to do with James Earl Ray?" Lyndon wasn't the only one to suspect the "suicide" of Warden Nash was a murder.

While in Jeff City, James was shocked and saddened by the death of our mother in 1961. By this point her liver had walked its last mile. Even on her deathbed she refused to see George. Two years after our mother's death, we lost our grandmother Mary "Mom" Maher in the spring of '63, and that fall was the untimely death of our younger brother, Franklin. Franklin died in an automobile accident when the car his girlfriend was driving careened off the bridge that crossed from Missouri to the Illinois side of the river. Franklin Dennis Ray was one of the younger children that was taken from our mother, because of her drinking, and put in a Catholic shelter in Alton.

My brother James's imprisonment at forty-seven-acre Jeff City was at first rather standard. The prison had initially assigned James to the cleaning plant. He attempted without success to escape the Walls on November 22, 1961. In June of '62 his prison job was changed to the vegetable room, but my brother refused to work there because it was considered the sex offenders' assignment area. He was transferred to the bakery, and worked there until late 1965, when he chose to be a cleaner in J and K halls.

At this time, for a nominal fee, an inmate could request job changes and cell changes, since other inmates were predominantly in charge of these assignments. If a new young convict, attractive to an older inmate, came into the prison, a $10 fee would guarantee the desirable cellmate.

It is from J Hall that James unsuccessfully attempted to escape in March of 1966. His failure mirrored our brother Jerry's failed attempt to escape Jeff City a few years earlier.

James's codefendant, Jimmy Owens, had pleaded guilty back in 1959 to the St. Louis Kroger grocery store robbery, but had been released earlier. Since Owens's criminal record made James look like a choirboy, his early release angered my brother. James was angry and wanted out of the Walls.

His 1966 escape plan went as follows: On movie night, James placed a makeshift dummy in his cell bunk, then pushed a broom around pretending to be cleaning J Hall as usual. He made his way into a rooftop tunnel which connected several buildings. At the end of the tunnel he planned to drop to the street from the administration building. The plan went bad when a gutter came loose, causing James to fall and injure himself. He was met by a gang of guards who took him to the hospital, where he first came face-to-face with the rather newly installed warden, Harold Swenson.

"Put this man in the hole immediately!" Swenson ordered. He also asked for additional time for James, which was rather typical, especially in those days. On April 14, 1966, James was delivered to the magistrate court in Cole County to be arraigned on attempted escape charges. His judge, Sam Blair, appointed a private attorney named Charles Quigley to defend my brother. Quigley decided James should plead insanity.

Since James was in the mood to escape, and since he thought the bughouse, State Hospital #1 in Fulton, would be less secure than the Walls, he went along with Quigley's idea to fake insanity. He thought that this plan might also give him an easy out from the charges against him if the escape plan from Fulton failed.

On Thursday, September 8, James's prison record states: "By order of Circuit Court of Cole County, this inmate has been taken to State Hospital #1, Fulton, Missouri, on an Out-Count." James would spend several weeks in Fulton; he would not be discharged back to the prison until October 21.

Whatever happened in State Hospital #1 in Fulton changed my brother; I had never known him to be so afraid. Another inmate rode along with him on the twenty-five-mile trip to Fulton, and this man was beaten by the guards during their first night in the facility. The next morning, James confessed to a doctor named Peterson that he was going to attempt to fake insanity at his trial in order to evade the charges. Even though he would eventually be found sane, James had to spend forty-four days in the bughouse in Fulton.

We know from James's book, *Tennessee Waltz*, that he was seen by the "Chief Bug Doctor," Dr. Donald B. Peterson, although Peterson's name is not found on any of James's paperwork from the state hospital. Although no libelous information about Peterson is contained in *Tennessee Waltz*, later publishers of the book removed his name. In Donald Peterson's November 1987 obituary in the *Fulton Sun Gazette*, it states that he was a career officer in the army and a psychiatrist, who completed his psychiatric training in Washington, D.C., at St. Elizabeth's Hospital. During the Korean War, Peterson was in charge of psychiatry for the army's Far East command. He was the chief of psychiatry for the U.S. Army at the height of the brainwashing era, 1954–1956, and supposedly left the army to return to his native Minnesota to head the State Psychiatric Hospital in Anoka, where he introduced the MK-Ultra associated drug Thorazine to the hospital. In 1962 Dr. Peterson left Anoka to work as director of State Hospital #1 in Fulton, Missouri. In 1965, while at Fulton, he co-wrote a book on hypnosis with prolific author George A. Ulett, titled *Applied Hypnosis and Positive Suggestion*. Peterson was the first of two army bug doctors Jimmy would see over a period of two years.

According to testimony given by my brother to the House Select Committee on Assassination investigators after the killing of Dr. Martin Luther King Jr., electroshock was used in Fulton, to the point that some prisoners developed bald spots where their hair used to grow. Electroshock was also routinely used in government brainwashing programs at this time. This can be verified by the CIA's release on Dr. Ewen Cameron of the Allen Memorial Institute in Montreal, who used this treatment to change patients' behavior.

Here is an excerpt from a 1957 document, released through the FOIA by the CIA as MORI 234481:

```
    After considerable experimentation, we
have developed a procedure which in the
most successful cases has produced behav-
ioral changes lasting up to two months. The
procedure requires: the breaking down of
ongoing patterns of the patient's behavior
by means of particularly intensive electro-
shocks (depatterning).
```

Dr. Cameron had other means of removing a person's initial personality, noting in a report: "We propose to use LSD 25 and other similar agents as a means of breaking down ongoing patterns of behavior."

Later, in a letter to Warden Swenson from B Basement at Jeff City, James would write about his experience in Fulton:

```
    I am writing you concerning my possible
release from B Basement. I have been here
eight months now, minus six weeks in Fulton.
One of the doctors there told me that I had
probably had a physical and nervous break-
down. I think if I would have had a doctor's
diagnosis when I first started having the
trouble in April of 1965, it's possible I
never would have been in this predicament.
```

James was not the vicious killer he was reported to be in the press; neither was he the type to have a nervous breakdown. He was generally a more stable man than this, even after his release from the army. James later states in a letter found in his prison file that he was "given medicine" that made him feel much better even in segregation or "the hole" (B Basement).

Lyndon Barsten has suggested that the CIA took advantage of my brother's unsuccessful escape attempt, and that they manipulated him into one of the many yet-unidentified brainwashing operations funded by the feds. He was not one to talk about his experiences with bug doctors, but it's a fact that these unusual activities took place. Addressing then Director of Central Intelligence Stansfield Turner in 1977, Senator Edward Kennedy described the CIA's mind control program during the Senate Select Committee on Intelligence Hearing on MK-Ultra:

> "...an activity which took place in the country that involved the perversion and corruption of many of our outstanding research centers in this country, with CIA funds. Where some of our top researchers were unwittingly involved in research sponsored by the Agency in which they had no knowledge of the background or the support for.
>
> "Much of it was done with American citizens who were completely unknowing in terms of taking various drugs, and there are perhaps any number of Americans who are walking around today on the east coast or west coast who were given drugs, with all the kinds of physical and psychological damage that can be caused. We have gone over that in very careful detail, and it is significant and severe indeed."

James described what he saw at Fulton in his autobiography, *Tennessee Waltz* (reworked by the current publishers as *Who Killed Martin Luther King?*):

> When the patients were not undergo-
> ing some type of examination, they were
> required to sit in rocking chairs in a
> large room. The chairs were positioned on
> either side of the room with the backs near
> the wall, so that the patients faced each
> other. Some patients had developed eccen-
> tric mannerisms, possibly from staring at
> one another all day. Many laughed most of
> the time. A non-laugher who didn't watch
> himself could be affected by the lunacy. All
> things considered, though, these patients
> didn't appear to be in any more need of
> therapy than many folks in prison, or on
> the outside.

A prisoner who supposedly sold drugs in prison with Jimmy, James Cooper Green, repeatedly claimed in interviews, "They kept several of the prisoners on Thorazine all the time." FBI documents claim that Green and my brother sold amphetamines together, but this is not true. Although he was an alleged drug dealer, the FBI would hire Green within just a few years; his Memphis FBI file verifies this fact. In the early 1970s, *Freedom* magazine wrote an article assert-ing that a mind control operation was being run in the Missouri prisons.

The following information is contained in my brother's Fulton State Hospital #1 file, dated October 17, and signed by a Dr. Tuttle:

> ". . . he [James] told staff he had
> some sort of a secret which he divulged
> in part to one psychologist, but would not
> reveal to the staff even after prolonged
> and repeated questioning."

I'll bet my brother told Peterson his secret.

Charges against James for the botched escape would eventually be dropped by the court. After his return from the lunacy that he had wit-nessed in Fulton, my brother was told by his lawyer, Quigley, "You don't have to accept the findings of the staff at the State Hospital that you are sane and competent to stand trial. We can petition the court to appoint a psychiatrist of our choice to examine you." A doctor was chosen, but oddly, the examination never came about. Something caused the court to change their mind, and the escape charges were abruptly dropped. It is my belief that someone in a position of power didn't want James examined by an outside psychiatrist.

The prison at Jefferson City had one resident physician, Dr. Hugh Maxey. Hugh Maxey's good friend was a man by the name of John R. Kauffmann. During World War II, Kauffmann had been a U.S. defense contractor, manufacturing gliders for the War Department. But in the 1960s, Kauffmann ran a company called Fix-A-Co, which manufactured a variety of legal drugs, and some illegal ones, including street amphetamines. In 1967 Kauffmann was busted for trafficking speed by the then year-old U.S. Bureau of Drug Abuse Control, the St. Louis office. The drug bust was international, since it included one Chinese citizen. It was Kauffmann's amphetamines that flooded into Jefferson City through a guard, and possibly through his friend, Dr. Hugh Maxey, along with a St. Louis mobster who had been James's cellmate, John Paul Spica. This assertion is not doubted by those who knew Dr. Maxey or Spica, and the relationship is even documented by the feds.

Wrongly convicted murderer Spica, called Sonny by his friends, was amazingly allowed out of the prison on weekends as early as 1966, and he hung out with Dr. Maxey and Kauffmann at Kauffmann's motel on the outskirts of St. Louis. It was almost certainly Spica who was in the pocket of the prison authorities and the syndicate who convinced James that there was a major deal waiting for him if he escaped.

In the late 1970s, the drug deal would be described as follows by the House Select Committee on Assassinations (HSCA):

> ```
> Testimony given at Kauffmann's nar-
> cotics trial reveals a link between his
> illegal drug operation and the Missouri
> State Penitentiary where James Earl Ray
> was incarcerated until his escape in April
> of 1967. . . .
> ```

During an interview with the committee, one of Kauffmann's codefendants disclosed that Kauffmann had arranged for an additional delivery to the Missouri State Penitentiary on the day of his arrest.

In addition, the HSCA received allegations that Maxey was involved with Kauffmann in the distribution of amphetamines in the prison. James himself wrote the following about the large amount of amphetamines floating around the prison: "After two or three days on speed, the user sometimes starts hallucinating or becomes paranoid. It wasn't unusual to be awakened in the early morning hours by a prisoner screaming his lungs out on amphetamines. In response the guards would drag the freak-out to the fifth-floor hospital, the floor referred to as the 'bug-ward.'"

Aside from the drugs flowing into Jeff City through nonofficial channels, there was also an official flow of experimental drugs of the psychological kind. This is James's description from his manuscript for *Tennessee Waltz*, concerning Hugh Maxey's open and stocked drug cabinet: "The main task of the technicians, it seems, was prescribing tranquilizing goofballs for every type of complaint. Often the goofballs were experimental drugs supplied to the prison free by pharmaceutical firms."

Not only were inmates used for drug experimentation, but Maxey also involved them in other medical experiments. In January of 1964, six inmates went public with the story that fifty inmates had allowed a substance, supposedly dye, to be injected into their spines the previous fall. The experiment had been conducted by Dr. Earl P. Holt of St. Louis. Inmates were given sixty days "good time" for allowing themselves to be experimented on.

The irregularities at Jeff City are obvious:

1. Federal operatives were put in place within the Missouri prison system over the bodies of two dead men, Warden E. V. Nash and Chief Engineer Wagner.

2. The prison system was fearful of James being examined by an outside psychiatrist.

3. Sonny Spica was allowed to walk out of the Walls on weekends.

Although I can't prove it, surely you can see why I have to ask: Was my brother being prepared for an escape by these feds, who climbed into their positions over the bodies of Nash and Wagner? Given what is known and documented about their environment at that time, it is a more than fair question.

In the late 1970s, a former inmate came forward and signed an affidavit which he sent in the mail for James, who was then imprisoned in Tennessee. The former inmate was Gene Barnes, a St. Louis native. After James's ultimately successful escape in 1967, Gene Barnes became a trustee and confidant to then warden Donald Wyrick, who had replaced Swenson. Wyrick informed Barnes that he (Wyrick), Wilkinson, and Swenson had allowed James to escape in 1967 so that the feds could later use him as the fall guy in the King homicide. The same information was given to the House Select Committee on Assassinations, which would "investigate" the King murder in the late 1970s.

Although James was considered perfectly sane just months before by the doctors at Fulton, his examination for possible parole by the late Dr. Henry V. Guhleman Jr., in November of 1966 produced a different result. Dr. Guhleman's report described a man with serious psychological problems, and it's likely that this report kept James a prisoner at Jeff City until his successful '67 escape—the one that was indirectly encouraged by the feds. There is no more vulnerable patsy or fall guy than an escaped prisoner, because no matter what, he cannot go to the police or any official source for assistance. Guhleman's description of James was downright silly: ". . . he describes a feeling of fear which can be alleviated if he takes a glass of water which he is drinking and sets it on the table and moving [sic] it back and forth several times."

Guhleman described James as "severely neurotic," and noted that doctors at Fulton had prescribed the drug Librium for James. Librium is listed in government documents as one of the drugs used to strengthen narco-hypnosis.

James Cooper Green, the federal operative who was in prison with Jimmy, complained that he couldn't remember a period of about two weeks during his time in the Missouri prison system. Green's prison medical file verifies this odd amnesia. He is now deceased, but Green frequently verified to participants at conferences and in interviews the odd situation of drugs flowing like water within the Missouri State Prison.

Just before his final successful escape from the Walls in 1967, James was conveniently returned to his bakery job, where another inmate was about to hand him a plan for escape from a bakery truck. Just months before his 1967 escape, another prisoner had successfully escaped, George Ben "Benny" Edmondson, who was in the Walls for armed robbery. This is coincidental in that very few convicts had ever tried to escape from the Walls. After his escape, Benny Edmondson trotted up to Chicago, then Montreal. Oddly, James was also sent to Chicago, then Montreal, a city which was Canada's hotbed of both Mob and intelligence activity. Edmondson was listed as an FBI top-ten fugitive, and was eventually captured on June 29, 1967, and returned to Jeff City, where he almost immediately was released on bond. Edmondson would then be allowed to leave the country, returning to Montreal to get married to a woman named Jinette, and to live under the alias "Alex Bormann."

A newly released document from the National Archives, which now controls the FBI file on the assassination of Dr. King, reveals that in August of 1970, Benny Edmondson was living under the Bormann alias in the eastern United States, and even felt comfortable going to the FBI to complain about the publication of William Bradford Huie's book, *He Slew the Dreamer*, because it revealed his alias.

Although I have no personal knowledge of James being talked into escaping from the Walls, James did write that he was talked into it by another inmate: "A fellow prisoner outlined an escape plan from there," James wrote in his book, *Tennessee Waltz*, referring to the bakery.

According to another inmate, J. J. Maloney, who became a reporter for the *Kansas City Star*, James was convinced to escape by inmate Ronnie Westberg. Westberg was generally known as a "crazy son-of-a-bitch" with a terrible reputation among the prison guards. It was Westberg who discovered that the large box that held bread—baked in the Jefferson City prison and delivered to two other locations, Renz and Church farms—was not examined closely as it left the prison.

Ronnie told James that he (Ronnie) was "too high-profile" to escape, but that James could get away by hiding in the bread box. Did someone in the prison management order Westberg to convince James to escape? Westberg is no longer around to be asked about it. He, too, "committed suicide" in his solitary-confinement cell in Jeff City, at the same time that Fred T. Wilkinson was retiring from the Missouri State Prison. Westberg hung himself. A couple of inmates told me in 1971 that Westberg had broken arms and broken legs at the time of his "suicide." Reportedly, the prisoners at Jeff City were making jokes about this: "Ronnie was so tough he even broke his own arms and legs before he hung himself."

Except for an inmate named Raymond Curtis (described by the FBI as having the mind of a child), who was trying to sell a story, all of the inmates James served with Jimmy at Jeff City said that my brother was surely innocent of the King homicide. While this is not proof that James had no involvement in the assassination, one must understand that inmates in close confinement get to know one another very well. Even if an inmate never talks, their general way of being—such as their propensity toward violence, quickness to react if provoked, tendency to either let go of anger or to store it and seek revenge—all of this is revealed by their behavior in prison. These other inmates had nothing to gain by faking their opinions. They were just speaking about another man's fundamental nature, as they saw it demonstrated, under the stresses of close confinement and over a long period of time.

On April 23, 1968, the *St. Louis Globe-Democrat* interviewed several of James's fellow inmates. "He didn't seem like the kind of guy that would kill anybody," said one man. Another inmate added, "They're just trying to pin it on him because he escaped from here. They think they've got to lay it on somebody, so they're trying to lay it on him." Another man claimed, "Nobody thinks it's him [Ray]."

The inmates were right.

In recent years investigator Lyndon Barsten phoned an eighty-something-year-old terminally ill Dr. Henry Guhleman in Jefferson City to ask him about the ridiculous report he wrote about James for the review board. He also wanted to inquire about a government behavior modification program at Jefferson City (or Fulton) in the 1960s.

The first time that Lyndon phoned him, Guhleman couldn't speak for long. The second time Lyndon called, Guhleman surprised him by actually bringing up the report. Lyndon had not mentioned James by name, but had only questioned Guhleman about behavior modification programs in the Missouri prison system and state hospitals. After much prodding, he got this out of Guhleman: "Well, ah, way back there they used to put these men on the fifth floor [mental ward of the Jeff City prison hospital] and leave them there, and the people from Fulton would come over and look at them and decide, 'Well, I'll take this one, and we'll take him over to Fulton, but, this one I won't.' And that's the way they did it then."

When asked, "Was this for therapy or work?", Guhleman chuckled and responded, "Well, presumably for therapy."

five

The Mole Flies the Coop

No real criminal organization conspired with Ray—the Mafia simply does not use small-time losers as hit men. Neither, by all odds, did any racist group like the Ku Klux Klan—which must now regard outsiders as stool pigeons of the FBI.

—"Ray, Sirhan—What Possessed Them?", *LIFE* magazine, June 21, 1968

It is difficult, so many years after the death of Dr. King, for many young people to understand that King was considered a threat to national security. But he was. His security file at the FBI was a file classification 100, meaning "National or Domestic Security issue." The vocal disagreements between Dr. King and the FBI had been in the news for three years before James escaped from Jefferson City. Dr. King had criticized the FBI in public for having been slow or inadequate in their investigation of crimes against black people, especially in the South. In 1964, FBI director J. Edgar Hoover, in retaliation, called King a "notorious liar" before two dozen reporters who scrambled to phone in the story.

King and his top lieutenants from the Southern Christian Leadership Conference (SCLC) met Hoover shortly after the "notorious liar" comment. Their relationship, while pleasant enough when face-to-face, broke down quickly, because nearly everything Dr. King said in a hotel or on a phone was recorded for Hoover's review. Much of the electronic surveillance from the SCLC wasn't flattering to Hoover's gigantic ego. Also, much of King's philosophy was considered "Communist" by Richard Helms at the CIA and the Joint Chiefs in the Pentagon, who all shared reports.

Contrary to how highly he is regarded today, in the 1960s Dr. King was controversial, especially to the conservatives and military types. This was true even before his criticism of the Vietnam War and his disagreements with Lyndon B. Johnson. Many of King's associates, including Stanley Levison, Hunter Pitts O'Dell, and Bayard Rustin, had actually been members of the Communist party. During the 1950s and '60s, Communists were feared the way terrorists are feared today. In the North and South from Siren, Wisconsin, to Baton Rouge, Louisiana, you would hear it said again and again, especially from whites: Martin Luther King was on the Commie payroll.

Even NAACP executive secretary Roy Wilkins was really in the FBI's camp at this time. Portions of Wilkins's FBI file that were released to my brother show a man who met frequently with Cartha DeLoach, who was then the number-three man at the FBI. Most of Wilkins's FBI material is still classified, and the released portions explain why. For example:

```
    Wilkins told me that he would be lec-
turing in California most of next week. He
stated that before he leaves for the coast
he will attempt to see King, along with other
Negro leaders, and tell King he can't possi-
bly win a battle with the FBI [redacted]. He
stated that he may not have any success in
this regard; however, he is convinced that
the FBI can ruin King overnight [redacted].
I told Wilkins this of course is up to him;
however, I wanted to reiterate once again
most strongly, that if King wanted war, we
were prepared to give it to him, and let the
chips fall where they may.
    —Roy Wilkins FBI HQ File, meeting with
Cartha D. DeLoach, November 27, 1964
```

In 1965 the FBI tried to get Dr. King to kill himself before he accepted his Nobel Peace Prize. They sent a blackmail tape of him, supposedly

cheating on Coretta Scott King in a hotel, to the SCLC offices. The note
with the tape recommended that King commit suicide before he collected
his Nobel Peace Prize. The meaning on the note was obvious:

```
"King, there is only one thing left for
you to do. You know what it is. You have
just 34 days in which to do (this exact num-
ber has been selected for a specific reason,
it has definite practical significant. You are
done. There is but one way out for you. You
better take it before your filthy fraudulent
self is bared to the nation."
```

Mrs. King would later claim that the tape was of such poor quality she
couldn't hear anything on it.

As the war in Vietnam continued to require more resources in South-
east Asia to be sent and more coffins brought stateside, Dr. King became
ever increasingly critical of the war. By March of 1966, Dr. King was publicly calling the Vietnam War a "social evil" and stating that the United
States had taken "a stand against people seeking self-determination." In the
Pentagon, National Security Agency (NSA), and CIA, these were fighting
words. The demonstrations at home were slowly beginning to dismantle the
Vietnam War, and the most effective spokesman of the antiwar movement,
Dr. King, was to live for only a few more months. I firmly believe that the
gears in the machine to take down Dr. King began to turn rapidly at this
time, and James—groomed by the army and the CIA as a patsy—was about
to be manipulated into the kill zone.

James escaped from prison on April 23, 1967. Nineteen days before,
on April 4, exactly one year before his death, Dr. King came out swinging
against the government's Vietnam policy at Riverside Church in New York.
The speech, "Beyond Vietnam," told a truth about war, a truth I was raised
to believe:

```
They watch as we poison their water, as
we kill a million acres of their crops. They
```

must weep as the bulldozers roar through
areas preparing to destroy their precious
trees. They wander into the hospitals,
with at least twenty casualties from American firepower for one "Vietcong"-inflicted
injury. So far we have killed a million of
them—mostly children. They wander into the
towns and see thousands of the children,
homeless, without clothes, running in packs
on the streets like animals. They see the
children, degraded by our soldiers as they
beg for food. They see the children selling
their sisters to our soldiers, soliciting
for their mothers.

"That goddamn nigger preacher's gonna cost me the White House," President Johnson said privately, according to the late Dr. Phil Melanson, University of Massachusetts Chancellor Professor of Policy Studies, author of *The Murkin Conspiracy*. Dr. King's early and strongly negative reaction to the war helped end LBJ's political career. Johnson didn't even bother to run for president in 1968. The opposition to the Vietnam War was growing stronger, and the government considered King the ringleader of the movement. The antiwar candidate in 1968, Robert Kennedy, would die in a similar way to Dr. King, just two months after MLK, shot in the back of the head by Sirhan B. Sirhan (who was actually standing in front of him at the time).

If James was convinced (indirectly) to escape from Jefferson City by the government, I was not told about it. But consider this: James had tried unsuccessfully to escape from prison several times, including the year before, in 1966. He was terrified of being put back in the bughouse, State Hospital #1 in Fulton. So why, just weeks before his chance to sit in front of the parole board, would he try to escape again? Unless someone could more or less guarantee that he would make it out of the Walls, there was no reason for him to attempt escape once again.

Did the guards assist James's escape this time? The guards were unfairly low-paid employees, as they still are today in many prisons. This is one of the reasons prisons are so corrupt.

The Sunday my brother escaped from prison in Jeff City, I was living on the north side of St. Louis in a three-room apartment on the second floor. I lived upstairs from my nearly toothless landlord, Clarence Haynes; his wife, Diana; and their newborn baby. Clarence was fifty-four, twenty years my senior, and Diana was a severely retarded teenager. Also living with Clarence at the time was his four-hundred-pound girlfriend, Ruby, who was married to someone else and had a six-year-old son named Johnny who lived with them. I had lived there for several months, and I usually used the phone downstairs, since I didn't have one in my own apartment.

I was waiting to go back to work, but being a union bartender, it was mostly seasonal work, golf courses and the like. I had worked all over the United States, from New York to California. During the summertime I mostly worked in Chicago. Just by chance I was in Dallas–Fort Worth when JFK was shot in '63 and in New York when Malcolm X was shot in '65.

When I communicated via mail with my brother James in the state prison at Jefferson City, I used my landlord Clarence Haynes's address. It was at this address in January that I received an encoded letter from James that said, "I will come out through the front gate through normal channels." If James underlined his name twice, the real message would be found by reading every seventh word, starting with the first word rather than the full text of the letter. Some of the mail I'd get from James would come from other prison inmates who had been released, and the envelopes would have a stamp cancellation from another place. This is when I'd know the message was more serious.

I received a short message from James which included the date of a possible escape, April 23. So I drove to Jefferson City to see him on the day before. I had a visitor's pass which said "Jerry or John Ray," so nobody actually knew which one of us was visiting James at Jefferson City. I have no idea why the prison did it this way, but anyone could use your visitor's pass. I had loaned my visitor's pass to a couple of people, including a friend of ours, James Drake. The way prison visits worked was if Jerry and I wanted to go in at the same time to see James, I would have to photocopy the pass and send one to Jerry in Chicago.

I took Catman Gawron down there to Jefferson City in case we needed some type of help. I was assuming James wasn't going to make it out, since he had attempted to escape before, to no avail. I didn't know that this time the prison authorities seem to be in league with the plotters of the assassination.

When we got to Jefferson City, I dropped Catman off at a tavern, since he said he didn't want to know anything about the escape that he didn't have to.

On Saturday, April 22, I went in to see James. He said he'd be out the next morning, and that he had help. James was reasonably certain of his escape being successful this time; this was before the great age of the prison stool pigeon. James explained to me that he was going to be hidden in a large bread box in a truck used to deliver bread to a nearby facility. He knew how many stop signs he would hit and where he would jump out before the truck picked up speed.

"I'll jump off at the stop sign in Jefferson City, but if I can't make it out of the box right away, I'll be under the bridge that crosses the Missouri River a few miles upriver," he told me. We certainly weren't going to drive onto federal property and be arrested. I agreed to pick James up if he made it, but I was still doubtful he would. Most of the time you can't escape prison, and if caught trying, you are punished pretty severely. I told him I would have Catman with me, who was his old crime partner from eight years earlier.

I left the prison and met Catman in the tavern, and told him what was going on. He was reluctant to get involved, and there was some talk about his taking a bus or a train back to St. Louis, but in the end, he decided to stay with me.

The next morning, I was ready to pick James up at one of the spots he had described, with a hot license plate on the car that I had gotten from Clarence Haynes (who always had them and always needed a buck or two). But James wasn't at the stop sign, or under the bridge. Catman and I saw some red lights in front of us, and as we got closer, we could see that it was a police car. We assumed James hadn't made it. I made a U-turn to avoid the police, and when Catman looked back, he said he thought he saw someone on the highway. We didn't know if it was a guy working on the highway or what, but to make sure we didn't leave James in the woods, we drove up a dirt road following the river. We still didn't see anyone.

James had said he would be "under the bridge," but I didn't know what bridge he was talking about. Catman and I looked all around the bridge we thought it might be, and didn't see anyone. We drove up this dirt road, then drove over near Columbia University. It was getting near nightfall, so we stopped to get something to eat. We parked near the University of Missouri, listening to the radio for any All Points Bulletin (APB) about a convict escape from Jefferson City. There was nothing. I decided the best thing to do was go back to St. Louis, to my place above Clarence Haynes. I didn't want to go near the prison and create a problem.

The next day, or perhaps the day after, I got a call at Clarence Haynes's place from James. I wasn't there, but he left a message giving specific directions for me to pick him up near the town of New Franklin. I went down there and met up with him in a tavern. He was limping from having jumped out of the speeding bread truck, but he was in one piece. He climbed into my car and we headed back to St. Louis. I gave him my picture ID and social security card in one of my legal names, John Larry Raynes, 318-24-7098; this was the social security number from my paper route in Galesburg, Illinois, when I was eleven.

We didn't know it until later, but the fingerprints the prison sent out after James's escape weren't his; they had been switched by Wilkinson and Swenson with another man's prints. If Jimmy had been captured, the police would have had to set him free, since the prints would not have matched up. This is not just my theory; I've heard stories through the criminal grapevine that this escape was orchestrated by Richard Helms and the CIA and their agents, such as Wilkinson, who ran the prison.

After James escaped, I took him to Joe Burnett's hangout in an attempt to put some money in his pocket. Burnett was an old friend, and would know how and where James could get some money. While they were talking I remained in the background, out of earshot, but I know that Joe Burnett sent my brother to see Obie O'Brien.

James asked me, "Do you know where Obie is at?"

I answered, "He's across the river on the East Side, at Buster Wortman's."

At this time Jimmy "Obie" O'Brien was running a gambling operation for Buster Wortman next to the Paddock Lounge and Restaurant in East St. Louis, which Wortman owned. On this particular evening, however, Obie was parking cars for the Paddock. There was a lot next to the Paddock, and next to that there was a two- or three-story building, known as a type of safe house. We spoke with Obie in the parking lot.

"Do you know of anything that could put a little money in Jimmy's pocket?" I asked him. O'Brien said that he would "check with Buster about things," including a possible diamond heist that was supposed to be going down. "I've got a couple of rooms above the card games. Why don't you take one of them until I get some details?" Obie said. James agreed, believing that O'Brien might be able to get him some work.

Over time, O'Brien started talking to my brother James about opportunities in these diamond heists. I wouldn't get involved with the Chicago outfit—the mob that controlled Wortman, so I refused to join in the conversation at all. James wanted to stay there in Wortman's safe house, with these card games on the first floor. My brother didn't really know these people, so I stayed there with him on the second floor in order to make him as comfortable as possible. He was happy to be out of Missouri, and the room was free. That night we went out to a tavern up the street, the Miami Lounge, and talked through much of the night.

Anytime I stay overnight in an unfamiliar place, I always prop a chair against the door, and I did this that night in the safe house. I even do it in my own home. I slept on the floor, since I like sleeping on the floor anyway, and James slept in the bed. That night someone twisted the doorknob of our room and gently twisted a key inside the lock, which could have been an innocent mistake, but James heard it too. It happened two or three more times during the night. We were both leery about this, so we decided to leave the safe house the next morning.

It was at this time that Obie got James a gun, a .38. James would later claim, once Catman was dead, that Catman had gotten him this pistol, but Catman was afraid of guns. He hated guns even before he went to fight in World War I in Europe, but what happened after he saw battle turned Catman fully against them.

After leaving the safe house, James and I took a Greyhound bus to Chicago to meet our brother Jerry, who was working near there. A couple of times James said, "I think I'm going to end up on the FBI's Most Wanted list." At that time, this list was broadcast each week on *The FBI* television show. I couldn't help but wonder where he was coming from. This was a nickel-and-dime escape, of the type that happens all over the United States on a rather frequent basis, since the United States has a lot of people in prison. In retrospect, James may have been thinking down the line a bit, or perhaps he just had some particular insight when he made the comment. Just over a year later, he would top the list.

Once James and I arrived in Chicago, we met our brother Jerry and we all had drinks at the Round-up Tavern by the Greyhound depot and the 808 Lounge on South State Street. Jerry's day off was Thursday, and we were all together by Thursday of that week. By the end of the month, James had a place to stay in Chicago. Since Jerry was already working at a country club near Chicago, James was going to take any job he could get there until this diamond deal was pulled together. I got a job at a restaurant called Bamberger's, on the near northwest side of Chicago.

James also applied for work at a restaurant, and on May 3, he would get the job. My brother, the supposed ultra-racist, started work washing dishes at the Indian Trails Restaurant in their very integrated kitchen, where nearly thirty African-Americans worked. The Indian Trails Restaurant was in the wealthy Chicago suburb of Winnetka. No matter what any fed operative might try to tell you about James having piles of money from the sale of drugs in Jeff City, it's not true. He never would have gone for that dishwashing job if he'd had a fat wallet at the time. Within days of his employment, the owners of the restaurant gave him a better job.

The Klingmans, owners of the thirty-five-year-old Indian Trails Restaurant, noticed that although James received no personal phone calls in May, toward the end of June, calls started to come in for him. By the third week in June, the Klingmans witnessed the appearance of a mysterious man at the restaurant. Immediately after that, on June 24, James quit. According to an FBI report, author William Bradford Huie would eventually tell the Klingmans that the mysterious stranger in their restaurant was the start of the plot to kill Martin Luther King Jr. The FBI interview with the Klingmans recorded in their Chicago testimony (serial or document 44-1114-37) verifies that Huie knew from his investigation it was a plot that killed MLK, as Huie tells the Klingmans, "The actual murderer of King was not Ray . . ." But Huie would change his tune before he published his book on the case.

When James left the Indian Trails Restaurant on June 25, he told them he had accepted a job on a boat, and he had his last paycheck sent to Jerry. No fugitive from the law is this brazen unless he feels the feds are on his side.

While James was in Chicago, he had kept in touch with Obie O'Brien in East St. Louis. James was waiting to hear more about the diamond deal they had discussed at Buster Wortman's. After the assassination of Martin Luther King, Obie O'Brien would go missing.

Common sense dictates that if James were determined to kill Dr. King, he would have gotten to it right after his escape from prison. Dr. King's home address was generally known. The church he preached at was well known. Why would James take so much of a chance traveling around the country when he was an escaped convict? Why would an escaped con wait from April 23, 1967, to April 4, 1968, to kill King, when each day was another opportunity for him to get caught? The government's case doesn't make any sense. Perhaps the feds were waiting for the one-year mark from Dr. King's "Beyond Vietnam" speech to send a message to the dissidents.

In July of 1967, James's job came through with the diamond deal. He was summoned by Obie of the Buster Wortman outfit to come later that month to East St. Louis. He would first spend some time in Illinois with our family in Quincy and St. Louis before eventually heading to Canada for the job. He saw our sister Melba in Quincy, and our sister Carol in St. Louis, then went on to the farm in Center, Missouri, to see our dad. It was also his intention to visit our aunt, Mrs. Frank Fuller, in Quincy.

James hung out in the Quincy area for just under two weeks. He stayed in two hotels, both located on Oak Street. It was at this time that the Bank of Alton was held up by masked gunmen. In an effort to explain where James got all his money in 1967 and '68, the blame for the Bank of Alton heist was placed squarely on the shoulders of the Ray brothers—James and me. This occurred a decade later when the House Select Committee on Assassinations, created to investigate the murders of JFK and MLK, issued their report. There was no truth to the bank robbery accusation. Nonetheless, the committee wrote the following:

> The Alton bank was held up by two masked
> gunmen at approximately 1:30 p.m. on July
> 13, 1967. One was described as a middle-
> aged white male, 5 feet 10 inches tall, 150
> to 160 pounds; the other, a middle-aged

white male, 5 feet 8 inches, 170 to 180
pounds. One was armed with a handgun, the
other with a shotgun; both wore stocking
masks and hats. Once inside the bank, the
one with the shotgun stood guard, while
the other collected $27,230 from behind
the teller's counter. The two men then left
the bank and walked westward to a nearby
church parking lot. No further direct evidence was developed in the FBI's investigation of the robbery or in this committee's
reexamination of the crime bearing on the
manner, or the direction, of the robbers'
flight from the immediate vicinity of the
bank. At the time of the committee's investigation, none of the stolen money had
been recovered.

The committee first examined eyewitness
and physical evidence bearing on the robbery. Because the bank robbers wore stocking masks, eyewitness descriptions were
imprecise. Nevertheless, none of those
that were given would eliminate the Ray
brothers as suspects. Moreover, the facts
developed in the FBI's investigation—in
particular, the apparent route of flight
taken after the crime and the location of
discarded evidence—provided some evidence
of the involvement of James Earl Ray.

The local police did not consider us suspects and neither did the FBI,
until it became necessary to explain the source of James's funds.

While in Quincy, James saw Ted Crowley, owner of the Gem Tavern
and the local Mob boss. James was being directed toward Memphis, though
he would not know it for nine months. I cannot say for sure that Crowley
was knowingly in on it, though he was one of the local crime bosses downriver that answered to the Chicago Mob which has ties to the CIA. After

this Quincy period, James returned to the Chicago area to pick up his last Indian Trails Restaurant paycheck from Jerry. James's salary had been raised rather dramatically. He was paid weekly, and his first paycheck on May 7 was $57.69; his last full check issued on June 18 was $95.19, so his salary had nearly doubled in that short period of time. James's last check that was sent to Jerry was for a partial week's work. In the short time James worked in the suburban Chicago restaurant, he had moved up from dishwasher to cook. He was an excellent worker, liked by all, including the black men in the ethnically diverse kitchen.

After picking up his check, James returned south to East St. Louis, Illinois, where he had been summoned by the Mafia to learn more about the diamond heist. On the way to East St. Louis, James developed car trouble with an old '59 Chrysler that he had bought while working in the restaurant. He stayed a night in East St. Louis, where he received his funds from the Mob through the Buster Wortman outfit—the funds that both he and the government would later lie about. Obie O'Brien handed the money to my brother. James was aware that the large amount of money he received was really from the Chicago syndicate and not their local representatives downriver. The money was given to him to do a job in Canada (even though he did not commit any crimes in Canada to the best of my knowledge).

The next day, Friday, July 14, 1967, he sold the Chrysler to a service station operator for approximately $45. On July 15, he purchased a red '62 Plymouth for $200 at Bundy Olds in East St. Louis. The newer Plymouth was purchased under my name (or one of its variations), John L. Rayns.

I think the feds and his former army "buddies," who were with him when he joined the CIA, set him up by turning him on to this diamond heist. Then, the diamond job suddenly disappeared, and they said, "Come on—we've got bigger things going on." James's job changed to gunrunning in the southern United States and they used this gunrunning and also the transportation of drugs to set him up with a rifle. Privately, he'd often show his anger about these army buddies who had settled in Chicago. They knew he had a predictable psychology, and this was something he said himself—that he was chosen because of his psychological makeup. There was a uniform dislike of Martin Luther King Jr., at that time among the higher-ups in the military and intelligence agencies, and they certainly wouldn't hesitate to sacrifice James to achieve their goal. What was supposed to have been a diamond deal ended up, in reality, being the murder of Martin Luther King Jr.

Once you become involved in the Mafia's operations and they pay you, you are indebted to them for life; you don't really have any choice. If you don't go along with everything the Mob asks you to do, you'll get killed yourself. James was caught up with the Mafia and the feds. He never should have gotten involved with them. I never crossed over to that side of the fence. I certainly had my chances, but I didn't trust either of them—the Mob or the feds. Probably if I had gotten involved with them, somebody would have blown my head off. When you go into the snake pit, your likelihood of getting bitten increases.

Sam Giancana, interim Chicago Mob boss from the time just before James's prison escape, called the CIA and the Chicago outfit "two sides of the same coin." The CIA—and to a lesser degree, the FBI—used the Mob for clandestine operations so that they could maintain plausible deniability if the operation went wrong. There had been a deal for years that the Mob would leave the families of the FBI guys alone if the syndicate was left alone. If the feds arrested anyone in the Mafia, it was the equivalent of dropping a dime in a phone booth. The Mafia, when they want to get rid of one of their own but would prefer not to kill him, set the person up for the state or federal authorities to arrest. The famous Roger Touhy case was an example of the rackets bosses "dropping a dime." Highly decorated Chicago police detective Frank Pape, who died recently, killed a lot of criminals at the request of the Mafia.

John Paul "Sonny" Spica may have had connections with the framing of James and the murder of King. James had been a cellmate of Sonny Spica's when he worked in the Jeff City hospital. James would later write about Spica: "He was said to have heavy Mob connections." Spica also had connections with Joe Burnett, who had connections with Obie, who was tight with the Chicago outfit's man in Central Illinois, Buster Wortman. Although my brother had connections with all of these men, the House Select Committee on Assassinations that investigated the King murder in the late 1970s would only call John Paul Spica to testify. Spica walked into his closed-door testimony with a newspaper over his head. He would not cooperate with the committee or their investigator in the St. Louis area, Conrad "Pete" Baetz.

Spica's Cadillac was eventually blown sky-high in suburban St. Louis on November 9, 1979. Maybe the government was behind the explosion, maybe not, but Spica died only about seven months after the committee had issued its final report, and shortly after meeting with our brother, Jerry. Spica met with Jerry at James's request in 1979 and told Jerry that he had secretly recorded former intelligence officer and committee investigator Pete Baetz. On the tape, according to Sonny, Baetz tells Sonny how he should testify before the committee, and also makes comments relating to Sonny's parole status. If such a tape existed, it would have made Sonny Spica a threat to the committee.

There is reason to believe the FBI was interested in this diamond deal. A few months after James became involved with the Mob, in late '67 and early '68, a guy by the name of Earl Sattlefield was released after having served time in Missouri State Prison with James. Every now and again he'd come around a tavern I owned with money from James, and he would try to get me involved as a getaway driver in some heist. Sattlefield always had a diamond heist of one kind or another going on, and this sounded much like what my brother James was involved in. Four years later, Sattlefield would be one of the main witnesses used by corrupt elements within the FBI to testify against me in a dummied-up case that would put me behind bars for a quarter of a century.

So why is this guy coming around talking about diamond heists that sound like James's operation? And why was he saying that he was under some kind of protection, as if I were going to kill him?

The purpose of Sattlefield's activities are unknown to me, but logic would tell me he is performing some function for some branch of the federal government. Perhaps he was trying to implicate me in the diamond operation to imprison me at the right time.

Two years after the assassination of MLK, while I was in jail, there was a guy known as "the flying bank robber." This guy would fly all over the United States, robbing banks, and he had a very big reputation. They put him in the jail where I was serving time, in St. Charles, Missouri. The federal marshals told me that he was an FBI snitch, so I should keep my eye on him. The famous robber had come in from federal prison, and he was involved in diamond heists, just like James was supposed to be. The marshals told me that he had a microphone and a radio in there with him that he really wasn't supposed to have. I started talking to him anyway, and every time I told him that I was going to be out on bail, he started packing his stuff up like he was getting out too. And then when I told him that my bail had fallen through, he'd unpack his stuff and say the Federal Bureau of Prisons told him he'd have to stay longer.

This incident, which took place well after James ended up in Shelby County Jail after the murder of MLK, made me think that the FBI was well aware of the diamond heists James was involved with, as this guy was obviously doing the FBI's work for them. He seemed to be talking about diamond deals just to get a response out of me. I believe certain individuals within the FBI were in on the assassination of King, and they hushed up this diamond deal because it might have also involved other federal agencies and the Accardo Mob, called the outfit in Chicago, and their subordinate rackets bosses downriver.

Let the record show that I have no specific information about the CIA, James's handlers, military intelligence, or the FBI. I'll just lump them together and call them the feds. This is also the term that my brother James used, because I don't think he knew specifically who he was dealing with most of the time. The most famous operative in this case is the man known internationally as "Raul" or "Raoul." James usually spelled this shadowy character's name Raoul, although he never saw his handler write it; however, when James's lawyer, Bill Pepper, and his investigators discovered the real Raul some time later, it was confirmed that he spelled his name without the "o." In 1968, when James contacted Art Hanes in Birmingham to be his lawyer, he knew that the feds were behind Hanes. They are all connected; they go to the same clubs, and they share documents. Most of them are moved into positions like U.S. attorney, state's attorney, or other positions of power. So when he got Hanes as a lawyer, as he had been told to, he must have known what the possibilities were. And William Bradford Huie, who wrote the government-line book, *He Slew the Dreamer*, had been in bed with the FBI for years. It was Hoover that said, "Once FBI, always FBI." I didn't know what the world was really like back then, but James did—he should have known what could have happened.

At the time, in 1968, I didn't know about these connections between organized crime and the feds, especially in Chicago. The only thing I knew about was James's connection to the syndicate. It wasn't until his answering my final questions on the case for me, years later, when we were housed together at the time of his 1974 evidentiary hearing, that I learned about his simultaneous ties to the feds and the Mafia.

I know for a fact that in 1967 and '68, James was convinced that he was getting in on a diamond heist. I don't know if the Mob and the feds changed their minds and decided to frame their associate, or if it was all figured out beforehand. But James was not involved with the Mob for the purpose of being a willing participant in the murder of King. He would have been scared and mystified and in the dark as to who was pulling his strings and where the puppet masters would take him.

six

Tricked into the Kill Zone

> Ray angrily denied it. "I've lived among col-
> oreds all my life," he said. "I don't have anything
> against them. It depends on the person. There's
> a lot of whites I don't like—it has nothing to do
> with color."
>
> —*An American Death*, Gerold Frank

After getting his money in East St. Louis, James started his trip to Canada, supposedly to do this diamond heist job that would never materialize. He stopped in Chicago again on the way because there was someone there he was supposed to meet, later in Canada. Presumably this was his handler, Raul. The meeting of Raul C. in Canada was not a chance meeting, as he would later state. He had to make that claim, since it would have been fatal to cross the Chicago Mafia.

I honestly don't know if James even counted his money from Obie before he gave me a portion of it, $25,000, as a gift. Of course, today, that's equal to more than three or four times that amount. My belief is he got about $50,000 in large bills from Obie. With that money I would be able to purchase a tavern, which would eventually be the Grapevine, along with a moving truck, which I planned to use in a new business venture with Clarence Haynes, who had spent his entire life working with moving trucks. However, James also told me that out of this $25,000, I must keep $10,000 aside for him to use for bail money in case of his arrest. By this time I had quit Bamberger's and was back down in St. Louis.

This also clearly indicates to me that my brother didn't intend to kill anybody. If he got arrested, he was expecting to get out on bond (and a fairly minor level of bond money, at that). Every ex-con knows that getting arrested is a distinct possibility, just for the bad luck of being in the wrong place at the wrong time. Once you're branded, the label tends to stick. As for me, James told me that Obie had informed him there was a criminal job looming for me in San Francisco that I would be paid additional funds for, if I took it. I was to be the getaway driver for an operation of some sort. Jimmy and I never had dealings with Wortman on any of these possible jobs; only Obie, never Wortman.

The day Jimmy entered Montreal for this job, he found a city alive with Expo '67, the Canadian Centennial. Over eight hundred new exhibitors had built buildings for it. The very educated early computer geek Benny Edmondson, who had also escaped Jeff City, was "coincidentally" working at Expo '67 under the alias "Alex Bormann." Edmondson/Bormann had also stayed in Chicago for a while, like James did.

Very shortly after arriving in Montreal, James met CIA asset Jules Ron "Ricco" Kimble. According to what Kimble told a BBC team working on a special about the King assassination in 1989, Kimble took James to an identities specialist at the Central Intelligence Agency, who gave James the cover identity of "Eric S. Galt." There was a real Canadian named Eric S. Galt who had a security clearance, and that could have helped the future patsy to walk away from any sticky situations.

The first question that Memphis attorney Wayne Chastain, who would become James's local counsel, would ask James when he met him was, "Who gave you the Galt name, James?" This is where you have to look at my brother's motivation. If he was given that name as a knowing asset of the federal government, he would be much less likely to divulge it, because he was already fearful of being murdered in prison. He knew that a sure way to shorten his life span was to let it get around that he was somehow aligned with the feds. This is why he held back on revealing information. The plot was much larger than one lone nut shooting a rifle from a bathroom in a flophouse.

In Canada, Jimmy was frequently in the company of CIA operative Ricco Kimble, who, as of this writing, is in prison in Texas, serving a double life sentence for murder. Kimble was supposedly a notorious racist, and he did have ties with the Minutemen and the Ku Klux Klan. However, it seems likely that this racist attitude was cultivated by the Central Intelligence Agency or the military. He may have been a backup to the main patsy, my brother James. In the mind of the public, it would take a racist to kill Martin Luther King, so it is more than coincidental that Jimmy would be in the company of another supposedly violent racist, even though nothing in his pre-military life showed him to be that way. According to what Kimble told Lyndon Barsten, he and James were both directed to a new Holiday Inn, built for Expo '67. It is here Kimble told Lyndon in a telephone interview that "an older man came out from McGill University's Allen Memorial Institute to hypnotize" both James and Kimble. Kimble would brag to his Montreal girlfriend, Marcelle Mathieu, that he was affiliated with McGill and the hypnosis programs there. This is verified in Royal Canadian Mounted Police documents, which show that Mathieu was interviewed about Kimble in June of 1968. According to Mathieu:

> He also told me that he could hypnotize
> people and that he helped a doctor curing
> people with it. I told him not to try it on
> me. He told me that he was studying psy-
> chology at McGill University, but I found
> out this wasn't true either.

Since there was no public knowledge of the CIA's Sub-project 68 at McGill University in 1968, Kimble must have had first hand knowledge of the goings on there.

When Ricco Kimble was maneuvered back to the United States from Canada, he was manipulated by private detective Joseph A. Oster of West Monroe, Louisiana. (Interestingly, in the early 1960s, J. A. Oster had shared offices in the Big Easy with Guy Bannister, where Lee Harvey Oswald had worked in 1963.)

At this time, the Allen Memorial Institute at McGill housed Subproject 68 of the CIA's notorious MK-Ultra mind control program. The Agency had data from way back in 1948 that James could be controlled. They called on Allen Memorial Institute boss, Dr. Ewen Cameron, to ensure that James was indeed a proper patsy. Who knows if it worked or not; I suppose it did. Dr.

Cameron's CIA file has been mostly shredded, but what remains is telling. A Freedom of Information Act request to the CIA revealed that Cameron's security clearance at the agency was bumped up a couple of notches as the machinery of the King murder plot began to turn. Cameron wouldn't live more than a matter of days after James left Canada in 1967. He died of a reported heart attack up in the mountains.

There is a false story James told after he was captured that supposedly happened at this time. James wouldn't cross the Mob, but he had to somehow explain away all the money they had given him. The first story that James concocted to account for his sudden wealth was that he'd stolen the money from a Canadian grocery store. When it was revealed that no such robbery had taken place, he had to concoct a second fabrication: the robbing of a pimp. He realized he had to come up with a story that could not be compared to a police report. So here is the second, revised story:

> That evening in Montreal on St. Cath-
> erine East, in a nightclub, I was accosted
> by a prostitute; subsequently I agreed to
> go to her place via taxicab. After we got
> located in her apartment, I gave her the
> requested $25.00 fee and she carried the
> money to an "office." When I left I wrote
> down the address of the building. The next
> day I rented an apartment in the Har-K
> Apartments, located at 2589 Notre Dame East;
> then later, I parked my automobile close to
> the building where I had the night before
> been with the prostitute. That evening I
> returned to the aforementioned nightclub
> and, meeting the same girl, again accompa-
> nied her via taxi to her apartment. Inside
> I gave her another $25.00, but this time I
> showed her the pistol Mr. Gawron had pur-
> chased for me and told her I would go with
> her to wherever she was taking the money.
> When she aroused the manager into open-
> ing the "office" door, I put the pistol on

him. We moved back into the office, wherein
I asked him for the money. Taking out his
wallet he offered me the small amount in
it, about 5 or 10 dollars. When I told him
I wanted the rest of the money, he spoke
about a cabinet nearby and motioned to a
container, before leaving the "office," I
had the manager lie on a bed and the girl
remove her stockings and tie his hands and
legs. I then had her get under the bed
before departing. Later I found I had taken
approximately $1,700.00 in mixed currency
from the manager's office.

This fabrication meant that there would likely be no record of where he had actually gotten the money: Buster Wortman and Obie O'Brien, who got it from the Chicago Mob, who got it from a select group of clandestine operatives within the Central Intelligence Agency.

Until the mid-1970s, most people didn't know that the U.S. government was working hand in glove with organized crime. James was aware of it, possibly as early as the 1950s, because he was part of that world in Chicago. He was certainly aware of it by the early 1960s, when the Chicago Mob was working with the CIA in trying to bring down Cuba's Castro.

In 1967, the Canadian Mob was centered in Montreal under the influence of Mob bosses Vic "The Egg" Cotroni and Luigi Greco. Cotroni and Greco answered to New York Mob kingpin Joseph "Joe Bananas" Bonanno, head of the powerful New York City crime family. It should be easy for anyone to make the connection here. Was James working for the Mob? Yes. Was he working for the government? Yes. Raul C., James's notorious Portuguese handler from this time, belonged to the shadow world between U.S. intelligence and the Mob. He came from Joseph Bonanno's territory, just outside of New York City.

In the meantime, I was directed by Obie to head to San Francisco, where they had set up a getaway job for me. I wanted to get fake identification for James so I could get my own ID back from him. I drove westward in the Rambler station wagon that I had gotten from my brother Jerry, who wanted to get rid of it. My first stop was in Wyoming, where I bought about a thousand dollars' worth of traveler's checks. Next I stopped in Nevada, where they were having a Butch Cassidy holiday, and drove west into San Francisco where I checked into a second-floor apartment on the side of a hill. The car had been driven hard, so I took it in to be serviced, then went down to Pacific Gas and Electric to get my utilities turned on. I stopped down to the Department of Motor Vehicles to get a California ID. I tried to get a new ID in San Francisco for myself, but the driver's license bureau wouldn't issue me one until I presented my birth certificate. The bureau did give me a 90-day permit, however.

I got a map of San Francisco and found streets in the Skid Row district where I could get false papers by bribing a drunken sailor. I got about three or four sets of ID while I was there. (As it would turn out, I wouldn't end up giving any ID to James, because in the meantime, he had obtained much better false identification.) It was while I was getting the ID for James that I heard the announcement: Martin Luther King was coming to town. He was getting a lot of publicity, but I didn't pay much attention to it. About a day later, I was talking on the phone to Obie in East St. Louis about my being a getaway driver.

Obie said, "You should watch out; the getaway driver job isn't going down as you think. You could wind up floating in the Bay."

I wasn't sure what he was talking about, even though I did know that on some jobs, the Mob kills all the participants involved in the crime, both to cut off their connection to the crime and to concentrate the loot. It's for those reasons that I didn't work with them, especially the Chicago Mob. So with Obie's warning in mind, I immediately checked out of my apartment and drove down the coast toward Tijuana, Mexico.

I called Jerry from San Diego, telling him to contact James and let him know I was headed south, so he might not get the ID right away. As I drove down Highway 101, a cop stopped me for driving too slow. I wasn't driving that slowly, and although I was having a beer while driving, he didn't even mention it. This whole stop struck me as odd, like I was being watched. I later dumped the rest of the six-pack into the Pacific, just in case.

At this time, I had to contact James through Jerry in Chicago. When I called Jerry about the IDs, he told me, "He don't need an ID any longer." The government must have given James the Galt ID by then.

I didn't spend long in Mexico, as I spoke no Spanish. I sat having a few beers, trying to figure out the best thing for me to do. Eventually, everything pointed to going back to St. Louis, so I turned the Rambler northeast and headed to Missouri on old Route 66. By then I couldn't get the air-conditioning in the car to work, and in Arizona, the heat climbed so high that I was overcome by heatstroke. I checked into a motel to get some relief from the heat. I bought a cup of coffee and a paper and passed out in my room. When I came to, I read the newspaper headline from August 26. It said that the notorious American Nazi Party leader George Lincoln Rockwell had been shot by an FBI informant. After a long rest, I continued my journey on old Route 66, by this time absorbed into Eisenhower's interstate system.

At this point in his life, my brother James wanted to be a bartender and run an Irish pub in Ireland. He really wanted to get out of the United States, but was too cautious to put all his eggs in one basket. So from Canada, he enrolled in a mail-order locksmith course at the Locksmithing Institute of Plainfield, New Jersey. As he moved around North America during the coming months, he had the locksmith materials rerouted to him. Someone who is plotting to kill Martin Luther King Jr., doesn't keep the hope alive that he will soon run a pub in Ireland or have a locksmith shop.

At about the same time that he enrolled in the locksmith course, James apparently decided to get out of his current situation and create a new identity aside from the one the feds had given him. He wanted out of North America, to get lost overseas, preferably in Ireland. For that, he needed a guarantor to get him untraceable travel documents. James decided to vacation at the Gray Rocks Resort in the Laurentian Mountains, and to seek out the help of someone who would act as his guarantor in his application for a passport out of Canada.

He drove to the resort and met a recently divorced woman named Claire Keating. At this time, he still had his older-model Plymouth, but had sprung for some new clothes, so he probably gave a nice enough appearance to a woman traveling alone. He later saw Keating again in the Canadian capital of Ottawa, where they stayed together from Friday, August 18, to Sunday, August 20. It was there in Ottawa that Jimmy learned Keating was employed by the Canadian federal government. He claimed that this ended his plans, but at this time, I also put pressure on him (out of fear of the Mob), to keep him from taking off to Ireland.

After the assassination of Dr. King, Keating was interviewed by the Royal Canadian Mounted Police. She told them that Jimmy never said a single racist thing to her, and never mentioned Reverend King. Now, a clever criminal might avoid saying anything about secret plans to a girlfriend, but a racist is a racist. What man is going to curb his racist speech when drinking and fooling around with a girlfriend? She never heard him make those kind of remarks because Jimmy was not that kind of guy.

It was about this time, when I was talking to him on the phone from St. Louis, that I got the feeling he was about to run off to parts unknown. If he had run off, I probably would have been killed, because it would have put a lot of heat on me. He had, after all, been paid for a job that he hadn't done yet. In St. Louis at this time, lots of guys died in exploding cars. I told him that if he didn't "stay on the job," I'd "put the Mob onto him." Sometimes, to get Jimmy moving, you had to poke him with a stick.

After he returned to Montreal, Jimmy met with Raul several more times. James was about to become a drug smuggler and gunrunner; at least, this is the type of thing he believed he would be doing. Personally, I think he was being programmed to do as he was told by getting used to the "routine" nature of these dangerous tasks.

This is where the Galt name came into play. Eric Galt of Toronto, whose name James was given, resembled James. They even had matching scars. Should James get arrested, he would be walked out of the situation by officials, and he knew this. The real Galt worked for Union Carbide and inspected proximity fuses for the use of the U.S. military. For this reason, Galt had a security clearance. It is likely that James was not the first man to be given the Galt name, because in 1965, according to FBI reports, while James was an inmate in the Missouri State Prison, a man using that name was living in New Orleans.

James agreed to smuggle contraband across the Canadian border, and later, to do the same thing at the U.S. southern border with Mexico. I believe this part of the story is truthful. He always told it the same way. This is how the programming of James Earl Ray started, getting him to do as he was told.

On August 21, 1967, at the railroad station at Windsor, Ontario, Canada's "sin city," the reddish haired short and slim Raul entered with an attaché case in his hand and found James sitting in his Plymouth. Raul entered the

Plymouth and said, "Let's go; find some side street." Raul then removed the backseat and took out the contraband (presumably diamonds) from his case and hid them behind the seat. Jimmy was then directed by Raul to the tunnel that connects Ontario with Detroit. But first, before he took off, Raul said, "Let me out of the car, and we'll cross separately. Pick me up on the U.S. side. I'll cross in a cab." James cleared customs with no problem, and picked up Raul in Detroit as directed.

On an American side street, Raul removed the diamonds from the seat of the Plymouth. "Take me to the Greyhound bus depot," Raul directed James. At the bus depot James was told, "Return to Windsor and wait for me at the same railroad station, like before." James drove back to the Windsor station as instructed, and soon Raul appeared again, with his attaché case in hand. They repeated the procedure from the first trip, except that this time, James traveled over the bridge at the border, rather than through the tunnel. Jimmy appeared to be doing as he was told, as many times as possible, with no harm coming to him. He would do this many more times. This is how you get a man used to danger and used to following orders—even illegal orders—without question.

On one of these trips, Jimmy became aware that the invisible hand of Intel may have been guiding him. The customs officer who was in the process of searching his Plymouth was stopped by another customs officer who appeared, then abruptly ordered the first man away from the car. At this point, Raul told James to get rid of the Plymouth, saying, "A new car should be purchased with your new Galt identity, and not with a name that could so easily be tied to you."

They were next to meet in Birmingham. Being a fugitive from justice, James hated to come back down over the border, but he thought he was safe as long as he wasn't in Missouri. There is a good chance the Birmingham address was chosen by the feds to put a racial spin on the case, making James seem like a Southern citizen, which he never was. Later, the feds would tell James to choose the former mayor of Birmingham, Art Hanes, to be his lawyer.

Raul gave James a New Orleans telephone number to use as a contact. New Orleans at that time was a major center of organized crime in the South, under the control of Carlos Marcello. In the 1960s Carlos Marcello, born a North African, had hand-in-glove ties to the Dixie Mafia. The Dixie

Mafia were more dangerous than most organized crime because they were not organized; instead, they shot from the hip, or anyplace else they felt like. The film *Walking Tall* is about Sheriff Buford Pusser battling the Dixie Mafia. The criminal specialties of the Dixie Mafia were normal syndicate activities, certainly drugs, which is likely where James Earl Ray fits in.

James left Canada and drove to suburban Chicago on August 25, 1967, to see our brother Jerry. James gave the Plymouth to Jerry and caught a train to Birmingham, as Raul had instructed. On August 26, James climbed off of the segregated train in Birmingham, the city that had jailed Dr. King four years earlier. James would spend seven weeks in Birmingham, where he signed up for five dancing lessons at $2.00 a night. He rented a room at 2608 Highland Avenue, under his alias of Eric S. Galt. Soon after, he picked up a general delivery letter from Raul. The letter asked James to meet him at the Starlite Cafe, which was across the street from the Birmingham post office. The two men discussed business at the Starlite, and it was here that Raul again directed James to buy a newer, more reliable car under the Galt name. The "springtime yellow" Ford Mustang that he would eventually purchase at Raul's insistence would become internationally famous.

Early the next day, Raul handed James $2,000 to buy the car. James was also instructed by Raul to purchase expensive camera equipment. It was at this time that Raul gave James a backup number in Baton Rouge, another contact that my brother could reach him through. Both numbers were in cities very close to one another in the same state, in the territory of Carlos Marcello. In Birmingham, Jimmy rented a safety deposit box to hide the ID with my name on it. He had a compulsion to not let go of stuff. He should have dumped that identification in the river. He was also hanging on to his radio, the one with his Missouri prison number scratched in it. While in Birmingham, James also went to see the elderly Dr. Schwartz, who prescribed pills of a psychological nature for him.

Now, here is an escaped convict who the government would later say wanted to kill Martin Luther King Jr., more than anything, and yet here he is laying around Birmingham for seven weeks, from August 25 to October 7, doing little more than buying camera equipment that he'd never take out of the boxes, continuing his locksmith training course, and taking dancing lessons—really, just wasting time and waiting for his next contact, which came by way of one of the plot's operatives, asking James to meet Raul in New Orleans, in early October.

Lying doesn't make you guilty. When Jimmy got caught in a tangle of lies, the mainstream media and government accused him of trying to hide his guilt. In reality, James altered his story in order to stay alive, and partly to protect me. One of the reasons that the truth has been successfully buried in this case is the sheer complexity of it. You need a highway map to help you understand the details. Here's an example from Jimmy's congressional testimony of what people might call an obvious lie about this period. You may wish to check your road map:

> On or about October 6, 1967, I departed Birmingham, Alabama, en route to New Orleans, Louisiana, intending to meet Raul in New Orleans. The next day, or the day after, upon arriving in Baton Rouge, Louisiana, I phoned the Baton Rouge number Raul had given me; unable to reach the party, I then phoned the New Orleans number and did reach this party.

Now, Birmingham to New Orleans is 345 miles, a five-hour drive. This wouldn't take anyone two days, let alone three. Birmingham to Baton Rouge, which is farther west, is 400 miles exactly, almost an hour farther west and north, and not on the way to New Orleans. These types of inconsistencies about Baton Rouge were used by the government in the 1970s to make Jimmy out to be a murderer, but I can tell you that he was just scared. Here's what the House Select Committee on Assassinations (HSCA) pulled ten years later:

> James Earl Ray maintained that, following his October 6, 1967, departure from Birmingham, he drove through Baton Rouge, La., and called a telephone number he had been given by his mysterious coconspirator, Raul. The subscriber to this number, according to Ray, was to give him instructions about his

next rendezvous with Raul. The committee hoped to identify and locate the subscriber to that Baton Rouge telephone number; however, Ray's conflicting accounts about this part of his journey cast doubt on the Baton Rouge story.

In a March 3, 1977, interview with CBS reporter Dan Rather, Ray indicated that his destination was New Orleans when he left Birmingham, Al., in October 1967. Ray claimed he called the number Raul had given him when he reached Baton Rouge, and the party that answered told Ray his next meeting with Raul had been changed to Nuevo Laredo, Mexico.

During the committee's third interview with Ray six weeks after the Rather interview, he indicated, however, that he knew his destination was Nuevo Laredo when he left Birmingham. Ray said he called a number given him by Raul while driving through Baton Rouge, but he never spoke with the subscriber of the number because the line was busy when he made the call. Ray later received more detailed instructions concerning his next meeting with Raul by calling a New Orleans number Raul had given him.

James's falsehoods don't mean that he killed Martin Luther King Jr., and was covering it up. They just show that he was in over his head, as he had been for many years already and would continue to be for as long as he lived.

In the late fall of 1967, I bought a building in south St. Louis near the Budweiser Brewery to house a tavern, purchased with part of the $25,000 from the Mob that James had given me. It was first to be called Jack's Place, but I ended up naming it the Grapevine, after the "prison grapevine." Although I purchased the building in the fall, I had to wait until after Christmas for the license to be issued in my sister Carol's name. The building is still there, over on Arsenal Street.

James at this time was involved with dangerous government operations. Because of that, in interviews and in his writings, he had a habit of identifying people in the plot, but making them sound less important than they actually were, dropping hints but not telling all he knew. He was playing with fire. A man in prison is a "sitting duck" for an attack. For the rest of his life he would try to cook his own meals for fear someone would poison him. One man he knew, and who was identified through Jerry, was Randy Rosenson (aka Randolph Erwin Rosen) of Miami. James met Rosenson in the Playboy Lounge in New Orleans with Raul, where Jerry identified him around 1970. Jimmy did actually find Rosenson's business card in his car, but he knew that he had met Rosenson with Raul. He did the same thing with Carlos Marcello, essentially dropping hints of his involvement.

This is the "official" James Earl Ray story about finding Rosenson's card on this drive to Los Angeles, as told to the HSCA:

> . . . in preparing to leave the motel for the United States, as was my practice, I searched the Mustang. Down between the front seat and the gearbox, I found a cigarette case with a pack of cigarettes in the case. Inside, between the case and the pack, was a business card. The name and most of the accompanying information had been inked out. What I could see that was still partly visible was the name "New Orleans" and the letters "LEAA." On the back side of the card was the handwritten name of Randolph Erwin Rosen.

I believe he was doing this same lessening of importance with a contact who lived in Baton Rouge. This conspirator was Edward Grady Partin, a corrupt union official of the Local 5. Partin had been a federal witness against Jimmy Hoffa. He had a mountain of blackmail evidence held against him by the federal government. Persons around Jimmy Hoffa figure into James's case more than once. Jimmy Hoffa's lawyer, Z. T. Osborn, would end up "committing suicide" after he agreed to represent my brother James. How did James make Osborn's acquaintance, and who would send my brother Jerry to ask for Osborn's assistance? It was none other than St. Louis Steamfitters Local Union #562 boss Larry Callanan, right-hand man to plotter Buster Wortman.

Ed Partin's arrest record includes kidnapping, armed robbery, and rape. This is the type of guy the feds like to work with, as they have some legal leverage over him. Partin, who used the aliases C. B. Johns and F. Alexander, controlled Herman A. Thompson, the man who would turn out to be James's contact in the Baton Rouge sheriff's department. That's right: The backup phone number James was given in Baton Rouge belonged to Thompson, an assistant chief criminal deputy of the East Baton Rouge Parish sheriff's department. The government has said that there is nothing to the Herman Thompson story, but the too-convenient Partin/Thompson relationship is documented in a federal lawsuit, Amant v. Thompson, 390 U.S. 727 (1968) 390 U.S. 727, which was argued before the Louisiana Supreme Court on the very day Martin Luther King Jr., was shot in Memphis. This is testimony from that trial:

> Now, we knew that this safe was gonna be moved that night, but imagine our predicament, knowing [390 U.S. 727, 729] of Ed's connections with the Sheriff's office through Herman Thompson, who made recent visits to the Hall to see Ed. We also knew of money that had passed hands between Ed and Herman Thompson . . . from Ed to Herman. We also knew of his connections with State Trooper Lieutenant Joe Green. We knew we couldn't get any help from there, and we didn't know how far that he was involved in the Sheriff's office or the State Police office through that, and it was out of the jurisdiction of the City Police.

This is the Louisiana arm—seemingly directed by Carlos Marcello—of a plot centered in Chicago. Marcello was very friendly with the Chicago outfit, which was now under the official control of John Cerone, though Accardo was still a powerful adviser. Cerone would go to prison shortly after the assassination of MLK, as I would.

But there is more.

On the day Dr. King was murdered in Memphis, local civil rights activist John McFerren was shopping at a produce shop, Liberto, Liberto and Latch. McFerren heard the shopkeeper Liberto scream into the phone, "Kill the son of a bitch on the balcony—you'll get your five thousand. Get the job done!" Later, he heard Liberto say into the phone, "Don't come out here. Go to New Orleans. You know my brother; get the money from him." Even the government had to admit in a series of FBI documents on the Libertos and organized crime in Louisiana that there were ties between Liberto's brother in New Orleans and Carlos Marcello.

After his Baton Rouge stopover, James was indeed directed to Nuevo Laredo, Mexico. He was told to get a "Mexican Tourist" sticker on his car. After the death of King, interestingly, the only U.S. border secured would be the southern U.S. border with Mexico. James drove into Nuevo Laredo, Mexico, on or about October 8. Raul and Jimmy were to repeat the smuggling routine from Canada to the United States at the U.S./Mexican border. As they did so, James saw an associate of Raul's sitting in the car. This operative was a bearded man whom James would later recognize. He was identified by James in 1979 as David Gravier Gitnacht, who had altered his name to just "David Gravier." At about the time of the King assassination, or shortly thereafter, his FBI file reveals that Gitnacht was a bagman for a terrorist organization in Argentina called Los Montoneros.

Amazingly, this same man would maneuver his way into a powerful position at New York's American Bank and Trust Company and into the social circles of Nelson and David Rockefeller. At ABT, Gravier looted the bank for as much as 30 million dollars. Some unknown force restrained bank examiners from moving on Gravier. Gravier's death appears to have been faked when a chartered jet airliner burst into flames in Mexico, because FBI documents have him alive in Florida after the plane accident. Many researchers, such as Mae Brussell and her protégé, John Judge, believe that banks are looted of billions by the intelligence community to fund clandestine operations. Nobody ever went to jail for the theft of millions from ABT, though remarkably, there were others involved. There are literally hundreds of firms that have connections to, or are directly owned by, the CIA, and American Bank and Trust had ties through Credit Suisse to Permindex.

For five years, in the late 1950s and early '60s, Clay Shaw, who was charged as a conspirator in JFK's murder, had been on the board of directors of Swiss-based Permindex, promoting free trade, essentially globalization, for American manufacturers. Charles de Gaulle would blame Permindex for an assassination attempt on his life. Permindex's sister organization, Italian-based Centro Mondiale Commerciale, was actually created in Montreal where James was positioned; it moved to Rome later. Jim Garrison's 1991 book, *On the Trail of the Assassins*, reveals that the Italian and Swiss governments expelled Centro Mondiale Commerciale and Permindex from Italy for "subversive intelligence activity."

Multiple sources reveal that the initial Permindex board had some interesting members in 1958. According to the incorporation papers in Switzerland, initial members included some Italian fascists; Canadian citizen OSS Major Louis Mortimer Bloomfield; Mob boss Joseph "Joe Bananas" Bonanno; and Clay Shaw—the usual suspects for activity that has one foot in Intel, and the other in the mob. More about them later.

With a few minor changes, James and Raul's southern border smuggling was a repeat of the earlier affair, though I believe it also involved gunrunning in Mexico for anti-Cuban, anti-Communist insurgents. As directed by Raul, James applied to Mexican customs for a Mexican visa. Raul gave James another New Orleans phone number and asked James to tear up the old number. James would spend nearly seven weeks in Mexico, arriving in Acapulco by mid-October. He only stayed days in Acapulco, but a month in Puerto Vallerta, where he checked into the Rio Hotel on the nineteenth. At this time his room was only $4.80 a night. He met a prostitute named Irma in Puerto Vallarta, and they developed as much of a relationship as they could, given that James spoke very little Spanish and Irma almost no English.

In spite of the fact that they couldn't communicate well, the authorities and the press would have us believe that Irma was aware that James made racist comments to her. It was reported that one night in Puerto Vallarta, four black men and two white men were laughing it up in a bar. Irma allegedly told authorities later that James was making racist comments to her about the black guys—even though she spoke very little English.

While in Puerto Vallarta, James saw an advertisement in a *U.S. News and World Report* asking for individuals interested in immigrating to what was then the white-run Rhodesia. He allegedly wrote to the people who placed the ad, and his inquiry about immigration to what is now Zimbabwe would further paint him as a racist. I have trouble believing he did this on his own, but he might have done it on the insistence of one of the plotters, or perhaps if he was given some phony reason to do it. I also find this hard to believe, knowing his strong emotional ties to Ireland and how he dreamed of living there.

Another girl that James met in Mexico, after Irma, was a single mother named Alicia. Alicia knew that James was smuggling marijuana, which was somehow involved in his gun smuggling job. Their relationship became so serious that James gave her money to get them an apartment. Instead, Alicia took off to Guadalajara with her children. She left James a note apologizing for leaving him, but she was afraid of his drug smuggling.

When James came back to the States, he came across the border with a spare tire loaded with marijuana. On November 19, 1967, James pulled the yellow Mustang into Los Angeles still covered with Mexican mud. He was thirty-nine years old, and the last time he had lived in LA, he was twenty-one. James first rented an apartment in a white Spanish stucco building at 1535 North Serrano Avenue, near Hollywood Boulevard.

Facts seem to dictate that he was under orders to deliver his tire full of marijuana to a fence, probably Charles J. Stein, who had been born and raised in New Orleans and had an extensive criminal history there. Charlie died in 2003, but he had the distinctive mixed-race look about him that is common in New Orleans. The fact that Charlie appeared to be of mixed race was almost never mentioned in the press, as it would have destroyed the racist legend of James Earl Ray. Charlie took James to the Sultan Room to meet his cousin, who was known by several names, including Marie Martin (her real last name was Tomaso). Marie had more aliases than Jimmy. Charlie's attractive sister Rita became part of James's inner circle, to a lesser degree. Both Charlie and Marie had extensive criminal histories. With Charlie's family, the mask of racism fell from James's face. The best the FBI reports on Rita can do is to state: "It is doubtful Ray would have considered her black." What an ignorant comment. James was familiar with mixed-race people, as anyone who has spent time in the South has to be.

Ten years later, the HSCA had to deal with the reality that there were several witnesses to the fact that James knew Charlie Stein before the two were ever supposed to have met. On this score, the government's disinformation would have the same motivation: to eliminate the signs of a major plot.

By this time, James was running out of money and was just doing things to kill time. He placed an ad in the help-wanted section for hotels and restaurants in the *Los Angeles Times*. He also contacted the Big Bear Resort in an attempt to do maintenance work there. He tried to sell vacuum cleaners, and applied for work directly at a couple of hotels. However, although James had some identification in the Galt name, he didn't have a social security card, and this held him back from regular employment.

At 10:00 A.M. on Monday, November 27, James phoned an American-born, Swiss-trained clinical psychiatrist specializing in hypnosis, named Dr. Mark O. Freeman. Later that day, James would see Dr. Freeman and ask to be hypnotized. He would see Freeman four additional times for hypnosis. It is impossible to know how James got hooked up with this bug doctor, since he didn't speak with me much about this other than to say, "The feds are messing with my mind."

Nearly twenty years earlier, while Jimmy was barely out of his teens, the government had gotten the desired behavior out of James, and now, the man who was put on drugs in Jeff City, who was given pills in Birmingham, was put under hypnosis. How he was maneuvered to Freeman, I don't know, but Dr. Freeman lived a long life—long enough to tell investigator Lyndon Barsten that he was with army intelligence during World War II, and that he had a relationship with the FBI after the war. Just as the government experimented with LSD, so did Freeman.

According to Lyndon Barsten, government documents clearly show that California has been one of the centers of mind control experimentation for many years. It is interesting to note that the two "assassins" who would grace the covers of magazines internationally were in the Los Angeles metro area shortly before the crimes were committed. Just a few miles from James at this time lived a young man who made a fool of himself by being too much of an excellent hypnotic subject during a hypnotist's act. His name was Sirhan Sirhan. Larry Teeter, Sirhan's recently deceased lawyer, believed this is how the clandestine operatives in the CIA found the other obedient 1968 patsy. Two months after James would supposedly shoot Dr. King, Sirhan would shoot Bobby Kennedy behind his right ear, even though he was in front of RFK at the time. Larry told Lyndon Barsten that Sirhan had no memories of his mind controllers, though he (Sirhan) was sure he had been programmed.

While he was in LA, James was still thinking about his dream for the future: running an Irish pub in Ireland. He wanted to take bartending classes, so he signed up for some in Los Angeles, and graduated on March 2, 1968.

James's sixth appointment with Dr. Freeman was never to be. The last time that he saw Dr. Freeman was on December 14, a Thursday. When he left, he made an appointment to see him the following Monday. But the next day, the fifteenth, James cancelled the appointment. He was going to New Orleans.

In early December, James had checked the general delivery section of the main LA post office, to see if Raul had sent him a letter. He hadn't. So on the fifteenth, James called the most recent New Orleans phone number that Raul had given him back in Mexico. The number, 866–3757, was the number of the Town and Country Motel in New Orleans, home base of Carlos Marcello. The intermediary at the Town and Country asked James, "Can you come to New Orleans in late December?"

So James, with hippie-attired Charlie Stein alongside him in the yellow Mustang, took off to New Orleans on December 15, 1967. While Charlie and James drove across the Southwest to New Orleans, FBI documents describe a man in Memphis who was also calling himself Eric Galt, or a similar variation of the name. This man, who was called "Stevie" by an associate, had been in Mexico; like James, he drove a pale-colored Mustang. Everything about Stevie matched James. Later, a great deal of effort was put into finding out who Jimmy called on this trip. Reporters paid Charlie for his recollections of the numbers. I can tell you right now—sometimes, he was calling me.

When James pulled into the heart of the French Quarter, he went right to the deluxe Hotel Provincial. James called the phone number at the Town and Country Motel that Raul had given him in Mexico, and Raul told James to go to Le Bunny Lounge on Canal Street. This club was part of the Playboy empire, and has since closed. As I said, although James never admitted it, Mob associate Randy Rosenson of Miami, whose card James supposedly found in the Mustang, was with Raul at this meeting. James tried to spin Charlie Stein as a crazy hippie, but he was more than that. Rosenson and Stein traveled in the same criminal circles and even had the same lawyer. Rosenson was in several places James was, and is up to his eyeballs in the sheep-dipping of my brother. During this and another meeting at Le Bunny Lounge, Raul told James that in May, he (Raul) again wanted to transport rifles in Mexico.

The meeting with Raul was leading up to a more important one at the Town and Country Motel, owned and operated by Carlos Marcello. Marcello had close ties to the Chicago Mob, and it was likely that Jimmy was being manipulated to do a variety of activities so he would not question his orders when the big one came down—the one where he was to be involved and implicated in the murder of Dr. King.

On December 17, 1967, James would reportedly meet with members of the Southern Mob. I have no personal knowledge of this meeting, but several people who have studied the case agree that it took place, including *LIFE* reporter William Sartor, who would become one of the mysterious fatalities in this case. Reportedly at this meeting were Charlie Stein, Salvatore LaCharda, and Sam DiPiazza. DiPiazza in particular has a very extensive FBI file and was tied to Carlos Marcello. Salvatore LaCharda was a juvenile probation officer in the pocket of organized crime in the St. Bernard Parish sheriff's office; he also committed suicide in 1968, two months after Dr. King's murder.

James left New Orleans driving westward on December 19, with Charlie's little nieces in his car with him. Back in LA, James decided to move about three blocks into the St. Francis Hotel (today, the Gershwin Hollywood Hotel & Hostel), above the Sultan Room lounge where Marie Martin worked. In the past, it was also home to the notoriously bad film director, Ed Wood. During this time James did some normal things, including seeing Sonny and Cher in concert and taking dance lessons.

James frequently used the pay phone in the lobby of the St. Francis and wrote the numbers he was calling in the phone booth. After the King assassination several residents of the St. Francis contacted James's lawyer, Art Hanes, to inform him that guys in ties and dark suits went into the phone booth in the St. Francis lobby with buckets of soapy water and brushes to scrub his phone numbers off the phone booth. When journalist Louis Lomax, author of *To Kill a Black Man*, examined the phone booth later, the phone numbers had been replaced with racist graffiti.

The operations put in place to perpetuate the racist myth of James Earl Ray didn't end in the phone booth in the St. Francis. They also took place in another club nearby that James frequented, the Rabbit's Foot Club. Located on Hollywood Boulevard, the club was filled with young starlet types. The drinking age was eighteen, then, and there was a largely black clientele, often half the crowd. At the Rabbit's Foot, the St. Francis, and the Sultan Room, James was patronizing places frequented by a disproportionately high number of African-Americans in the 1960s—very odd behavior for an alleged racist.

One night James pulled his Mustang into a parking spot across from the Rabbit's Foot Club. A man inside supposedly saw James's Alabama license plates and began to pick a loud fight with him on racial politics. James quietly answered him in a rather neutral way. James left the bar, only to be mugged outside. Although James left the club quietly and had his car keys stolen in the parking lot after being mugged, a false story was created as to events that took place that day. FBI reports claim that Jimmy hit a female patron named Pat Goodsell and dragged her to the door, allegedly because she was "defending Negroes." The fight between the two was supposedly broken up by customers. *LIFE* magazine also repeated the story. Ten years later the HSCA would track down Bo Del Monte, one of the two bartenders on duty that night. He would tell them that there was "no truth at all" to the stories told of my brother's racist ranting that night.

On January 4, 1968, James walked into the Long Beach office of "Reverend" Xavier von Koss, another hypnotist. Von Koss was born in Germany around 1905, and appears to be someone brought over by the U.S. government after the war through Operation Paperclip. Von Koss ran a business called the International Society of Hypnosis. Although James supposedly saw von Koss only one time, he wrote on the application for his locksmith course that he was taking a course through him. Von Koss was James's second Los Angeles hypnotist, at the very least. If you check the remaining MK-Ultra documents, you will find that the government had these people in every major city in the United States. When James was arrested in London, he was carrying three books about hypnosis. Von Koss admitted in interviews that he recommended these books. I cannot say for certain how many times James saw von Koss, but it certainly appears to be more than once.

About this time, in early 1968, James began writing certain phrases over and over on paper. These are included in the FBI file on the assassination. Sirhan did the same thing. One of the phrases James wrote was, "Now is the time for all good men to come to the aid of their country."

During this time in early 1968, James received a letter from Raul asking James to meet him in New Orleans in March, for a trip to Atlanta. James called the number he had been given to the Town and Country Motel in New Orleans. James decided that if he was ever going to escape this madness and get to Ireland to open his pub, he'd have to disguise himself. James's most distinguishing features were his ears, which stood out slightly from his head, and his pointy nose. James decided to have rhinoplasty at the offices of Russell Hadley on Hollywood Boulevard, but before he could have his ears done as well, the plotters called. They were all to meet in New Orleans.

Local FBI special agents would later believe that the plot to kill King thickened about this point in time. Former marine Allan O. Thompson, fifty-three years old, was managing the St. Francis and working the switchboard. He received at least one call for Eric Galt from a man named James C. Hardin. James called this man "J. C."

Hardin identified himself to Thompson over the phone. Within a few days he showed up at the St. Francis to haul James out of California. The instruction was left for Galt to "call collect." Although by all accounts the FBI never positively identified J.C., they believed him to be FBI informant James C. Hardin, born April 10, 1938. A special agent from the Atlanta FBI office verified the informant status of J. C. Hardin for James's friend and investigator, author and former Department of Justice employee Harold Weisberg. The agent told Harold, "Oh God, he's one of our snitches." As soon as the investigation of J. C. Hardin became active, FBI headquarters shut it down. Regular FBI agents began to identify Hardin in preparation for an arrest, realizing this was now a conspiracy. But orders must have come down from above, as Hardin's name has been lost in history.

James called me frequently, especially after he got back to the United States from Mexico. About this time I got a call from him saying that he was "heading east." On March 17, 1968, James changed his address to General Delivery, Atlanta, and departed Los Angeles for New Orleans. As James filled out his change-of-address card, Dr. King was speaking just three miles away. Dr. King coming to town was always in the news. Did Jimmy even bother to show up to stalk his supposed prey? No.

When James arrived in New Orleans, his contact at the Town and Country told him to drive to Birmingham and meet Raul back at their old haunt, the Starlite Cafe. From the Starlite they proceeded on to Dr. King's hometown, Atlanta, Georgia.

At that point, Dr. King had just over two weeks to live.

In Atlanta, James located what the FBI would call a "hippie joint" to stay at, located at 113 Fourteenth Street, Northeast. Raul met James there, and they went to a restaurant on Peachtree Street to eat. This is important, because the receipt for that dinner exists today, and it clearly shows two persons, and not one "lone nut." At this meeting Raul was asking James to purchase rifles in Atlanta to be later shown to prospective buyers, a continuation of the Mexican gunrunning.

The next day, as planned, Raul came to the room that James had rented, and repeated a plan he had spoken of in the Peachtree Street restaurant. Raul wanted James to drive him to Miami, Randy Rosenson's hometown, but for some reason, Raul never showed up for the Miami trip.

Raul finally reappeared after about a week, still talking about purchasing rifles. Jimmy wanted to buy rifles in Alabama because of his identification. So the two of them, Jimmy and Raul, drove to Birmingham. James checked into the Travelodge there. Since Raul's cover story was the purchase of rifles, they flipped through the Birmingham yellow pages, looking for a gun shop. James would later learn that the rifle, eventually purchased from Aeromarine Supply, was the "throw-down" rifle in Memphis—not the real murder weapon, but the "official" murder weapon. The FBI called the rifle "Q2." James purchased the rifle of his own accord, under the name "Harvey Lowmeyer," to keep the Galt alias out of the shenanigans if possible, in an attempt to protect a good alias and to ensure there was no paper trail.

At first, James purchased a .243 caliber rifle and telescopic sight at Aeromarine Supply on March 29, 1968. Donald Wood, an Aeromarine salesman, made the sale. When Raul saw the gun, he said it was not powerful enough, so James called Wood to try to exchange it. Wood would later state he was aware that someone else was bossing my brother around while they were on the phone.

It was on March 29 that Jimmy called me, asking me about guns. In hindsight I always wondered why Raul didn't give him more strict instructions, unless something was communicated to Raul after the fact. I guess Raul did so after the purchase. I told him on the phone, "I can get you guns, because I know a soldier from Fort Campbell, Kentucky, who can get you anything you want." He never took me up on it.

The next day, March 30, James exchanged the .243 caliber rifle for a more powerful .30-06 Remington Gamemaster slide action rifle, model 760, with a Redfield variable telescopic sight, serial no. A17350, and Weaver sight mount. After the purchase, Raul gave James the name of a motel called the New Rebel, on the outskirts of Memphis. James was given instructions to bring the rifle to the motel and meet Raul there on April 3. Raul claimed he had to make a business trip to New Orleans, in the meantime. James would claim that he stayed in motels in Florence, Alabama; Corinth, Mississippi; DeSoto, Mississippi; and other motels prior to his arrival on the outskirts of Memphis on the third of April. He was adamant that he did not return to Atlanta, and he did not. It was, however, important for the government to place him in Atlanta at the time that the Atlanta papers announced that Dr. King was traveling to Memphis.

Logic and fact do not suggest that James went back to Atlanta before running off to Memphis in a hot sweat to murder Dr. King. The newspapers announced that Dr. King would be in Memphis on April 2, and might be gone soon after. Atlanta to Memphis is 389 miles, and the trip takes about 6¾ hours. If James knew on April 1 that MLK would be in Memphis and he wanted to kill him, he would have been there that night, finding out where the Lorraine Motel is and preparing for the assassination, rather than leaving everything until the last minute. This is just another reason why the government position makes no sense.

Here is James's version of his travels:

March 30: James leaves Birmingham in the morning, travels from Birmingham to Decatur, Alabama: 82 miles—about 1 hour and 20 minutes of driving—then rests for the night.

March 31: James travels from Decatur to Florence/Tuscumbia, Alabama: 48 miles (50 minutes)—then rests for the night.

April 1: Florence/Tuscumbia to Corinth, Mississippi, and the Southern Motel: 60 miles (1-hour drive). According to the guest list of the Southern Motel compiled by the FBI, some Mob operatives in this case were likely at the Southern Motel.

April 2: Corinth, to Tennessee state line near Memphis metro area: 97 miles (2-hour drive). The overall distance from Birmingham to Memphis: 243 miles (4½ hours).

Are these the travels of a man looking to kill? I say no. And I have personal knowledge of his state of mind then, because I spoke to him during this time. It was early April, probably the second, when I got another phone call from James. He wanted to see Obie O'Brien about something that was going down, something that he felt was important, but that he knew nothing about. To say that he was in a panic would be too strong, but he felt it was urgent. He was scheduled to be a getaway driver, as I had been in San Francisco, and nervously said, "I want you to set up a meeting with Jimmy O'Brien—Obie—immediately." James gave me the name of a tavern in West Memphis. He asked me to meet him the next night

The next day, I put a machine gun in the trunk of my Thunderbird and stuck a couple of handguns under the front seat on the passenger side of the T-Bird in case they were needed, just in case something was going down. James was involved with serious people. On the phone, Jimmy made it clear to me that he was still in the gun business, so I decided to take some along just in case. I had bought the machine gun from a soldier stationed at the military base in Kentucky. This soldier had also given me a list of armories around the country, which were easy to break into, to get any type of weapons. One of the armories was located in Chipley, Florida.

It was now the evening of April 3, 1968. Down in Memphis, violent storms had moved into the Delta. Raul was attired in a wet trench coat, looking like a true spook when he showed up at James's room, #34 at the New Rebel Motel. Raul told Jimmy, "We're staying for a few days in Memphis. There's a place located near the waterfront where we will rent a room." Raul ordered James to meet him at an address he wrote down: 422½ South Main Street. They were to meet around 3:00 in the afternoon the next day. Raul said if he were not in a room in the South Main flophouse, he would be in Jim's Grill, on the street level; he also wrote down these instructions. Raul took the boxed-up rifle that was purchased in Birmingham and left.

As Raul walked into the interior parking area at the New Rebel, James secretly took photos of him. He preserved these, and sometime later James would give the film to investigative author Harold Weisberg, who was a friend to James as well as his investigator. Astonishingly, Harold hung onto the film and did not attempt to get it developed until much later, when it had gone bad.

Not far away, on stage in Memphis at the enormous Mason Temple, Dr. King seemed to acknowledge what Charles Cabbage, a member of the black militant group, the Invaders, had told him: Rumors were flying among the Memphis police that he would not leave the city alive. Dr. King therefore concluded his impromptu speech with these prophetic words:

> Like anybody else I would like to live a long life. Longevity has its place. But, I'm not concerned about that now. I just want to do God's will. And he's allowed me to go up to the mountain. And I've looked over, and I've seen the Promised Land.
>
> I may not get there with you. But I want you to know tonight, that we as a people will get to the Promised Land.
>
> So I'm happy tonight. I'm not worried about anything. I'm not fearing any man. Mine eyes have seen the glory of the coming of the Lord . . .

As Dr. King was speaking, just across the Mississippi River, I was walking into the West Memphis Tavern to meet Jimmy. The bar was on the right, and several tables were on the left; Jimmy was sitting at one of the tables in a trench coat, sipping a beer. That seemed odd to me, because he didn't like beer. He claimed that it gave him a headache, but he said he was sipping it to kill time. In all of my years, I never saw him drunk, and I never saw him smoke a cigarette.

My brother said that he was "going to do a job," but didn't know what was going down. He wanted to see Obie to find out if he could get some information about it. He did not have a good feeling about the job. I told him, "Obie's out of town, and sometimes he stays out of town for several weeks, sometimes months." We agreed that Jimmy had to pay back the Mob for the money they had given him. In fact, if Obie vouched for us, then both Obie and I could have a problem with the Mob. I told him what Obie had told me about floating in San Francisco Bay, and James stated that he didn't want to be floating in the Mississippi River. We sat there for a couple of hours, trying to figure out what was going down, and whether there was going to be a double cross. But there was just not enough information to make sense out of the supposed job that was waiting for him. We then came to the conclusion that our imaginations might have been getting the best of us.

It was the mistake of our lives.

James told me that he had to leave to meet a couple of people back across the river. I told him about the guns out in the car, but he was not interested in them anymore. I walked outside with him, wishing him well, and watched while he disappeared down the alley. Once he was out of sight, I went back inside the bar. I felt better when I made it back across the state line into Missouri. But the "safe" feeling of being back in my home state was not to last.

seven

Kangaroo Court

> . . . Jerry told me how much James Earl
> and he [Jerry] liked everything I had written and
> how James Earl regarded me as "his only real
> friend."
>
> —William Bradford Huie, from
> *He Slew the Dreamer*

On April 4, 1968, James didn't check out of the New Rebel Motel until around noon. He then went out for breakfast at a restaurant. James didn't know Memphis—he hadn't been there in years—and he was very casual about the possibility of getting lost or never seeing his supposed prey.

With the assistance of a policeman, James located Main Street and drove south to what is considered South Main. While he was trying to locate the 422½ South Main Street address of Jim's Grill, he accidentally went to the wrong "Jim's," an establishment he later believed was Jim's Belmont Cafe. There, two operatives looked him over. One of these men appears to have been James Cooper Green, now deceased, a government operative who had been in Jeff City with James, where the FBI claims my brother was selling amphetamines with him. James did not recognize Green, as Green had been a juvenile at the time both were incarcerated at Jeff City and therefore segregated from James. It would have been virtually impossible for the two to have sold amphetamines with each other while segregated from one another, as the FBI claims.

When Lyndon Barsten later met Green, he asked him, "What were you wearing on April 4, 1968?" He knew that buried in the congressional

111

volumes of the HSCA, James had described the clothing of the men he had seen eyeing him earlier on April 4. Green described his black T-shirt and pants perfectly to Lyndon. Green was a native of Caruthersville, Missouri, a town with an East St. Louis–like Mob structure that also answered to the Chicago bosses. Green claimed he was chosen to be a backup shooter to kill my brother if the police didn't kill him, like in the Oswald case. Strangely, Green became a bona fide Justice Department employee shortly after his release from prison. He also claimed firsthand knowledge that Buster Wortman was a King conspirator.

When a waitress told James that he was in the wrong spot, he took off to find the correct Jim's Grill, owned by Loyd Jowers. He entered, looking for Raul. He didn't find him, but Jim Green and an associate were there too, and according to James, they were "noticing me more than was necessary." James ordered a beer, but shortly went upstairs to inquire about renting a room. According to an FBI interview with Bessie Brewer, the proprietress of the rooming house, she told James she had two rooms to let, and showed him both. Brewer later verified to the FBI that this took place "between 3:00 p.m. and 3:30 p.m."

A killer who does not know Dr. King's agenda would have been in place hours before, and wouldn't have been drinking. Jimmy took the second room he was shown, 5-B, which was only a sleeping room (no cooking facilities). He paid the $8.50 for a week's rent with a $20 bill, under the name "John Willard." The Willard alias was borrowed from a gunrunner, Dr. Gus Prosch, who James had known in Birmingham. The place was a real alcoholic's flophouse, and didn't even have doorknobs; instead, the doors had leather straps with metal hasps for padlocks. A death had freed up room 5-B when the prior tenant, Commodore Stewart, was taken to the hospital. Stewart died there on March 14.

At the Lorraine Motel, Dr. King's brother, the Rev. A. D. King, had come to visit. The local black militant group, the Invaders, was the closest thing to security that King had that day. However, Dr. King was being spied on by the feds and local police from the fire station across Mulberry, next to the flophouse.

After paying for his room, James went back to Jim's Grill. There were fewer people in the restaurant, and this time, Raul was there but Jim Green and his associate had left. Almost immediately, Raul wanted to go check on James's room. Raul suggested that James bring the personal items he had in the Mustang up to the room, saying with his Portuguese accent, "We may have to be here a few days." Raul also wanted my brother to purchase a few things—items that would eventually be used to incriminate my brother in his role as the patsy.

Raul gave James directions to a nearby sporting goods store, York Arms, with instructions to purchase infrared field glasses. James was told that the buyers they were supposedly meeting up with later might want them. He was unable to locate the sporting goods store the first time. On the second trip, James located the York Arms Company, but found that the store didn't sell infrared field glasses, just regular binoculars. The salesman, Ralph Carpenter, first showed James a pair of binoculars for $200. In 1968, this was easily the equivalent of about $1,000 today. Instead, James chose a pair that cost $39. The salesman suggested an army surplus store for infrared attachments. On the way back to Bessie Brewer's rooming house, James stopped at a drugstore on the ground floor of the Chisca Hotel and ordered an ice cream. Again, hardly the actions of a murderer with time running out.

Back at the flophouse, James went to his room where Raul was waiting and told him they would have to get the infrared attachments at an army surplus store. James went downstairs into Jim's Grill and ordered another beer. The waitress on duty was owner Loyd Jowers's young girlfriend, Betty Spates, who would later become famous—and somewhat controversial—for her role in the case as she would later serve as an important witness for the King's lawyer, Dr. William Pepper.

At this point, James still believed he was to be the getaway driver for some job, so when he was instructed to sit in the car and wait, that's what he did. He sat down in the front seat of the Mustang and waited for Raul. But then he heard a shot, and shortly afterward, Raul ran down the steps and leaped into the car. Once in the backseat, Raul threw a sheet over his head. This is James's earliest record of his actions after the assassination. When he realized at a later point it might make him legally guilty of aiding and abetting, he lied and instead placed himself at a gas station rather than in the vicinity of the murder. It may be that an incriminating bundle containing his Jeff City transistor radio (with the prison number etched into it), the Remington he had purchased, and other "evidence" was dropped very shortly before, and not by Raul. Witnesses at the Canipe Amusement Company believed that a bundle was dropped by the door before the shot rang out. The rifle in the bundle was the "official" one—the one Jimmy had purchased—and not the real murder weapon. After riding with Jimmy a few blocks, Raul jumped out of the Mustang and fled.

Modus operandi (MO) is the term used to describe the mode of operations of a person, or even a company. When James was sticking up grocery stores, his usual MO was to use a switch car. Now, here he was, supposedly killing a Nobel Prize winner, *Time* magazine's Man of the Year. For this job, at a time when he had more money than he'd ever had before, why wouldn't he have used a switch car?

When a crime such as the murder of Dr. King is committed, the authorities often block all cars at the state line. Downtown Memphis sits on the Mississippi River, and just across the river is West Memphis, Arkansas, where Jimmy and I had been the night before. This means that Jimmy could have been out of the state almost immediately. Instead, he took the long way, through northern Mississippi. Are we to believe he wanted to sightsee by Graceland on his way out of the State of Tennessee?

And then, what does the alleged "murderer" do? He throws items bearing his fingerprints onto the sidewalk, incriminating evidence that would easily identify him, like the Remington .30-06 and the radio with his Missouri prison number scratched into it.

Authors who claim that James shot Dr. King always leave out the story of the late sheriff's department lieutenant, J. E. "Bud" Ghormley. Ghormley and others had pulled into Fire Station #2 on South Main for a break at 5:50 P.M., with Tactical Unit #10, leaving a patrolman named Douglas in the command car to monitor the police radio.

When the shot that killed Dr. King rang out, most officers jumped down over the retaining wall onto Mulberry. But Ghormley had a bum leg and turned around when he reached the railing. Rather than jump the eight feet to Mulberry, he turned around and ran back to South Main, along with a patrolman named Gross. In Ghormley's sworn testimony, it took him less than two minutes to reach the flophouse door from the back door of the fire station. When James's attorney, Jim Lesar, and investigator Harold Weisberg walked the Ghormley route, it took them under forty-five seconds, allowing for Ghormley's bad leg. Ghormley saw nobody running from the flophouse, even though it surely would have taken James longer than two minutes to put his bundle together—containing the rifle, radio, cans of beer, and other assorted items—and exit the south wing of the flophouse. This enhances the possibility that the bundle was dropped seconds earlier. Six years after the crime, Bud Ghormley, then working for the public defender's office, testified on James's behalf during an important evidentiary hearing in Memphis. A network of conspirators was likely working in that flophouse to ensure that there were no screwups.

It was decades later before James or anyone else knew that the rifle contained in the bundle at the scene of the crime was not the murder weapon. Robert Hathaway, a ballistics expert hired by James's lawyers, testified in 1997 that twelve of the eighteen bullets fired from the "bundle rifle" had an identical "reference point" that was not to be seen on the actual slug that had entered Dr. King's jaw. In other words, the rifle at the scene was test fired, and those bullets did not match the bullet taken from Dr. King's body.

After leaving Memphis, it was James's plan to phone the Town and Country number in New Orleans to find out what had happened at the South Main rooming house. But as he entered Mississippi, he heard over the car radio that Dr. Martin Luther King Jr., had been shot in Memphis. About a quarter of an hour later, another news bulletin on the radio stated that police authorities were looking for a pale Mustang and a white male subject for the murder of Dr. King. James quite justifiably feared the worst and turned east toward Atlanta. Shortly afterward, he pulled the Mustang over and emptied the trunk, including all of the camera equipment, still in their original wrappings, that Raul had ordered him to buy.

James arrived in Atlanta at approximately 7:30 in the morning. Fearing the worst, he abandoned the Mustang in a private parking lot near Capitol Homes. James hated to leave that Mustang, but he did so, wiping it down for prints. James then returned to the rooms he had rented on Fourteenth Street, Northeast, and waited for a while, but nobody contacted him. He walked to the Piedmont Laundry, where he had previously dropped off items of clothing to be cleaned. Our familial mistrust of the government, which was a firm part of James's character, now kicked in; he decided he had to leave the country right away. The plotters had wanted him to have a "Mexican Tourist" sticker, so he chose Canada.

James phoned the Greyhound station and found that a bus was leaving Atlanta for Detroit, Michigan, in a few hours. So he returned to the Fourteenth Street rooming house for his suitcase, then caught a taxi to the bus station, where he bought a ticket to Detroit. As we all know, his escape to Canada would be a temporary one.

Although I had my suspicions, I would not know for several more days that the man wanted in this horrendous murder was my brother, and that he would be caught in the crooked web of deceit that is the MO of our military and intelligence agencies.

On April 4, I was back in St. Louis in the Grapevine Tavern, tending bar. It was dinnertime when some guy poked his head into the Grapevine and screamed that somebody had shot Martin Luther King Jr. This same man poked his head into my friend Margie's tavern up the street, screaming the same thing.

At first, law enforcement announced they were looking for a John Willard. A few days after that it was announced they were looking for an Eric Galt, and that the name "Willard" was likely an alias. I was unaware at this time that Jimmy's alias was Galt, since he'd never told me about it. But when it was announced that the suspect was Galt, our brother Jerry called me at the Grapevine and said, "Jimmy is Galt." I immediately hung up, fearing that the phone could be bugged.

Jimmy was involved with the Mafia, but logically I couldn't see how the Mafia or Jimmy could be involved in the shooting of Dr. King. I saw no connection. The Mob only gets involved with something that directly involves their organization. In the Kennedy brothers' assassinations, it's easy to see why they would become involved, because there was a lot going on under the table with the Kennedys, the Department of Justice, and the Mafia.

I became more confused when the FBI started coming around during their investigation. In the first visit, they were celebrating, and even ordered a drink in the Grapevine called the "Ruddi, Tuddi, Tuddi with Flem Flam Sauce," which is a drink that is mostly preferred over in the Kansas City area. One of the agents even danced a little jig, singing, "For He's a Jolly Good Fellow." I didn't know whether he was singing about Boss Hoover or James Earl Ray, and I didn't ask him.

During the FBI's second visit, they were upset with all the hoopla coming from the mainstream media. They were under the impression that the King killing was just another nickel-and-dime civil rights killing, and that public outrage would quickly dissipate. They claimed the media was "whipping up the public into believing that King was some kind of saint, and that Hoover was some kind of devil."

In another visit, the FBI agents told me they thought the CIA might be involved in the King killing, and that Boss Hoover was taking all the heat. In one of their visits, they asked me to give them some type of statement relating to my connection with Jimmy after he had escaped from the Missouri State Prison, because someone in Washington wanted a record of my involvement. I told them I wasn't sure it was me who had visited Jimmy the day before he escaped from Jeff City, because I often let other people use my visiting permit, including our brother Jerry. I also claimed that I wasn't even aware James was an escapee; I had thought he was still serving time. I told them, "Yes, I took a trip out to San Francisco to see about going to work on one of those passenger ships that caters to tourists. However, I had no luck because I couldn't get seamanship papers, due to a problem with my birth certificate. So I came back to St. Louis to help my sister Carol run her bar."

By the time the authorities knew about the Galt alias, James had made it to Toronto, Canada. Once I'd left Chicago for San Francisco, and Jimmy had left for Canada, we did not see each other face-to-face until that meeting in the West Memphis bar in Arkansas. We kept in contact with a few letters, but mostly through phone calls. I still couldn't figure out if Jimmy was Mafia and why the Mafia would be involved in the King shooting, so I collected all the information that I'd received from James, information which he had also told others, and put it down as follows:

The plotters gave James two additional aliases to use if he ever got into trouble, but after the assassination of Dr. King, he didn't trust them enough to use those names.

James entered the offices of the *Toronto Evening Telegraph* to research names of persons slightly younger than he was, since he had been told that he looked younger than forty years of age. He would later assume the identity of either Paul Bridgeman or Ramon Sneyd. Both of these men were born a month apart in 1932. If James was going to apply for a passport to fly out of

Canada on the Bridgeman or Sneyd name, he would have had to make certain that these men didn't already have passports. A call verified that Sneyd had never applied for a passport, meaning his photo was not on file in the passport office. (Ironically, Sneyd was a police officer.)

James rented two simultaneous places, one in Toronto on Ossington Avenue, and one on Dundas Street. Anna Szpakowski managed the Ossington Avenue place, and Mrs. Sun Fung Loo, the place on Dundas. During this time James also made a trip to Montreal for a few days; I believe it may have been to see Mob elements there. (James didn't realize that these people had such concrete connections to the U.S. federal government.)

In magazines at the time, the real Galt was described as a warehouse supervisor, but this was not an accurate description; it does not take into account the sensitivity of his real position in defense work for the military-industrial complex.

It would take until April 18—fourteen days after the shooting—to identify the prints on the rifle and bundle items as those of James Earl Ray. The alleged murder weapon was delivered to FBI labs in Washington on the morning of April 5, but according to Cartha DeLoach of the FBI, the team assigned to identify James's fingerprints on items from the scene of the crime didn't begin their work until April 17. This would mean that while cities burned from the riots which followed King's death, the FBI had other more pressing things to do for thirteen days than to identify Dr. King's alleged murderer's prints.

According to William Sartor, an investigative journalist from *LIFE* magazine who looked into the case shortly after Dr. King's death, money hadn't changed hands on the Mob side of the plot, and it was for this reason that James wasn't killed. The original plan was to kill James near the scene of the crime. We will never know if emergency meetings were taking place to decide what to do, but I suspect they were. What other reason would there be for not even officially trying to identify "Dr. King's killer" for nearly two weeks?

It appears likely to me that the FBI labs, headed by George Bonebrake, had their scenario for the King case shortly after the murder of King took place, altered from the original plot only by the fact that James survived Memphis, which wasn't in the original plan. In 1993, Bonebrake testified that the FBI did nothing to identify the other men's prints in my brother's Ford Mustang.

The FBI could never get it together in their efforts to dummy up the identification of James's prints, which they had from the rifle, the binoculars Raul asked him to get, and a map of Mexico. One FBI report, HQ File 44-38861 Serial 2034, claims that the identification of the prints on the new NCIC computer took only "two hours' machine time" to search 25,000 records, and that if the search "had to be done manually, it would have possibly taken several weeks." Another report relating to fingerprints in the case, HQ File 44-38861 Serial 5818, claimed the prints "had been compared during the eleven days following the murder with approximately 400 suspects."

Dummied-up case or not, the fact remains that James was afraid of the feds and the Mafia. He had reasons to fear a trial because of their kangaroo courts, and he was, of course, afraid of being killed before a trial could even take place.

On April 18, the FBI made James's identity public, and he abruptly moved to the Dundas Street address full-time. Six days later, Raul—or someone else with reddish-blond hair and weighing approximately 125 pounds—showed up at the old Ossington Avenue address. He showed the landlady, Mrs. Szpakowski, an envelope with a list of names (aliases) on it, and she recognized one name: Paul Bridgeman. "He's no longer here," she explained.

In Toronto, on May 2, James was given a letter and, I believe, money by a man known in the press at the time as "the Fat Man." His name is Robert McDouldton, and early in the day, McDouldton was picked up by a cab driver named Reis across the street from James's Dundas Street address, and driven just three blocks to a bank. He was in the company of another man during the cab ride. The actual man who lived across the street, at the address given the cab driver by McDouldton, didn't call the cab. Later, the Fat Man dropped off an envelope marked SNEYD.

A story would be concocted later that an envelope containing a job application of James's was found in a phone booth, and that the Fat Man was just bringing it to its rightful owner. This "rightful owner" story was repeated by Posner in *Killing the Dream*, but when professor Phil Melanson of Southeastern Massachusetts University found McDouldton in 1984, their very tense meeting went like this:

From Dr. Melanson's book, *The Murkin Conspiracy*:

Prof. M: I'm a professor of political science, and I'm interviewing a number of persons like yourself who had interesting encounters sixteen years ago.

RM: How did you find me? What's going on with this case?

McDouldton immediately knew that Melanson meant the King case. McDouldton told Professor Melanson that he feared for his life.

RM: They [the FBI] wanted me to go to be a witness [in 1968]. I refused. Why go and get a bullet in my head?

McDouldton told Professor Melanson that the delivery of the envelope was a job he was given.

RM: I've never told . . . It was a job, all right.

When called by researcher Lyndon Barsten, McDouldton became quite frightened and agitated. This conversation is on tape. This was not a man who found a job application or the like in an envelope on the street. McDouldton was likely afraid of the Mob, unaware that the U.S. government has worked hand in glove with the Mafia since World War II. McDouldton knew he could end up like Louis "Lepke" Buchalter, executed at New York's Sing Sing Prison after Charles "Lucky" Lucciano decided to drop a dime on his partner in crime.

McDouldton had to stick to the implausible story that James would apply for jobs in Canada when he'd actually booked a flight to London for May 6. James paid for his ticket to London later on May 2, after the Fat Man dropped off his package. James later claimed that the Fat Man also brought identification papers. James's passport would mistakenly be issued in the name of "Sneya" rather than "Sneyd."

The pressure that the news media placed on the FBI seemed to change their attitudes as time went on. By this time our family was being investigated.

The FBI was illegally bugging us in my tavern and my apartment. They also bugged my sister Carol's house. Attorney general Ramsey Clark refused to give Hoover permission to bug us, but they just went ahead and did it anyway.

On May 7, 1968, with false identification in the name of Ramon George Sneya, James flew from Canada to England. As he landed at Heathrow Airport, he was met with the eerie image of his own face on the cover of *LIFE* magazine, accompanied by a story meant to create the impoverished racist legend of James Earl Ray.

While in Europe, James noticed that he was being followed by U.S. federal agents, but they merely watched him and didn't arrest him. It was his impression that he only lost them twice while in Europe. Almost immediately, he flew to Lisbon, Portugal, in an attempt, I believe, to find the family of Raul, his handler. James used the remaining portion of his round-trip ticket back to Canada to pay for the ticket to Portugal. Additionally, James also tried to go to Nigeria in Africa from Lisbon, and it was in Lisbon that James got a new passport in the corrected name, "Sneyd." It created a bit of a stir at the time, that newspapers and magazines knew so much about his Lisbon travels, so soon. Readers felt he must have been followed in order for the police and reporters to know so much.

By the middle of May, James was back in London, with three more weeks of freedom before it would all end for him. Although it would later be reported that he flew from Lisbon to London on a TAP Portugal flight, I believe this is not the case. There is extensive documentation of other flights in the early documents and the British documents, but not this flight; there are no witnesses listed in any document I have seen, and the tickets seem to have materialized much later. According to New Scotland Yard, the person who claimed that James was on a flight from Lisbon to London was Mrs. Doris Westwood, the proprietress of the Heathfield House Hotel, where James stayed upon his return to London. This lack of evidence of any official flight from Lisbon to London would botch up the feds' arrest scenario in the worst way.

During this last stint in London, James stayed at three hotels: Heathfield House Hotel, New Earl's Court, and the Pax Hotel. While at New Earl's Court Hotel on Penywern Road, James called a reporter, Ian Colvin, who seemed to know something about passage to Africa. By this point James was hoping to get lost in the world. Colvin told him to go to Brussels and research what was transpiring in Africa. It is an interesting fact that the British researcher on the John F. Kennedy assassination, Peter Dawnay, was staying only one hundred yards away from James in London at this time. I can't prove that this detail is significant, but the fact that one of the early experts on the JFK murder was a stone's throw from Jimmy is another of the many strange coincidences surrounding my brother's alleged involvement in Dr. King's murder.

New Scotland Yard documents verify that the murder of Bobby Kennedy had a very unsettling effect on James. "It was happening again," he thought. In the middle of a horrific storm, James heard the news about Robert Kennedy. He ran from New Earl's Court to take refuge in the Pax on June 5, after trying to get a room at the YMCA youth hostel on Warwick Way, which was full. When he stopped at the YMCA, I believe that Raul C. was with him; the man with James was said to be a 125-pound man with reddish-blonde hair—like Raul.

The proprietor of the Pax, Mrs. Anna Thomas, later told reporter Ian Colvin that James was "nervous, furtive, locked his bedroom door at night and stayed in bed most of the day." And according to a New Scotland Yard document, while in room 3 at the rather small Pax Hotel, James received calls from an American-sounding woman. Contrary to speculation, this was not our sister Carol.

At this time James was in contact with British and American intelligence. A deal was struck, and he was supposed to walk free. So on Saturday, at 6:15 A.M. on June 8, 1968, my brother gave himself up at Heathrow Airport in London. He was supposed to get off on charges relating to the murder of Martin Luther King Jr. The feds were true to their word; they initially tried to get him off after only serving a few years.

A great deal of controversy was created at the time, because the feds obviously had a double of my brother flying to Heathrow Airport from Portugal. Two very different scenarios were reported in the press and verified by the airlines. Since he went from Lisbon to London by covert means, they were providing a double to fly in from Lisbon and be arrested in transit to Brussels. The only problem was "secrecy, and need-to-know tactics screwed up their operation," Lyndon has been told by an intelligence operative with some knowledge of the case. Someone on the ground in London must have decided that too many witnesses had seen the real James in London for three weeks, and that the London James should be captured.

The United Press International article, which has been quoted all over the world, stated, "Ray was seized at London's Heathrow Airport shortly after he arrived on a flight from Lisbon, Portugal, in a culmination of an operation that involved top detectives of the U.S. Federal Bureau of Investigation, the Royal Canadian Mounted Police, and Scotland Yard." This is how all the early reports read. The only problem was that the real James Earl Ray had been in London for some time.

Additionally, passengers changing planes didn't need to go to the immigration desk where James was supposedly caught. A passenger on a flight from Lisbon would stay in the safety of the transit lounge and not have to present a passport—the act that supposedly led to James's capture. More than one author or researcher on this case has come to the conclusion that the feds' own security measures made it look as if there were two Sneyds (or Rays) at Heathrow Airport, which in a way there were, in the form of body doubles.

Peter Dawnay saw the confusion in the press and wrote New Scotland Yard to inquire if James had been in London at the time of his arrest, or if he was flying in from Lisbon, with a ticket booked to Brussels, as reported in the press. New Scotland Yard wrote back to Mr. Dawnay, who still lives north of London, to inform him: "The man was in transit through Immigration on arrival from Lisbon on his way to another country." British Overseas Airways (BOAC) only added to the confusion by claiming that they assumed James had just arrived from Lisbon, but they had no record of his ticket. Plans had been made for a double to be arrested, but the operatives messed up the "capture."

There was a purported deal made in London among the feds, author William Bradford Huie, and lawyer Art Hanes. Essentially, the deal would allow James to walk. Since James was nearly penniless, he would supposedly pay for his representation by feeding Huie information about the case, for a book to be published after the trial. In reality, there was plenty of federal money available to pay for Art Hanes and his son to represent James. Huie had been tight with the FBI since the 1930s, which is why he was brought in to control the story.

If a deal hadn't been worked out, James would not have come back from London to possibly face the death penalty. Because of British law, he didn't have to return. At first he wasn't going to come back to the States, and at this time, James was represented by Michael Eugene of the British law firm Michael Dresden and Company. The young solicitor had been appointed by the court.

I wrote Jimmy in London to tell him that the State of Missouri was going to reverse his case. This is what he wrote back:

> Dear John,
>   I will just write you a few lines to let you know everything is all right. I will probably be back shortly. Anyway, don't come over—for one, you couldn't get in; Attorney Hanes couldn't. And two, it's too expensive.
>   About Judge Casey wanting to reverse my case—I don't want it reversed. I will explain later, but you know their things are not doing anything to benefit me.
>   If you could, I would like you to give attorney Art Hanes six hundred dollars; you can get some of it off Jerry, and I will straighten it up with you when I get back . . .

He knew that I had quite a bit more than six hundred available to assist him.

The first book to be written about the King assassination was *The Strange Case of James Earl Ray* by Clay Blair. The book was first issued as a fast paperback. Blair was a government-friendly author who supported the official case, even though he obviously believed the case was strange. I cannot prove the Blair book was written at the request of the government, but others were. The FBI has released documents which verify that Gerold Frank wrote *An American Death* at the request of the FBI leadership, and that the FBI gave reports to George McMillan prior to the existence of the Freedom of Information Act. Though this may be unbelievable to many, even released CIA documents speak of "our propaganda assets." When Clay Blair went to see our old man to interview him, Dad was already shaken by the feds' helicopters flying overhead, conducting surveillance. When Blair showed up, my father pulled a pistol on him and told him to get off his property.

I was working on getting a flight to London when it was announced that James was returning to the United States. Although he didn't trust the feds, James had been told to contact former FBI man and CIA contract agent Art Hanes. According to recently released documents from the CIA, Art Hanes was on their list of "cleared lawyers." James also contacted F. Lee Bailey, who declined to represent him.

By June 16, Hanes told reporters he had accepted James as a client. Three days later, he flew to London. Before he left for Europe, Art Hanes and his son had been contacted by author William Bradford Huie. Huie offered to pay Hanes up to $40,000 for the story from James. Hanes's room in London was arranged and paid for by Huie's publishers.

The authorities in London refused to let Hanes see James, as there were decisions about James's extradition being made which would change Hanes legal standing as James's lawyer. Hanes flew back to the States. However, two weeks later, he flew back to London. On this trip, Hanes had a two-and-a-half-hour meeting with James, where legal contracts were signed, giving Art Hanes complete power of attorney and 40 percent of all monies received from William Bradford Huie after the publication of his book.

Hanes hired an unlicensed local Memphis detective named Renfro Hayes, who worked under the supervision of local attorney Russell X Thompson. Thompson has the unusual distinction of serving as an attorney for both James Earl Ray and Martin Luther King. Thompson, who worked in the first integrated law firm in Memphis, had extensive files relating to the Renfro Hayes investigation. Russell X Thompson would not represent James for any period of time; he was only temporarily on board.

When Hanes came on board, it put a racial spin on the case. He had represented the segregationists who killed civil rights activist Mrs. Viola Liuzzo. Even Art Hanes, who had been the mayor of Birmingham when Dr. King protested there, would say in Harold Weisberg's book, *Frame-Up*, that he believed James was told to ask for his (Hanes's) legal assistance "to put a racial spin on the case." Hanes would also claim that he had "received advance assurances of the availability of an enormous fund for his fee."

I was against the choice of Hanes from the start, and Hanes knew it. In spite of this, contracts were signed which would provide James with money for the trial from the publication of Huie's book. On September 3, Huie wrote James a letter in which he pressed James to confess—and Hanes delivered the letter. Something was clearly going wrong with James's defense.

The Memphis newspaper the *Commercial Appeal* ran a story by Huie on September 12 that was unflattering to James. That same day, James wrote to the judge in the case, Preston Battle, to complain about Huie's conflict of interest. The next day Hanes was quoted as saying that James might never take the stand in his own defense. By the middle of October, James wrote Huie that he wanted to get out from under the contracts he had signed. James felt that he would need money if his case went into appeal. Art Hanes wasn't licensed to practice law in Tennessee, and James would need an additional lawyer.

About this time the FBI's St. Louis agents showed up at the Grapevine to question me, asking, "Did you ever hear any plans about King being killed in San Francisco, or Atlanta?" The FBI's last visit with me was when the heat came down; it started up again later when Jimmy told author William Bradford Huie that he was working in Chicago, using my name and social security number right after he had escaped from prison. Huie reported the story of James's use of my old social security number in the now-defunct *LOOK* magazine.

The mainstream media made it appear that Huie was a better investigator than Boss Hoover; thus, I was waiting for the FBI when they showed up at the Grapevine. I told them another false story—that James had been using my social security number for years—to keep it from looking like I was aiding and abetting James's escape. They stated that the Justice Department was considering putting our father George back behind bars for being a fugitive from justice, as an escapee from the Iowa State Prison. They were also considering moving against our sister for supposedly fraudulently getting a federal tax stamp to operate the Grapevine Tavern, and against me for withholding information in a murder investigation.

I did not blame the FBI or Huie for my new problems; instead, I blamed James, because there was not one reason for him to bring out the fact that he was working in Chicago using my name and social security number. One of the first things I said during my first visit with him in the Shelby County Jail was to "keep my name out of it."

In November of 1968, articles written by Huie began to appear in *LOOK* magazine. The information provided by James was supposed to have been kept secret until the trial, but it was becoming public knowledge. The articles were deliberately describing an unclear plot. James also found out that Huie's publishers said James was "not going to be allowed to testify in his own defense." The publishers were supposedly worried about this, because if James testified, the story would end up in the public domain, and Huie's sole ownership of the story would cease. In reality, I think the feds were frightened by what James would have to say on the stand.

Just days before James's trial was due to start, word reached Huie that James wanted to take the stand. Huie called Jerry to Hartsville, Alabama, and offered us an additional $12,000 to keep James off the stand. Huie told Jerry, "Since my publishers are footing the bill for your brother's defense, Art Hanes and James are to perform according to my instructions." This meant that the total story, and James's chance at freedom, would be under the total control of Huie, the publishers, or the government—whoever was pulling the strings.

James clearly needed more help. Obie O'Brien told me that Percy Foreman, who was a local household name, would be a good lawyer for James. Obie also told me that I could try to get Morris Shenker, the Mob lawyer who had defended Buster Wortman and other well-known Mob figures. I contacted Shenker, who didn't want to get involved. It had something to do with the Jewish community to which he belonged, but he didn't go into detail about it. Shenker then put me in touch with Percy Foreman (who sometimes took Shenker's mother to dinner, so they had to be pretty good friends). Foreman agreed to come to Memphis from his home in Texas. Since Obie was part of the plot, in retrospect, I probably shouldn't have taken his advice.

However, on November 10, I met Percy Foreman at the airport with my brother Jerry and drove him to our hotel by the airport. He was a big man, about seventy years old. "Call me the Texas Tiger," the big man would say. I thought this was a really peculiar thing to call someone, but we played along. In the Carriage Hotel, the "Texas Tiger" looked at the contracts between James's first lawyer, Art Hanes, and Huie. Foreman claimed, "They're not worth the paper they're printed on." So Jerry drove over to the Shelby County Jail with him. Prior to being in Foreman's company, they wouldn't let me in. The first time I tried to see James down in Memphis, the sheriff made me go back to St. Louis to get "special permission." But somehow, Foreman waltzed right in.

I should have seen that things were being orchestrated, but you want to believe the best. Foreman would later claim that James had sent a letter giving him (Foreman) permission to visit, but James denied that. The outgoing mail log kept by the guards proves that Foreman was allowed in without permission from James. After their two-hour meeting, it was Foreman's opinion that Hanes was selling James out. "There's no evidence that Jimmy killed King," Foreman said. He told us that he didn't even think there would be a trial. "If there was evidence, the feds would have used it in the extradition proceedings, and there was no evidence," Foreman told us. He was adamant that it had been months since James had been arrested and there still was not a shred of evidence. Foreman told us that he had represented several thousand criminal cases and had never had one of his clients go to the chair except for his first case.

When Foreman agreed to represent James, he planned to show tapes of Martin Luther King Jr., and the violence that he inspired in the antiwar movement, especially in the black ghettos. Foreman told us, "By the time I get done, the jury will be shooting niggers on their way home, they'll be so upset."

Foreman told us that a deal had been swung before the Brits sent James from London to Tennessee. But I doubt if he really knew about that. I now believe that Hanes and Foreman were working together for the government to frame James, even though at the time, it appeared that the two lawyers were bitter adversaries. As we sat at the Carriage Hotel, Foreman didn't have a single decent thing to say about Hanes, though it was not long before Foreman would take his place in every way, shape, and form.

On November 12, the Texas Tiger filed a motion with the court to be recognized as James's counsel. For his retainer, James had to sign over the rifle that allegedly killed Martin Luther King, plus James's 1966 springtime yellow Ford Mustang. Foreman was obligated by a promise to James to retain licensed Tennessee counsel, but he never did. The date of the trial would be pushed ahead to March 10, 1969—James's forty-first birthday.

When Foreman took over the case, he wanted me to go to the Memphis Holiday Inn on the Mississippi River. This was the same Holiday Inn that

Dr. King was taken to by the Memphis police department when his protest march of March 28, 1968, turned violent. Hanes was staying there at the time, and Foreman wanted me to hand Hanes a note saying that he was fired. Percy Foreman wrote the letter up while he was in the Carriage Hotel and asked me to deliver it. But I told Foreman that it was up to James to decide who his lawyer would be, and I wasn't going to get involved.

When Percy Foreman came in, he said, "All James will have to say is that somebody stole his car and they used it, and that they stole a suitcase out of the car and threw it on the street. There's no evidence," he said. The Texas Tiger was emphatic. "When you get back to St. Louis, get ready for some big money; there's gonna be some big money in it for you, for the King family, for the Rays and everybody." We went back to St. Louis thinking everything was all right.

But of course, it wasn't.

Over the course of two months, from November 12, when Foreman was first recognized as James's lawyer, until the middle of January, Percy Foreman met with James for a total of one hour and fifty-three minutes. Six days after Foreman came on board, without James's consent, Judge Battle appointed public defender Hugh Stanton Sr., as cocounsel for James. Later that same day, after he spoke with Foreman, Stanton went to speak with district attorney general Phil Canale about the possibility of a guilty plea. The public defender's office, by their own admission, didn't interview their first witness until forty-eight days later. Foreman was so divorced from any action of the public defender's office that Hugh Stanton was "amazed and surprised and astounded" to learn three days before the trial that James would plead guilty.

I think it was in December of 1968 that Foreman called us and said that he wanted to call a Ray family meeting in the St. Louis area. So Jerry and I picked Foreman up at the airport, he checked into a hotel, and we all drove to my sister Carol's house in the suburb of Maplewood, not far outside of the city. Five of us were there: our father, Carol and her husband Albert, Jerry, and me. Foreman told us that he was concerned. "The feds got into this, in some way. This is no longer a state's case. We need to convince James to plead guilty, because he now needs to escape the death sentence."

I told Foreman, "I'm not going to get involved in James's decision. He has to make up his own mind." My father agreed, as did the rest of the family, except for Jerry, who was in shock. I couldn't get any details from Foreman. I knew there was no real evidence against James, but since Foreman had just switched his position by 180 degrees, I went down to Memphis to have a talk with James. This was not long before he entered his guilty plea, which took place on his birthday, March 10.

I was let into the Shelby County Jail and entered a special cell block built just for James, according to specifications from the Federal Department of Prisons.

"What are you doing?" I asked him. "Are you pleading guilty?"

"They have me boxed in," he replied. "There's something that's come out." He was nervous, because the whole cell was on video surveillance, and everything was recorded. The "something that's come out" would turn out to be the shooting of the soldier Washington while James was in the army. James explained to me that the feds had gotten frustrated with him. The CIA (or other intelligence-related officials) had come to see him and had offered to get him off within a few years, perhaps three or four. In order for this to happen, he had to lay the blame for the plot on a specific group of fall guys—namely, the Bronfman family of Montreal.

This is an odd turn of affairs, which I can't explain. The wealthy Bronfman family of Montreal was famous for their liquor company, Seagram's. The Bronfmans were a peculiar choice for fall guys, since it was close to the truth. James was told by the feds that the Bronfman family financed left-wing causes. The Bronfmans' lawyer at the time was former American OSS major Louis Mortimer Bloomfield. Many who have researched the assassinations of the 1960s believe that at least part of the internal functions from the period can be blamed on Bloomfield—certainly the assassinations of JFK and MLK. Bloomfield was on the board of CIA-linked Permindex, which was associated with ultrawealthy individuals such as H. L. Hunt.

James told the feds he wouldn't lay the blame on the Bronfmans. As the King assassination plot was under way, Permindex and its subsidiaries were under the microscope because of Jim Garrison's prosecution of Clay Shaw for conspiracy in the murder of JFK. After James refused to lay the blame on the Bronfmans, the feds came back with another proposal. The revised plot would lay the blame on Kirksey Nix of the Dixie Mafia. Nix was in prison and was expected to spend the rest of his life there, so they thought James would go for this. The Dixie Mafia was an interwoven group loosely associated with Carlos Marcello, Mob boss of New Orleans. But this also seemed a strange choice, since the Dixie Mafia had an association with Marcello, and Marcello had ties to the Chicago Mob, and Marcello surely was involved himself. The very left-leaning Nix would later be my cellmate. Perhaps this was the feds' way of reminding their own people who is boss. James didn't go for the plot of laying the blame on Nix, who, as of this writing, is still in prison.

So the feds got fed up with James and decided he was going to "go down." This must have been around December of '68. You can trace the feds' interaction with James in Huie's articles in *LOOK* magazine. Huie published the first two articles in November. The articles speak of a nebulous conspiracy involving maybe the Bronfmans, maybe Nix. Huie's November *LOOK* articles were titled: "The Story of James Earl Ray and the Conspiracy to Kill Martin Luther King" and "I Got Involved Gradually and I Didn't Know Anybody Was to be Murdered." By the following April, *LOOK* published its third and last article by Huie: "Why James Earl Ray Murdered Dr. King." Huie's orders had changed.

By the time the Texas Tiger told James that he had to plead guilty, James had been in the specially constructed jail cell in Memphis for seven months. He was breaking out in rashes and having nosebleeds, and he was kept under video surveillance full-time (except when the feds visited). Jerry and I told everyone we knew in St. Louis that there was no way James would plead guilty for that crime—that there was no evidence against him. We both felt like surprised fools when he abruptly changed his plea to guilty. The day before the guilty plea, Foreman stopped by the jail to see James, bringing along with him a couple of letters he had written to my brother.

Foreman's first letter contained this passage:

```
You have heretofore assigned to me all
of your royalties from magazine articles,
books, motion pictures, or other revenue
to be derived from the writings of William
Bradford Huie. These are my own property
unconditionally.
```

> However, you have heretofore authorized
> and requested me to negotiate a plea of
> guilty if the State of Tennessee through
> its District Attorney General and with the
> approval of the trial judge would waive the
> death penalty. You agree to accept a sen-
> tence of ninety-nine years.

At one point James had tried to fire Foreman, asking him for a mere $500 so either Jerry or I could get him another lawyer. Foreman twisted this in the second letter and offered to loan Jerry $500 and add it to his bill, which, according to him, was now up to $165,000:

> . . . I am willing to advance Jerry $500
> and add it to the $165,000 mentioned in my
> other letter to you today. In other words,
> I would receive the first $165,000. But I
> would not make any other advance—just this
> one $500. And this advance is contingent
> upon the plea of guilty and sentence going
> through on March 10, 1969, without any
> unseemly conduct on your part in court.

In court, a very uneasy James, afraid for his life and the well-being of our father—our old man was still legally vulnerable—attempted to protest. The transcript of the plea bargain went like this:

> JER: Your honor, I would like to say
> something too, if I may.
> The Court: All right.
> JER: I don't want to change anything
> that I have said. I don't want to add any-
> thing onto it either. The only thing I have
> to say is, I don't accept the theories of
> Mr. Clark.
> Texas Tiger: Who is Mr. Clark?

```
JER: Ramsey Clark.
Texas Tiger: Oh.
JER: . . . and Mr. Hoover.
Texas Tiger: Mr. Who?
JER: Mr. J. Edgar Hoover. The only thing,
I say I am not—I agree to all these stipula-
tions. I am not trying to change anything.
I just want to add one thing to it.
     The Court: You don't agree with those
theories?
     JER: I mean Mr. Canale, Mr. Foreman, Mr.
Ramsey Clark. I mean the conspiracy thing.
I don't want to add something onto it which
I haven't agreed to in the past.
     Texas Tiger: I think what he is saying
is that he doesn't think that Ramsey Clark
or J. Edgar Hoover is right. I didn't argue
them as evidence in this case. I simply
stated that underwriting and backing up the
opinions of General Canale, that they made
the same statement. You are not required to
agree or withdraw or anything else.
```

After James plea-bargained guilty on his forty-first birthday on March 10, 1969, he was shipped to a state prison somewhere in Tennessee, during the night. He had become Tennessee State Prisoner #95477. The officials wouldn't tell us where he was.

Foreman wanted Jerry and me to meet with the media and to state publicly that this was the right thing to do. Jerry was ready to talk to the media, but I said, "We're not going to do this for Foreman." I couldn't get over the fact that James was pleading guilty with no evidence that suggested he was guilty. So I steered Jerry out the back door. Before James's trial, Percy Foreman was one of the most famous attorneys in the United States. He was known for saving even obviously guilty men from prison sentences. So clearly, in my brother's trial, Foreman had either been bought off or threatened.

That night Foreman called Jerry and me at the California Hotel and asked us over to his room at the Sheraton. We went over there and met Foreman, who was sitting on his bed, half tanked on Scotch. He told us that he didn't generally take on criminal cases since "criminals don't have any money." The only time he'd take criminal cases was if it was a high-profile case and the publicity would give him "free advertising." Civil cases and divorces of economic elites were Foreman's standard practice. "With James's case, I had to put my whole practice on hold," Foreman claimed. But while Jerry and I sat with him, he got a couple of phone calls from prospective clients, one from the Boston area, and the other from his home state of Texas.

On March 12, James wrote Huie and told him that he had fired Foreman, and not to give him any more money. On that same day, Memphis lawyer Richard Ryan was retained as counsel by James.

Jerry and I went to Memphis to try and get information as to what James was going to do now that he had gotten rid of Percy Foreman. While we were there, Huie came in to chat us up, wearing a southern gentleman's white suit. While he was there, he threw a hundred-dollar bill down on one of our room's tables. Huie had a habit of letting money talk for him. I think this was the only time I met him, but William Bradford Huie had maintained a relationship with Hoover and the FBI since the 1930s. He was only one of the many authors writing a book about my brother's case in 1969.

At the same time, Gerold Frank, who had written the infamous 1966 book, *The Boston Strangler*, was in Memphis. Frank checked into the Peabody, the luxury hotel where Dr. King had often stayed when he came to Memphis.

Later I discovered that Gerold Frank is mentioned in FBI documents released through the FOIA as being the FBI choice to write a book on the King case. Frank's name was first mentioned in a memo to Hoover from Cartha DeLoach on March 12, 1969. DeLoach says about Frank, ". . . our relationship with him has been excellent."

As soon as James was transferred to prison in the segregation unit in Nashville, he began writing to Judge Battle and others in an attempt to overturn his guilty plea. At first he thought he would have to wait a couple of years until he had enough money to afford a real lawyer. But watching Foreman defame him on television had instilled the very real fear in him that he would never get a fair trial.

On March 14, James wrote Mississippi senator James Eastland, who had spoken of opening an investigation into Dr. King's murder. James told Senator Eastland, "I will cooperate in any such hearing."

Jerry had contacted attorneys J. B. Stoner, Robert W. Hill, and Richard Ryan of Memphis. In late March, Mr. Ryan drove from Memphis to Nashville to see James, but was not permitted in. At this same time, the prison stated publicly they planned to keep James in isolation indefinitely. Denied an attorney, James personally wrote a handwritten letter to Judge Preston Battle on March 26. He was requesting, as he had the right to do under Tennessee law, a hearing to petition the court for a new trial before a thirty-day grace period had expired. The next day, Robert W. Hill wrote a letter to Judge Battle, informing him of the unethical contracts that had been signed and of James's request for a new trial.

The judge, who had been nervous from all the riots associated with the case, had been on vacation. On March 31, Judge Battle returned to his judicial duties. He had received James's letter, and asked assistant prosecutor James Beasley to call the prison and have them ask James who was going to represent him. Unfortunately, by the time the dapper Beasley would get back to Judge Battle around 5:00 P.M., the judge was dead of cardiac arrest. He would not be the last person associated with the case to die in such a manner. Battle followed Buster Wortman, who died in late 1968, supposedly during cancer surgery.

Judge Battle was given an autopsy by Jerry Francisco, the same man who performed Dr. King's autopsy. Francisco is best remembered as the man who would later claim that Elvis also died of a heart attack, rather than the drug overdose that actually killed him. In this case, Francisco also ruled that Judge Preston Battle had died of a heart attack.

In the fall of 1974, James participated in an important evidentiary hearing. Through the process of discovery, he received a box containing materials relating to his case from the desk of Judge Preston Battle. The papers had been placed in the vault in the office of the clerk of the criminal court, on the very night of Judge Battle's death. One of the papers, hidden away for nearly six years, revealed that Judge Battle was about to grant my brother a new trial. Under Tennessee law in 1968, if the judge dies while considering a motion such as my brother's to vacate his plea, the motion would be granted.

This was true for at least one man we know of—but not James Earl Ray. For the next twenty-nine years, James would do everything possible to get a fair trial. It never happened.

In 1969, James sent Jerry to see Buster Wortman's right-hand man, steamfitter Lawrence Callanan. Jerry was looking for assistance and information from Callanan, who referred Jerry to Jimmy Hoffa's lawyer, Z. T. Osborn Jr., in Nashville. But soon after Osborn decided to help James with his case, Osborn abruptly committed suicide. Jerry had first contacted Callanan around Thanksgiving, and attorney Osborn was dead by February 1. Osborn supposedly shot himself in his garage in Nashville, but his wife didn't believe that Osborn had committed suicide. She issued FOIA requests for all of his extensive FBI surveillance files. The number of files on Osborn was so high that they made the wife pay up front for duplication costs. Osborn's death is just one more on the long list of what many would call mysterious deaths associated with this case.

The feds were so on top of the Ray family that they even developed Jerry's girlfriend, Marjorie Fetters, as a confidential informant. Jerry eventually became aware of this and dumped her because of it. Fetters lived on Arnold Street in Camden, New Jersey, which lies on the Delaware River. Camden is usually considered one of the most dangerous cities in the United States. Although the FBI could have put Jerry in prison for aiding James, an escaped convict, they most likely used him for information instead—information they funneled through Fetters.

There was one man in St. Louis at this time who must have felt empathy for the Rays, and who fed me information indirectly; this was police chief Eugene Camp. He'd funnel information to St. Louis Police Department detective sergeant Frank Cavanaugh. They knew the FBI was trying to get the St. Louis Police Department's assistance in framing me and putting me in prison—and they eventually succeeded. Why was the government trying to frame me? Because I knew too much about the assassination of King. I knew my brother was being framed and that he had joined the CIA earlier and had connections to the FBI in Chicago. I also knew of the deal made in the shooting death of solider Washington.

Most of the time, when Detective Cavanaugh wanted to funnel information to me, he would go to my friend Margie's tavern up the street from the Grapevine. Margie, who was twenty-three years old and very attractive, was his former girlfriend, and Cavanaugh must have known that she and I had a friendly relationship. A few years later Margie would die of a heart attack, in her mid-twenties. It is almost unheard of for anyone to have a heart attack at this age, especially a young woman in fine health. The heart attack gambit is an old one in the intelligence community, and I couldn't help but wonder if the CIA got rid of her—if her death was one more to add to the growing list.

The list continued to grow with the death of Dr. King's brother, the Reverend A. D. King, who was found dead at his home in an apparent swimming pool accident. The government undercover operative, the late James Cooper Green, would later claim that he, Green, was with the intelligence squad that killed A. D. King for the feds. Unfortunately, A. D. King would not be the last King family member to die violently. The cover-up of the King assassination left a pile of corpses in its wake.

eight

Kangaroo II

John held very few straight jobs through
the 1960s.

—Gerald Posner, *Killing the Dream*

My youthful life of petty crime, unfortunately for me, was the perfect fuel for the government to use in continuing to persecute anyone who might be able to assist James in his claims of having been deceived and manipulated into pleading guilty to the shooting of Dr. King. I managed to make a lot of good decisions in avoiding one federal trap after another, traps that had been set for me with the intent of keeping me in prison and incommunicado for most of my life. Unfortunately, I also made a few foolish decisions, and the feds saw to it that those mistakes would come back to haunt me in spades.

James never got any money from the literary deal worked out between his lawyers—Hanes, and later, Foreman—and William Bradford Huie. Our brother Jerry wasn't in the best financial situation either, since he had been fired from his job in Chicago due to FBI meddling. For the time being, Jerry was tending bar at the Grapevine. Since James didn't receive any of the money Huie had promised him from the book deal, I became a loan shark to earn some money. I'd lend a person some money, say $100, and they would pay me back double the amount. This is what the FBI calls "a juiceman." I don't feel it's criminal if someone like me loans somebody cash; many people lend cash. If the World Bank and the IMF loan money to developing countries and bleed them dry, they don't call them juicemen, though they should.

At this time, 1969, an ex-con named James Russell Rogers, known as "Foolbird," came by the Grapevine. You may ask how a man gets the nickname "Foolbird." It's a fair enough question, and I should have made a point to get an answer before I hired him to remodel my tavern. Foolbird Rogers was supposedly a carpenter, but he wasn't very good at it. He had served time in prison in Illinois on the old, corrupt "one-year-to-life" sentence after being convicted of robbing banks. He was released from prison in order to enter the service during World War II, with promises that his army stint would pay his debt to society. When they put convicts in the army, they put them in the front lines. After the war ended, the government reneged on the deal they had made with many of these convicts, including Foolbird Rogers. He had to go to court to be let out of prison.

I became a juiceman for Foolbird once he was released from prison. And although it sounds like the title of a Delta Blues song, I know that the FBI found out about our relationship through their wiretaps and informants in the Grapevine. The feds knew I was just loaning money, and nothing more, because they had me watched. For a long time I remained unaware that the feds were trying to frame me, though my ignorance wouldn't last the whole year.

James Benney, a guy whose uncle would eventually buy the Grapevine, also started coming around my tavern around this time in 1969. Benney had been in the St. Louis jail with a guy named Jerry Lee Miller, and together, they had broken out. The two of them joined forces with an ex-navy guy named Ronald Goldenstein. I lent Benney money because I knew his uncle—and his whole family—was the type to pay me back. At this time I lent Benney $2,500. Benney lived somewhere out on Interstate 70, which links St. Louis with Kansas City.

Things were getting hot by this time. I wasn't being watched by just the government; I'd also noticed cars hanging out on the street outside the Grapevine. From the looks of it, these cars were filled mostly with African-American guys who probably believed the lies in the media about our racist ties and the murder of King. The FBI was also putting a lot of heat on my sister Carol, who owned the Grapevine with me. The feds were telling her that they were going to put her behind bars due to criminal activity. The FBI's accusations of her criminal activity were ridiculous; Carol was working as an assistant teacher of little children for the Catholic Church. At one point Carol and I had to shut the tavern down for a week to let things cool off.

The feds were going to try and take down the family of James Earl Ray. Logic would tell you that this would do several things for them. One, it would make us look like hardened criminals, which would further implicate Jimmy. Two, since I was the oldest and knew Jimmy's secret life the best, they wanted me out of the way.

Beginning in 1969, a string of bank robberies was committed by men who were meeting one another in the Grapevine. None of these robberies involved me. A few months after I'd loaned Benney the $2,500, in late October of 1970, I fell into a federal trap. Benney and Goldenstein—we called him "Goldie"—had been in the Grapevine, joking around. Although they were talking about their plans to rob the Bank of St. Peters, I didn't have any specific information relating to their impending heist. St. Peters was a suburban community of just several hundred people. The bank was located where I-70 meets State Route 79, which runs up to Hannibal, Missouri. This was a good twenty-minute drive from the Grapevine on Arsenal Street.

At approximately 1:20 on the afternoon of October 26, 1970, Goldie, Benney, and Jerry Lee Miller entered the Bank of St. Peters armed and wearing masks, hats, and gloves. The heist took only three minutes. Goldie had learned a few tips from Foolbird Rogers, including how to hide in the woods after a robbery. That was the plan after this robbery, but unfortunately, Goldie wrecked the car while driving it into the woods.

I would later learn that Benney's girlfriend was also in on this job. She was supposed to come out and pick them up after she got off work that afternoon, but she was delayed. (Although I didn't know it at the time, I found out later that Benney's girlfriend was married, and her husband was high up in military intelligence.)

Since Goldie had wrecked the car, and Benney's girlfriend couldn't get there right away to pick them up, as planned, they needed some other method of escape. They naturally feared a massive shakedown, so they called me from a farmhouse near the crashed car. When they called the Grapevine and asked me to come and pick them up, my barmaid took the message and delivered it to me. I had two witnesses to the fact that their call came in after the robbery had taken place. They didn't say that they had robbed a bank—only that they had crashed the car and needed a ride.

In the meantime, the FBI had put out an All Points Bulletin on me; they must have known what was going down from their informants or wiretaps. So, like a dummy, I was driving around looking for these guys, walking right into the trap they had set for me. I never actually picked them up that day. The feds would have had me dead to rights if I had done so, but I couldn't find them. They were not in my car that day at all. The FBI, however, would later claim that I was the getaway driver. The police had found the wrecked and abandoned car, and they had a description of a supposed switch car: a two-tone, white over maroon '66 Olds—my car. They put out an APB to stop me. The FBI said that my license plates were the reason I was stopped while I was driving around out there.

The guy who arrested me, Evan Thebeau, was a deputy sheriff for the St. Charles County sheriff's office. Thebeau broke open the trunk of my car and tore the car apart; he didn't find any money, or anything else, for that matter. At first Thebeau was concerned because he had torn up my car. In front of me, on the police dispatch radio, he said, "Why did the FBI have me arrest this guy?"

Since the sheriff's office wasn't going along with the plan, the FBI came and picked me up and took me to jail. The special agent in charge of the St. Louis FBI office at that time was the notoriously high-profile J. Wallace LaPrade. I was picked up and thrown in jail for robbing the bank in St. Peters, Missouri, a heist of over $53,000. Once I was arrested, the FBI told the state and local law enforcement to call off the search for the actual robbers. The state police didn't understand, because they assumed the actual robbers were somewhere in the woods with the bags of money, but they did what the feds told them.

A few more minutes of searching and they would have captured the actual crooks. As a matter of fact, the robbers were preparing to stand up out of their hiding places and surrender—that's how close law enforcement actually got to them during their search. Instead, the bank robbers waited for Benney's girlfriend to get off work, and then they took off.

The authorities put me in jail, incommunicado, even though there was nothing to connect me to the robbery—no money, no guns. The real bank robbers all went their own ways. Benney was later killed in Portland, Oregon, while Jerry Lee Miller actually went to California and got married in Fresno.

The case against me would claim I was aiding and abetting the criminals. They had too many bank robbers in the picture, so I couldn't be made a robber. This is why I got it for aiding and abetting, driving a supposed switch car. So under these conspiracy laws, I was also pronounced guilty of whatever charges would have been filed against the actual robbers.

Clarence Haynes—my old landlord back when James had escaped Jefferson City in a bread box—wound up behind bars. He was implicated in a June 11, 1970, bank robbery in Laddonia, Missouri. When Haynes got arrested, part of the deal was to implicate me in the Laddonia heist. He was also told to implicate a guy by the name of Ernest Turley in these bank robberies. Turley is someone I never knew, but he was a friend of Haynes. Initially the feds wanted both Haynes and Turley to testify against me, but Turley wouldn't have anything to do with it, so they needed to discredit him. Haynes and Turley were initially held together in the St. Louis jail. The FBI and the Justice Department eventually offered Haynes immunity, and moved him from the St. Louis jail. They transferred him to the St. Charles County jail, and locked him up a floor below me.

So, Haynes decided to testify against me and Turley. This would shock Ernest Turley in the courtroom. The feds rehearsed Haynes, and by the time they got done with him, he sounded like a college graduate, which he was far from being. The U.S. marshals told me about how they were preparing Haynes. The other guy Haynes was going to testify against, Turley, was more or less a rehearsal, so he could practice before his higher-profile testimony against me later on.

Haynes claimed I was in on this heist in Laddonia, which started a frenzy of lies in the press. Most notable was Patrick Buchanan, an editorial writer for the *St. Louis Globe-Democrat*, who got in on the action. Later, as a member of the Nixon White House (he was a speechwriter), Buchanan was responsible for suggesting dirty tricks against left-leaning groups. FOIA releases later tied his writings to the FBI.

Haynes's testimony at Turley's trial didn't remotely stand up to cross-examination; he got caught in lie after lie. Turley's lawyer was obviously not in on the fix. In practically everything Haynes said, he got caught perjuring himself. The feds got mad about this. Also, Turley had witnesses who placed him hundreds of miles away from the crime at the time the bank was robbed, buying auto parts. Haynes was eventually charged with perjury, and Turley was found not guilty. The FBI and Justice Department immediately double-crossed Haynes, tried him, and shipped him off to Marion Federal Penitentiary, known as New Alcatraz, for fifteen years.

When Turley was found innocent, the media snakes crawled back into their holes, and the story was dropped. The federal propaganda assets did not print or speak one word about how the feds had snuck Turley out of federal court in St. Louis to retry him in Laddonia. One main purpose of the initial Turley trial was to spew pretrial publicity against me, and it failed.

The feds still wanted to get Turley, even though they knew he was innocent. Turley, like me, knew too much in the eyes of the feds. The FBI wanted to put Ernest Turley behind bars for several reasons, despite the fact that they knew he had no part in any bank robbery. Among the reasons was that he wouldn't give false testimony against me. But worse, he had embarrassed the Justice Department, the FBI, and the mainstream media when he was found not guilty of robbing a bank.

They rearrested Turley outside the courtroom, and they set up a state kangaroo court in the city of Missoula to get him. This is as unusual as the rest of the case against me, as you would nearly always be charged first with state charges, and then later, with federal charges. The marshals told me what was happening with Turley. They couldn't figure it out themselves, because rarely will you get a conviction in a state case when the feds have a 98.6 percent conviction rate. The feds seemed to have a plan.

They had no real witnesses against Turley. Their one witness, Haynes, was in the slammer for perjury. In the Turley case, they rehearsed before a corrupt cop from St. Louis and concocted a story relating to Turley's previous federal trial, where he supposedly bragged to his relatives about outsmarting the jury in the federal trial. The authorities placed this cop who had testified directly outside the jury room. This trial got Turley twenty years. The St. Louis media, including the *St. Louis Post-Dispatch*, hushed up this case.

On November 28, just over a month after the St. Peters bank robbery, the bank robbers came to light. Benney and Goldie checked into the Cornelius

Hotel on Southwest Park in Portland, Oregon. Benney used the alias "Michael Wolf," and Goldie chose the not-very-believable assumed name, "Robert Wagner." Goldenstein didn't have any money because he had buried his take in Minnesota. Benney did have his money, packed into a suitcase: twenties and fifties with verifiable serial numbers, directly from the bank.

Once they were in the hotel, Benney called down to the desk clerk and asked for a prostitute to be sent up to the room. The hotel clerk obliged, and when the girl came up, she noticed all of the money that Benney had. Once Benney fell asleep, the prostitute tried to leave in the middle of the night with the suitcase full of money, but Benney woke up in time and slapped the girl around. The prostitute later told her pimp about the money Benney had up in his room. The next night, the pimp approached Benney as he walked through the hotel lobby. An argument erupted between the two, and the pimp shot Benney, killing him. What the pimp didn't know was that Benney had taken his money, $12,876, neatly stacked in the suitcase, to Goldenstein's room for safekeeping.

When Goldenstein came downstairs to the hotel bar, he saw what was going down and hid in a back room. After the shooting, the police arrived, and detectives were brought in. The cops didn't know who all the people were, so they arrested five black guys who just happened to be there. The police also arrested Goldenstein, who they found still hiding in the back room. Since they thought Goldie's behavior was odd and there was a rumor of a gun in room 728, Goldie's room, his room was searched. Patrolman David M. Ueland found Benney's money in Goldie's room. It was at this point that the FBI got involved.

The suitcase had identification saying that it was Benney's, and since Benney was dead, the authorities couldn't introduce this money into court. Miller had not yet been located, so the principal becomes Ronald Goldenstein. Meanwhile, Goldie is indicted on bank robbery charges back in Missouri with me aiding and abetting. Once he was in custody, the FBI tried to coerce Goldie into admitting that the money in the suitcase was his own by threatening to charge him with a more-serious crime of partaking in the conspiracy to shoot Benney if he did not cooperate. And as for the pimp who actually shot Benney? The FBI offered him immunity if he testified against Goldenstein, if Goldie didn't cooperate. What did the FBI want so badly that it would grant immunity to known murderers? The eventual prize was me, behind bars because of my knowledge of James's CIA connections and the connection to the Washington shooting.

Goldie was transferred from Oregon to Missouri, bypassing federal court in Oregon, and bypassing any federal testimony before federal magistrates in Oregon. The feds wouldn't let Goldie testify, as that might have thrown a wrench into their plans for my trial. Goldenstein had little choice but to go along with the feds, as he was facing conspiracy to commit murder charges. The feds had to manufacture a principal—a main defendant—in order to get me convicted for aiding and abetting; thus, they had to manufacture a deal with Goldie.

When they searched Goldenstein's room, it was an illegal search. To circumvent the law, and to justify the search and seizure, the cops claimed Ueland chased Goldenstein up to his room. If Ueland was in hot pursuit of Goldie up to his room, this would provide the only legal justification for entering the room without a warrant, because it would fall under the "Hot Pursuit Doctrine." This is where Goldenstein had to keep his mouth shut and go along with the FBI's plan; the FBI needed him to testify that this is how everything went down.

The feds would have to doctor up the evidence they had, because the confiscated money belonged to Benney, and there was no physical evidence against Ronald Goldenstein. Authorities instructed Goldenstein not to take the stand. The FBI and police removed the suitcase that could be linked to the deceased Benney and said that the money was Goldenstein's. They had to have a reason to put Goldenstein on trial. In order to convict me, they had to have a principal I could aid, since I was not at the scene of the crime. So, Goldie kept his mouth shut, and although we would be tried together, we were not in the same boat.

Homicide detectives take over murder cases in all states. No homicide detectives testified at my trial, just this cop, Patrolman Ueland. Since Goldie was deliberately held in a separate jail from me, I couldn't find out what was going on, although the marshals were warning me about the legal shenanigans that were transpiring. They let me know that my trial was being fixed. The reason the marshals were willing to help me was because they were angry. King's murder had just happened; they had information about the hit, and they didn't like the corrupt FBI ordering them around. I was able to find out the truth of the FBI's maneuverings through them.

Once the feds made a deal with Goldie, they didn't want any of the true information to come out until after my conviction. Because of this, the five or so men arrested at the Cornelius Hotel—including the pimp, the actual shooter—had charges against them dropped by the State of Oregon. That's right: Charges were dropped against at least one real murderer in order to put me behind bars.

Goldenstein and I pleaded not guilty under indictment charging violation Title 18, Section 2113. I would go to trial before Judge William Hedgecock Webster in U.S. District Court, Eastern District of Missouri. To call Webster a snake is to defame snakes. The man I call "Willie the Bender" is a former U.S. attorney. Many innocent people who have spent time behind bars will tell you that these U.S. attorneys are good at fixing trials.

During my trial for aiding and abetting the St. Peters bank robbery, I was represented by three lawyers sent by my brother James. The proudly racist J. B. Stoner; Richard Ryan, the former head of the Wallace campaign in Tennessee; and local lawyer Richard Hamdy. Hamdy entered a pretrial motion on my behalf. Stoner disliked the FBI and had represented my brother James free of charge until their association became too controversial. Jesse Benjamin Stoner was clearly trying to get publicity from representing us for his segregationist party, the National States Rights Party (NSRP). Now I can't help but wonder if Stoner was my brother's payback after I had sent him Percy Foreman. I had three lawyers and still ended up in prison, whereas Goldenstein had only one court-appointed lawyer and eventually walked.

Family associate Catman Gawron, then seventy-four years old with a forty-three-year history of being behind bars, also testified. Officially he was there to testify for the feds, as he felt he had to, but he attempted to limit his testimony as much as possible to just Goldenstein. I was arrested on October 26, 1970. Catman's St. Louis FBI file was opened on November 2. Catman's citizenship, which had been revoked due to his felony conviction, was reinstated by the feds by November 30, 1970. Catman was a sitting duck for the feds, and because of his past, he had to cooperate with them.

Catman had been coming into the Grapevine and was well acquainted with Benney, Goldie, and Miller—the players in this string of bank robberies. As a matter of fact, he had to be told by the robbers to keep his fingerprints off a potential getaway car on several occasions. He didn't accomplish this very well, because his fingerprints are what brought the authorities to his apartment at Eleventh and Soulard, armed with riot guns and gas guns. On the stand Catman would later claim, "I didn't know if it was a holdup or a pinch!" The cops got a good feel for Catman within seconds, because he wandered out to the street and announced that he was "just going to head to the store," and they responded, "Okay, go ahead—get out of here."

When the police searched Catman's house, they found his burglary tools and confiscated them. Catman announced from the stand in Webster's court-room that this annoyed him, because he "had to go out and buy new ones." As Catman left the witness box, he looked at the stacks of money from the St. Peters heist and asked Judge Webster, "Can I help myself?" When asked why Webster allowed this in his courtroom, he responded, "I thought the court was in recess."

Catman's testimony against Goldenstein is something that angered my brother Jerry. Jerry and Catman never got along well, and Jerry didn't believe in testifying against anyone. Catman would eventually go to the FBI because Jerry beat him up on Market Street in St. Louis for testifying at the trial.

At the time, I felt Goldenstein's lawyer, a man named Sacks, might have been in on the fix because I felt he asked all the wrong questions in court. He also had the inventory list of Goldie's property from the Oregon hotel in his possession, and refused to let my lawyers see it until it had been altered. The inventory list of property would have shown that the suitcase of money was Benney's instead of Goldenstein's. If there hadn't been any evidence against Goldie, there would not have been a trial, and I wouldn't have gone to prison. At this same time, St. Louis right-wing journalist Patrick Buchanan was still writing editorials and going on television shows, painting me as guilty, and in the same breath maintaining James was guilty in the assassination of Martin Luther King Jr. It was revealed later, through releases made under the FOIA, that the FBI was handing Buchanan the false derogatory information about me.

I believe my case sent a message to the feds that Willie the Bender was willing to go along with their program. Cases like mine only come along once in a while. I believe Webster legalized illegal search in my trial. Evidence was recovered by an illegal search and seizure, which was a clear violation of my Fourth Amendment rights. I've heard that Webster was aware the money did

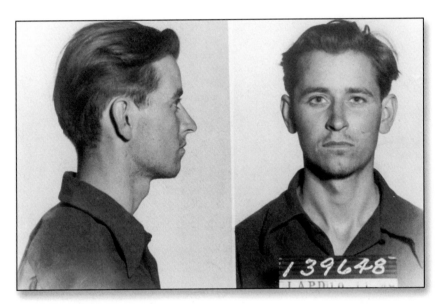

Twenty-one-year-old James Earl Ray's first arrest, Los Angeles, 1949. The arrest, just months after his general discharge from the army, appeared to be a possible extension of behavior modification experiments from the army. James would later claim to have blacked out either from drinking too much or having been slipped "a goofball." (Photo courtesy of the FBI)

Two dapper young men in custody: James Earl Ray (left) and Walter Rife.

(Photo courtesy of the FBI)

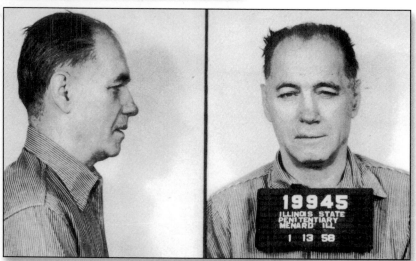

A photo of mob-tied Jimmy "Obie" O'Brien, taken during his time in Menard Prison, where he was incarcerated with John Larry Ray through much of the 1950s. O'Brien would later go missing after the murder of Martin Luther King Jr.

(Photo courtesy of the FBI)

East St. Louis rackets boss Frank "Buster" Wortman. Wortman was a subordinate to the Chicago Mafia. Deceased government operative James Cooper Green corroborated John Larry Ray's assertion that Wortman was part of the King murder plot. Wortman reportedly died of natural causes just months after the King homicide. (Photo courtesy of the FBI)

Charles Stein and his cousin Myrial Tomaso (aka Marie Martin), constant companions of James Earl Ray in Los Angeles. (Above: photo courtesy of the FBI; Below: photo courtesy of the U.S. National Archives)

James Earl Ray's "flop" in Los Angeles. The St. Francis Hotel housed the Sultan Room where Marie Martin was a barmaid. The FBI described the St. Francis Hotel as an "integrated den of iniquity." **(Photo courtesy of the FBI)**

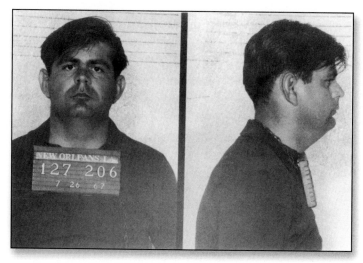

Arrest photo of CIA asset Jules "Ricco" Kimble. Although the House Select Committee on Assassinations would claim, "Kimble also denied meeting Ray or a person using any of Ray's aliases," Kimble claimed to investigator Lyndon Barsten in a taped interview that he and James Earl Ray were in Montreal, Quebec, together and were victims of narco-hypnosis by an employee of McGill University's Allen Memorial Institute. In 1967–68 the Allen Memorial Institute was Subproject 68 of the CIA's MK-Ultra mind control program. **(Photo courtesy of the FBI)**

Outside Dr. King's room at the Lorraine Motel in Memphis, the evening of April 4, 1968. (Photo courtesy of the Shelby County Archives)

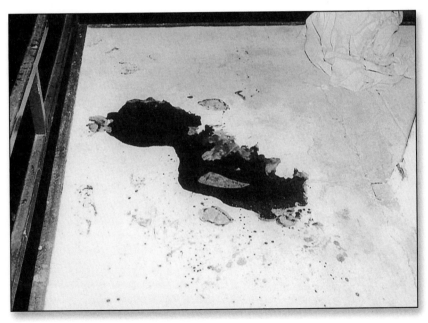

The blood of Dr. Martin Luther King Jr., on the balcony of the Lorraine Motel in Memphis. (Photo courtesy of the Shelby County Archives)

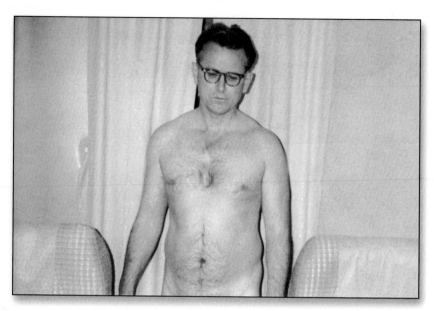

James Earl Ray in transit from England to Tennessee to await his trial in 1968.
(Photo courtesy of the U.S. National Archives)

SHERIFFS DEPT
MEMPHIS TENN
39794
8 2 6 68

Myself, photographed upon entering Shelby County Jail to visit James.
(Photo courtesy of the U.S. National Archives)

Jerry Ray in Memphis, 1968. (Photo courtesy of the U.S. National Archives)

Author of *He Slew the Dreamer,* William Bradford Huie. Huie's publications were to pay for the defense of James Earl Ray in 1968. In 1969 Huie testified that the original title of his book was *They Killed the Dreamer.*
(Photo courtesy of the U.S. National Archives)

Myself and my brother Jerry at the memorial service for James in 1998.
(Photo courtesy of the author)

not come out of Goldie's suitcase. They would have had no reason to legalize an illegal search, because he had a private investigation done of the case.

I would later learn that FBI Headquarters would be closely watching my trial. St. Louis FBI document 91-5279-36 to Headquarters on April 2, 1971, stated: TRIAL PROCEEDING SMOOTHLY. This same document verified that Headquarters would send someone (whose name was redacted) to St. Louis, in relation to my case. The feds' own documents make it clear that mine was not a normal bank robbery trial.

During his testimony, the hotel desk clerk denied that the police had chased Goldenstein upstairs (the feds hadn't anticipated this coming up), at which time William Webster piped up and said that he didn't believe the desk clerk's testimony. Remember: The money in Goldie's room could only be used as evidence in court if it was discovered in hot pursuit, which it wasn't. If Benney's money hadn't been made to look like Goldie's money, then they would have lost their principal in the case. Without a main defendant, they wouldn't have been able to put me away. To sum it up: Goldstein had to be convicted if I was going to be convicted of aiding and abetting—and that was ultimately their goal.

I had two witnesses that placed me at the Grapevine while the bank robbery was taking place. The FBI discredited the witnesses' testimonies and developed false evidence against me with rubber gloves. The bank robbers wore green rubberized gloves, the same kind used by the barmaids at my tavern for washing glasses and cleaning. The FBI went and bought a pair and cut the fingertips off and planted them in my car, presumably so they wouldn't have to match any fingerprints when they were presented as evidence at trial. Their conclusion: If the bank robbers had worn these gloves, and the same gloves were found in my car, then I'd be found guilty. Not only was this silly, since the gloves were sold all over, but why were the fingertips missing? Apparently, I had cut them off to be sure and leave my prints all over! It must run in the family, since my brother had made sure to throw down his rifle at the site of the King murder.

Not only was the trial fixed, but the jury room was also bugged—pretty typical of the feds. I know this because the federal marshals saw another judge, a former FBI employee, dancing and celebrating because he had information from the electronic surveillance of the jury room that it was not going well for me. The truth about my brother being a CIA asset was not even known by his lawyers, and the other family members were too young to have seen what I saw. Goldenstein, the actual bank robber, got thirteen years, while on April 23, 1971, I was sentenced to eighteen years. Goldie's sentence would later be overturned, just as the feds had promised him. Later, despite the fact that the statute of limitations had run out, members of the corrupt HSCA tried to pile additional years onto my sentence by convicting me of perjury. HSCA lawyers went to the U.S. attorney general, Griffin Bell, and asked him to waive the statute of limitations. It's my understanding they went to him three times. I believe the reason Bell did not prosecute me was because he knew the members of the HSCA were the ones engaging in criminal misconduct. Also, if I was put on trial for perjury, the shooting of soldier Washington may come out, which would open a can of worms for the Justice Department. Maybe the HSCA wanted the Justice Department to make public the Washington shooting since they couldn't do it themselves—who knows? What I do know for sure is that Bell wrote an almost unheard of forty-page opinion as to why he was not going to prosecute me. He said to prosecute me would be a boot-strapping type of prosecution.

When a client obtains a lawyer, the lawyer should work for the client—not the other way around. James got himself convicted by listening to his lawyer, and I wasn't far behind. If I knew then what I know now, I wouldn't have served a day of those eighteen years. The feds later tried to get me behind bars on the attempted murder of lawyer—and eventual adviser to former president Bill Clinton—Vernon Jordan, but after having spent ten years in solitary, with nothing to do but think, I knew how to get around their kangaroo courts. By June of '71, special agents from the St. Louis FBI had been working on my brother Jerry's girlfriend, Ronnie (Rhonda), threatening her with a situation similar to mine. Federal agents threatened to arrest her for being a getaway driver if she didn't implicate Jerry in a series of bank robberies under investigation. Jerry, who had been given a job by J. B. Stoner and was living in Savannah, sent copies of a letter to the media to try to circumvent legal action against him by the feds. He seems to have been successful, as the two-inch-thick FBI file prepared against him was never used in a court of law.

Webster became the darling of the mainstream media after my conviction. Rumors floated among the federal marshals about behind-closed-door deals in the works, which put Webster on the road to becoming FBI and then CIA chief—the only man ever to hold both positions. Willie the Bender was appointed a judge of the U.S. District Court for the Eastern District of Missouri in 1970 (just in time for my trial) by right-wing Republican president Richard Nixon and Democratic senator Thomas Eagleton. This was very unusual, to have a very progressive Democrat appointing a right-winger like Webster to the bench. By the late '70s, Congress decided to look into the murders of MLK and President John Kennedy. By this time, William Webster was the director of the FBI. Later, Webster became a government troubleshooter and was sent to hot spots like the Rodney King riots and the massacre at Waco.

An interesting thing happened in the St. Charles County Jail just before my being shipped off to the St. Louis City Jail at the close of the trial. The St. Charles County Jail lies in the city of St. Charles, Missouri's first capital, located about thirty miles west of St. Louis on I-70. St. Charles was built up on the Missouri River, while St. Louis was built on the Mississippi. I was held there, in the St. Charles jail, for about six months, until I was sentenced. At this time the St. Charles jail was all white, totally nonintegrated. St. Charles was mobster George Walsh's territory. Just prior to my arriving there, a Mob hit man had reportedly escaped by using a carved wooden pistol, like John Dillinger did; turns out this was really just a cover story.

One of the jailers, nicknamed "Blackie," had written a book no publisher would touch, about how the FBI had set up people for crimes they had not committed. He had years' worth of information on the feds. He told me that if I gave him $1,600, he'd let me out the side door. Blackie had already done this for the Mob hit man; the wooden pistol story was a cover for the real escape, made possible by Blackie. At this time my education about all these fixed trials had just begun, but it was this jailer, who was born in Mississippi and knew the background on myriad cases, who let me know the score.

Once I was sentenced, Judge Webster ordered me to be locked up in the nearly all-black St. Louis jail. Webster waited until I was sentenced, hoping the inmates believed the hype about the Ray brothers and would beat me up, or worse.

In the St. Louis jail I was housed with nineteen black guys and three white guys. The white guys were more than what a lot of men would call "sissified." To say the least, they were not men who could easily defend themselves against others. I would find out later on through official sources—usually the marshals—that this was a game to the FBI. They were trying to put pressure on me, get me to go on the record with some phony story about where James Earl Ray had gotten his money after his escape from Jefferson City. They reportedly didn't care what kind of story it was that I concocted; they just had a problem creating a believable story that accounted for Jimmy's funds. And they wanted to get a headline out of it. The chief probation officer, J. Allen McDaniels, was trying to make a deal with me for the same reason. There was only one problem: I don't make deals.

The St. Louis jail was everything the feds had hoped. The black jailer would call each inmate for his mail. Mine was called whether or not I had mail, but he wouldn't use my real name; he'd cry, "James Earl Ray, no mail for you today!" Or for medicine call, "James Earl Ray, do you need any medicine today?" He was under orders from the feds to stir up the inmates. At this time Jerry was trying to see me, but I was kept incommunicado. Jerry went to Judge Webster, attempting to get a court order that allowed me to have visitors. Webster said he would sign the court order, but when Jerry came back, the FBI was there; Webster refused to sign the court order, saying, "I don't want to offend anybody."

Stories were floating around the jail that I thought I was Jesse James, robbing all these banks. There was a six-foot-seven black inmate who must have weighed over three hundred pounds. Once he got inside his cell he started hounding me about the fact that I thought I was Jesse James. I knew this was going to be trouble, so I had to make up my mind what I was going to do to this jailer who was stirring all these people up. I walked up to the jailer and said: "I know you're an FBI bitch and they put you up to this racial trouble here. You call me by one of those names one more time, and I'm going to have somebody put a bomb under your car. The next time you pull this shit, your ass'll be blown all the way to the FBI field office."

The jailer didn't know much about me except all the stuff that had been made up by the media, so he didn't know if I was nuts or if I actually did have connections to the Mob. After the jailer had stewed for a couple of hours, he had changed his tune to a more agreeable one. Convicts always talk, and news spreads fast. It was all a bluff; I wouldn't have bombed anybody, even if I had known someone who could, or would, do it.

While I was in the St. Louis jail, two men, both Vietnam vets, refused to share a cell with me. These men had murdered a guy so they could have his wife for themselves. They wanted nothing to do with me because, based on the media reports, they believed I was too violent. While I was still there, the feds moved in a federal prisoner named Carmel who was taping Stoner and me with a concealed tape recorder. On almost a daily basis, this prisoner spoke of diamond heists or deals like the ones the Chicago Mob had involved James in.

A nineteen-year-old black man named Washington came into the jail, charged with being the getaway driver for several other guys who had allegedly robbed a loan company in St. Louis. He was to testify for the feds against his cohorts. The young man was very sick with asthma. When the other prisoners heard he was going to testify against the others, they wouldn't help him with his asthma attacks and refused to share a cell with him. Washington was scared to be locked in his cell alone because his asthma attacks were so bad, he feared he wouldn't be able to take his lifesaving medicine.

I asked the marshals to leave our cells open at night so I could give him his medicine. I was told, "No way—to hell with Washington." I asked if I could move into Washington's cell, and they agreed. Several times I gave him his medicine, and a couple of times I had to lift him back into his bunk. This frightened teenager told me that I had saved his life at least a few times. Even though Washington testified against his partners in crime, he still got six years in the maximum-security prison at El Reno in Oklahoma. This is one hell of a prison for the feds to send a sick teenager to. I heard later the young man only survived for a few months; he died in El Reno from his severe asthma condition.

In June of 1971, I was transferred to Leavenworth. My brother, James, had been in Leavenworth during the 1950s. About the time I started serving my eighteen years, Judge William Webster—Willie the Bender—made a public statement, to the effect of "Sometimes you have to bend the Constitution." Was he talking about Goldenstein and me? When you bend the Constitution, you often end up with innocent men and women on death row. The bending of the Constitution has turned the purported leaders of our criminal justice system into murderers of innocent people.

Leavenworth, known to convicts as the "Big Top," is a very old prison. Its walls are forty feet tall and sunk forty feet underground. When I first got to

Leavenworth, the caseworker called me to his office and said, "The U.S. attorney told us that he was going to try to get you for income tax evasion. They're going to say that you've been stealing for ten, nearly eleven years since you've been out of prison." Usually convicts are only out of prison for months, but I had been working honestly for years, contrary to what author Gerald Posner has written in *Killing the Dream*.

In June of 1971 I was placed in quarantine for about two weeks, which is routine. They had a top, fifth tier in the prison in a cell house. I was placed there, where they put most of the prisoners who are considered antigovernment or related to ultra–right-wing activities. These prisoners are deliberately put into ethnically integrated cells. These cells are integrated for the wrong reason—not because they want everybody to get to know one another and get along. They are hoping that you actually irritate one another.

The different groups—Aryan Brotherhood, Blackstone Rangers, Nation of Islam, and so on—have contracts against each other. Sometimes one group can't get next to you, but another group can, and that's how murder contracts are executed. There were several attempts made to kill me in prison. The first time, the Black Muslims sent a message, warning me through an inmate pal from Quincy, Gerald Wheeler. The second time, I was warned by Mafia boss Jackie Cerone, front man for the Chicago Mob in the late '60s, who was in the joint for tax evasion.

Prisons are dangerous places. A couple of years after I went to Leavenworth, when I was living on the first floor in B cell house, I was nearly killed in a plot perpetrated by two black guys who worked early shift in the kitchen. Both of these men were short and small. These guys were let out of their cells early in the morning to work in the kitchen, which was in another building. They figured they would sneak down the back steps, cremate my roommate and me with a Molotov cocktail, and be back in the kitchen before anyone knew anything. If not for my crazy cellmate, who was knitting at 4:00 A.M. and murmuring about the Mormons, the two guys would have burned me alive. My cellmate, Mitchell, screamed so loud when he saw them that they dropped the bomb and took off running back to the kitchen.

I took action to protect myself from these men. I had asked a fellow inmate, Arman Kiliyan Jr., to take care of them for me. A native Armenian, Kiliyan was a powerfully built man with a fanatical hatred of Communism.

He had been used by the feds, until he feared a double cross. Kiliyan will enter the story again later.

Goldie was in Leavenworth with me for a while. This was because of a mix-up between the U.S. attorney, the FBI, and the Federal Bureau of Prisons (BOP). A certain inmate from St. Louis, named Turnbolt, was always on Goldenstein. Turnbolt was a joker anyway, but Goldie didn't like it. Again and again, Turnbolt would joke about Goldie carrying his money around in a suitcase because he was a Jew. Finally, around August of 1972, Goldie said, "That wasn't my money in the room, and I can walk anytime. I can get my case reversed." When I heard that, I was stunned, even though the marshals had essentially told me the same thing. So I went to Goldie to get an affidavit from him documenting what he had admitted. I had my caseworker, James O'Connor, by my side as a witness. O'Connor went somewhere to get permission, and when he returned, he said, "I don't know if I can do this."

I should have known what would happen. The next morning I was working in the shoe shop, repairing shoes. The regular guard was missing from the shoe shop, and the guy I worked with was also missing. So, a new guy shows up who happens to be a black guy. I'm not alarmed to work with a black man, but the two regular guys were gone, and I knew how the feds wanted to maintain this "racist Ray" myth. When I inquired what was going on, I was told to shut up and get back to work. So, I went to my cell to think about what they might be trying. The next thing I know, I was collected by the prison goon squad and thrown back into solitary confinement. I was held there for sixty-plus days.

The *Kansas City Star* had written about my case, and the reporter had tried to see me, but assistant warden O'Malley wouldn't let him do it. I was told O'Malley had given the reporter a phony racist story about me as a cover. This activity all stemmed from the affidavit I wanted from Goldenstein. Unfortunately, the reporter believed O'Malley's fable and decided to print a story repeating the racist garbage.

A death perfectly timed to make certain that Goldie got off was the death of Catman, one of the main witnesses in the case. Catman Gawron's body was found in his home by the Third District St. Louis Police Department on January 23, 1972. On July 27, 1972, the Eighth Circuit Court scheduled Goldie's retrial.

John Eugene "Catman" Gawron died of a heart attack, one of the most common methods used by intelligence agencies for murder. In the weeks before Goldie's new trial, Catman had been beaten in front of his house by attackers, and his next-door neighbor had been shot. In the first incident, Catman was beaten up when he stepped outside his front door. When I asked him, "What were your four dogs doing when you were being beaten?", Catman said, "They sided with the attackers." The second incident involved a new neighbor from Arkansas who had moved next door to Catman. This neighbor stepped out of his front door about the same time that Catman was regularly known to go outside, and he was pumped full of bullets and killed. Catman stopped stepping outside at night after the shooting. When Catman died, his cats reportedly ate from his face and body.

In April of '72, the Eighth Circuit Court of Appeals stated that the money found in Goldie's room could not be used as evidence against him because it had been found during an illegal search of his hotel room. But, the money could still be used against me, the "aider and abettor," since I had no connection to the hotel room. In August, Goldie was found not guilty in what I believe may be the Eighth Circuit's first and last reversal of a bank robbery conviction. (Ironically, I was still accused of aiding this "innocent" person.) The facts must have been clearly laid out for the jury, which deliberated for less than an hour. The state did not prosecute as they had with poor Ernest Turley. Goldie was having the kind of luck that only the U.S. federal government can deliver. Once Goldenstein was released after having served eighteen months, I was free from solitary.

While I was still in solitary, however, I tried to get Willie the Bender and attorney Sacks to give me a copy of the inventory of items taken out of Goldie's hotel room in Portland, to see if the list had been altered. They both refused. I then contacted the clerk of court, who told me the document had been lost. I told the clerk that the feds had a history of changing transcripts to fit the Department of Justice cases on appeal, and if I didn't get a copy of the list, I'd soon be filing motions for it. I got the so-called "lost list" in a few days, and as I suspected, it had been altered to meet their legal needs, to make the money appear as if it was Goldenstein's, which it wasn't.

About this same time, I got a letter from author George McMillan. He offered to pay me $1,000 if I would correct names and dates for a book he was writing. I agreed to do the work, but the BOP wouldn't let me keep the money. They wanted to keep me poor because they knew I could hire an investigator with the money, which was indeed my plan.

Two years later, the feds claimed they had found the last bank robbery suspect, Jerry Lee Miller, in Fresno, California. They secretly transferred his court documents from St. Louis to Fresno. Represented by a lawyer named Nunez, Miller pleaded guilty in U.S. District Court in Fresno, California, to robbing the Bank of St. Peters. On January 9, 1973, the judge presiding over the case gave Miller three years; he served a year and a half. The feds did not want Miller to stand trial in St. Louis because he surely would have been found not guilty. They needed someone actually to be convicted in the St. Peters bank robbery to justify my incarceration, as up to this point, I was guilty of aiding and abetting someone who had been found not guilty. Reporter Harry Jones of the *Kansas City Star* brought the transfer of the court records to Fresno to my attention. The feds didn't mention Miller's extensive previous criminal record at trial.

The judge who did the sentencing in Miller's case was Judge M. D. Crocker. The *St. Louis Post-Dispatch* didn't mention one word about the feds and the Miller deal. I only found out about it because the *Kansas City Star*, the paper where J. J. Maloney, who had been in Jeff City with James, worked, carried the story of Miller's arrest.

Negative information in my BOP files would follow me for years. Later, when I was sitting alone on a transport plane that was to fly me from Marion in Illinois to Oxford Prison in Wisconsin, I spotted a cart as large as a grocery store cart and similar in design outside the plane. It was filled with dozens of stacked files. Seeing the files I assumed that I would be joined by several more inmates. When the plane took off I asked the marshal, "Where are the other prisoners?" When he looked puzzled, I told him about all the prison files. He told me that the massive amount of material I'd seen was my BOP prison file, and mine alone.

From Leavenworth, I was transferred to the federal prison in Marion, Illinois. In the summer of 1973, the feds kicked someone off the bus that was heading to Marion and replaced him with me. They came and got me at night. As I went by Arman Kiliyan's cell, it was obvious I was being transferred, and he asked me, "Do you still want me to kill those blacks?" I said,

"Let it go." He didn't like them either; he knew them from working in the kitchen. I saved those men's lives with three words.

Prior to his death, the feds would come to Kiliyan to try to get him to finger an innocent man in the bombing of telephone company executive Philip Lucier. They wanted to look good by solving the case, even if the innocent fall guy got the electric chair. Kiliyan refused.

They call Marion the "New Alcatraz" because after U.S. attorney general Robert Kennedy closed down the old Alcatraz, they were looking for a new maximum-security prison to take its place. I was there from 1973 to '78, until I testified for the House Select Committee on Assassinations.

Life in prison is a shock for most people and more of a shock if your last name is Ray. There was a lot to learn in order to stay alive. I knew better than to carry a shank (handmade knife), which, if discovered, would give the feds the perfect excuse to keep me locked up forever. Being a Ray, I couldn't defend myself as other prisoners could. I'd have to wait to get attacked and then make certain I had witnesses. If I were to have defended myself too soon or too aggressively, I would have gotten life, as the authorities pile years onto your sentence for such an offense. The couple of times I was attacked, it was by black men. If I had protected myself, the government would have made a racial incident out of it. So I had to use others to protect me, because the parole board would have taken the realities out of context and used this against me.

The biggest courthouse west of the Mississippi was built not so long ago in St. Louis, named after Thomas Eagleton, who died at the age of seventy-seven in March of 2007. Eagleton's niece, Elizabeth Eagleton Weigand, once had to face a federal grand jury to explain Eagleton's charges that she had tried to extort a quarter of a million dollars from him to give to the Church of Scientology. The niece was threatening to reveal Eagleton's closet bisexuality if he didn't pay up.

During this time frame, the early 1970s, there were two journalists who were investigating the murder of King: *LIFE* magazine stringer Bill Sartor and Dr. King's friend, Louis Lomax. Sartor was working on a book that would implicate Carlos Marcello, the New Orleans Mob boss, along with many of his subordinates. Lomax had written *To Kill a Black Man* in 1968, which dealt with the conspiratorial aspects of both Dr. King's death and the death of Malcolm X. Both journalists died under suspicious circumstances in the early months of the 1970s. Sartor died of an alleged drug overdose, which has since been ruled a murder. Lomax was killed in a single car crash in New Mexico in August of 1970. Their deaths joined the growing list of convenient and mysterious deaths that permeate this case.

DNA evidence recently showed that several death row inmates in Illinois are not guilty of their crimes but were put on death row by "benders of the Constitution," like Judge Webster. The Associated Press reports that since 1973, eighty-one men and one woman previously sentenced to death have been freed, the use of DNA testing being largely responsible. It may even be that Illinois governor George Ryan, who commuted all of these death sentences, did so to cover up the fact that so many of these kangaroo courts existed.

Down in Tennessee, my brother James was running into his share of kangaroo courts, trying to get a new real fair trial. When he plea-bargained guilty, he put himself into a legal tangle from which he'd never be able to get free. As soon as the Freedom of Information Act was passed, he began to send out request after request, trying to find the government document that would free him. At this time, in the early 1970s, James was also trying to get his own psychological records from the army, but the government would never give them up. This is the modus operandi of the Mafia and the feds. When James joined the CIA in peacetime, he joined a growing world Mafia whose grip now appears to be strangling the country that Americans call home.

nine

No Justice in Dixie

> McMillan claims that Ray was a Nazi sym-
> pathizer who used to give the Nazi "Heil Hitler"
> salute around his home (this was one of the
> reasons he requested duty in Germany); that he
> was an anti-black racist; and that he developed
> an intense hatred for King.
>
> —"The King Assassination Revisited,"
> *Time* magazine, January 26, 1976

In October of 1974, James got the closest thing to a fair trial that he would ever see. Represented by Jim Lesar and Bud Fensterwald, with Harold Weisberg as a researcher, he got an evidentiary hearing in an attempt to force a new trial. Jim Lesar, one of James's lawyers, would also represent me three years later before the House Select Committee on Assassinations (HSCA). Harold Weisberg, James's researcher, had been a brilliant employee of the Department of Justice until he was fired for being too liberal for the right-wing DOJ. The hearing was termed James Earl Ray vs. James H. Rose, Warden. The judge in the hearing was Judge Robert McRae.

I was taken out of the Marion federal prison in Illinois and brought to Memphis to testify on behalf of my brother at his evidentiary hearing. I was looking forward to the meeting, especially since I would get answers to the two questions that only my brother could answer: Why did the Mafia want King dead? and Why did he plead guilty to the shooting of King?

The marshals took me to Shelby County Jail, where six years earlier, James had occupied a special cell block put together for him by the Federal

Bureau of Prisons. I got there before James. I was brought to the third floor, where James had been the only prisoner, with metal plates over the windows and twenty-four-hour intense light. They must have known he was coming back because the plates that were over the windows in '68 and '69 were still there. However, the cell block now housed multiple prisoners, as it was built to do. Inside the first cell to the left was a guy called Fat Man Williamson. This Fat Man Williamson was not the same "Fat Man" as Robert McDouldton in Toronto. He was put in there by McRae, the same judge who was going to hear James's case. It was my understanding that he had been there for at least eighteen months. Fat Man Williamson was from Mississippi, and had been written up in *The Wall Street Journal*.

In the next cell there was a guy who had been arrested for a bank robbery just days before the seven-year statute of limitations had run out. In the third cell was the bank robber's codefendant. In the fourth cell was a guy who was in there for threatening a witness. In the fifth cell they housed me, and later James. They brought James in the next day. He was now closer to fifty than forty. I had turned forty-one the previous Valentine's Day. There was only one cot in each cell, so I let Jimmy have the cot, and I slept on the cement floor, as we had often done in the past.

Once the first day passed and we were locked up in our cell for the night, I asked him my first question: "Why did the Mafia want King dead?"

James stated, "It was not the Mafia, but the feds behind the Mafia, who wanted King dead. The feds were the ones footing the bill, and King started biting the hand that fed him."

I testified on James's behalf, and my testimony made it to the front page of the *Commercial Appeal*, which was the main paper in Memphis. Much of my testimony focused on how James was legally boxed in by his lawyer, Foreman, in 1969.

Herb MacDonell, the well-known crime scene investigator who is known today as the father of blood spatter analysis, had come on board as James's scientific witness. He testified about the crime scene evidence against my brother, and proved that the case prepared by the FBI was fiction. The defense proved that the shot couldn't have been made unless James had hung out the window of Bessie Brewer's rooming house. The angles were all wrong. The bathroom wall was too close to have allowed the Remington rifle enough room to sit at an angle that could fire to room 306 at the Lorraine. To angle the rifle sufficiently, James would have had to hang out the window or smash a ten-inch-deep hole in the wall for the rifle to fit into.

If you go to the flophouse today, it's part of the National Civil Rights Museum, dealing with the assassination. But if you examine the re-created bathroom and period photos of it from 1968, you will see an inaccurate re-creation that looks as if the shot could have been made without hanging out the window. However, the crime scene photos clearly show that the rifle would have had to have been inside the wall in order for the shot to have been made.

MacDonell had also analyzed the murder of black activist Fred Hampton, called a "shootout" by the feds and police. MacDonell counted one bullet fired from the Hampton residence in Chicago and a pound of lead fired in. "I don't call that a shootout," MacDonell said. "I call that a shoot in." Many will remember Herb MacDonell from the O. J. Simpson trial, and his testimony for Sirhan Sirhan.

As I talked to James in his cell, it was clear that he couldn't pinpoint specific governmental agencies responsible for the death of King. He didn't know who was FBI or part of their notorious Division Five, or who was CIA or military intelligence or Defense Intelligence Agency. Talking to him in that cell in 1974, I was astonished by how much in the dark he still was, even after all the years that had gone by since the crime.

In that cell I asked him my second question: "Why did you plead guilty to killing King?" He replied, "I had no choice. Because they were going to bring all this stuff out about the shooting of [soldier] Washington [from his army days] and they were going to make a race case out of it."

They were going to shift the weight of this murder, and one way or another, it would get him killed in the joint. It is deadly in prison to be identified as a federal agent, and Southern rednecks especially hate federal agents. The bottom line was that the feds would have fixed the trial, and he already knew what they could do. Jimmy still thought he was going to get a new trial, and there was no doubt from the evidence that Jimmy was innocent. There was also no doubt that the evidence had been twisted to make a case against him, but Judge McRae came up with technical legal reasons that nobody in the Memphis power structure or their counterparts in Washington would argue with.

As Bud Fensterwald, Harold Weisberg, and Jim Lesar prepared for the evidentiary hearing, news had reached us of the brutal murder of Alberta King, Dr. King's mother. Since the King family also did not believe the federal version of Dr. King's assassination story, this led me to believe the feds were nervous and would stop at nothing. Two months prior to the hearing, this eerie occurrence almost seemed like a warning or message to Coretta Scott King—who was now openly and publicly beginning to discuss her suspicions of government conspiracy in her husband's death, and in the death of her brother-in-law.

Consider this: On Sunday morning, June 30, 1974, a twenty-three-year-old black man named Marcus Wayne Chenault walked up to an usher at Dr. King's old church, Ebenezer Baptist Church, on Auburn Avenue in Atlanta. He asked, "Will Mrs. Coretta King be attending church services today?" The usher, expecting Mrs. King, told the young man that she would. Coretta King would, however, be absent that day. Coretta's father-in-law, Martin, Sr., who would normally have been preaching, was seated in the back of the church.

The young man was welcomed into a front row by retired teacher Mrs. Jimmie Mitchell, who shook his hand and told him, "We enjoy having visitors." He was seated just a few feet away from Martin Luther King's mother, Alberta King, who would move to the organ in front of the church when the service started.

The young man, who looked closer to fourteen than twenty-three, told Mrs. Mitchell and Mrs. King, "I am Mr. Chenault; I'm from Dayton, Ohio." He asked Mrs. Mitchell about Dr. King's family. The congregation began to sing "The Lord's Prayer," and the first shots rang out. Oddly, at first nobody thought the shots came from Chenault; this tends to imply a second shooter, and perhaps a trigger for Chenault to move.

Mrs. King was just feet away from Chenault. She and Mrs. Mitchell heard a gun, but didn't see it. Mrs. Mitchell said, "It sounds like a bomb." Alberta King, from her organ, responded, "It surely does." Within seconds, Marcus Wayne Chenault leaped up onto the pew, screaming, "I am in charge! I am in charge!" Chenault, just five-foot-two with thick glasses, waved two pistols, a .32 and a .32-20. Chenault shot Mrs. Jimmie Mitchell in the neck, which threw her off the pew and onto the floor. He next shot Edward Boykin, an elderly deacon of the church, followed by Dr. King's mother, shot through the cheek. Mrs. King died fifty minutes later.

Chenault then ran up to the podium of the church, waving his two guns, while pandemonium broke out in Ebenezer Baptist Church. When he tried to make his way out of the church, he was tackled and subdued by the wounded woman's grandson, Derek King. Derek would later describe the murderer as having some type of seizure, acting delirious, repeating the words, "The war did this to me, the war did this to me."

Sound familiar?

When taken by the authorities, Chenault gave his name as Yahweh (in English, "Jehovah"; or in the Old Testament, "God"), and he claimed that he was from Jerusalem, rather than Dayton, Ohio, his real place of origin. He claimed to be a Jew who hated Christians. Atlanta mayor Maynard Jackson told the press, "It's almost as if someone were testing this family. The Kennedy family and the King family are probably the most tragedy-ridden families in the country." Government clandestine operations are obvious to most African-Americans. Only the Kings, and if I might say, the Rays, have had the strength to fight back.

By the time Chenault got to court, he seemed to have no memory of the shooting. Chenault told the judge, "I assume that I shot someone. I'm not sure." Chenault's family in Dayton knew him as a shy, quiet, normal guy who was dedicated to his Sunday school classes. His classmates at Ohio State in Columbus, Ohio, knew a different man. The two Chenaults seem almost like the James Earl Ray who went into the army hoping to make a name for himself and the hard-drinking man with a criminal record who exited the service two years later.

Back in Ohio, Chenault had come under the spell of an elderly black man named Hananiah Israel, really Stephen Holiman, who admitted to being Chenault's "spiritual mentor," claiming, "I showed him the way." But Israel said that in the nine months prior to the shooting, Chenault had changed. It is a mystery as to how, under normal circumstances, a period of nine months could bring about such drastic personality changes.

The FBI found Chenault's list of black leaders who were to be murdered presumably by him. It included Ralph Abernathy and Hosea Williams. When Daddy King took his grandson, Dexter, to see Chenault in his cell, Chenault told Martin Luther King Sr. that he would "kill you when I get out of here, too." In six years, three members of the King family had died violently, including Martin's brother, A. D. King, who died in a swimming pool accident.

The jury sentenced Chenault to the electric chair, but he later died three weeks after having suffered a stroke in prison at just forty-four years of age. The Christian, non-violent King family refused to have him executed. In the courtroom, Chenault giggled and blew kisses at the jury while his distraught parents sobbed. Wayne, as they called him, refused to meet with them during lunch breaks. As he sat in the courtroom he pretended to throw grenades at his family. "I was ordered here by my God, my father and my master," Chenault said.

It is hard to believe that any young adult coming under the spell of an older person could have this much of a personality change in nine months. Is this as it seems—another drugging case by the feds? It certainly seems as if the King and Kennedy families were targeted. And I say that it is too much to accept, that this person would just happen to take a bus to Atlanta from Ohio and kill Martin Luther King's mother, just two months before my brother would get a well-publicized chance to win a new trial and walk free.

Nothing came of the evidentiary hearing, but a few months later, James did indeed get a chance at a retrial. In January of 1976, an appeal was filed with the Sixth Circuit Court, and on February 3, lawyers for James presented their case before a three-judge panel. It included Judge William E. Miller, whom James told me he considered to be an ethical man. The other two judges, Anthony Celebrezze and Harry Phillips, were considered by him to be reliable to the powers that be.

Somebody must have been nervous about the very real chance of a new trial being ordered for James, because a new book by George McMillan, *The Making of an Assassin*, hit the shelves in 1976. This was a book which had been "in the can" for some years. The book was promoted by a ridiculously scathing article, titled "The King Assassination Revisited," which put James on the cover of *Time* magazine's January 26, 1976, issue.

In his book, McMillan claimed that James would sit in front of a television in the Missouri State Prison in Jefferson City, and go into a wild, racist fit every time Dr. Martin Luther King Jr., would come on television. James refuted this accusation, saying that it never happened, and that furthermore, televisions were not allowed until three years after his escape, except for special occasions. The so-called (in CIA documents) "propaganda assets" then called James a liar, claiming that he would burst into a rage whenever he saw King on television.

This question was settled by reporter J. J. Maloney, who had been in Jefferson City prison with James. This is what Maloney wrote in September 1997, just two years before his death, about James in an online magazine called *Crime*:

> In his book, *The Making of an Assassin*, published in 1976, McMillan wrote: "In 1963 and 1964, Martin Luther King was on TV almost every day talking defiantly about how black people were going to get their rights, insisting they would accept with nonviolence all the terrible violence that white people were inflicting on them until the day of victory arrived, until they did overcome. . . . Ray watched it all avidly on the cell-block TV at Jeff City. He reacted as if King's remarks were directed at him personally. He boiled when King came on the tube; he began to call him Martin "Lucifer" King and Martin Luther "Coon." It got so that the very sight of King would galvanize Ray.
>
> [I agree with James that this] is utterly untrue. There were no cell-block TVs in Jefferson City while Ray was there. Three years after Ray escaped, they finally began to sell televisions to the convicts. I knew a lot of racists in Jefferson City, but James Earl Ray wasn't one of them. Although McMillan's book was gravely flawed, *Time* promoted the book heavily, and what McMillan wrote later permeated much of what was written about Ray.

The feds' fear of James getting a new trial was put to rest on April 12, when Judge Miller was found dead in his chambers. He suffered a fatal heart attack the month before his opinion on the King case was to be issued. Like Judge Battle seven years earlier, he was another suspicious demise, found dead on James's paperwork, as was Battle.

There would be no new trial for James Earl Ray.

ten

House Select Cover-Up
on Assassinations

"I suppose I am about to represent Judas
Iscariot," Mr. Foreman said softly as he visited the
shrine erected in the memory of Dr. Martin Luther
King Jr. at the Lorraine Motel on Mulberry.

—"Foreman Concerned of Brand as Traitor,"
Commercial Appeal, November 14, 1968

I didn't know it at the time, but attorney Mark Lane, my brother James, and to a lesser degree, several members of the Congressional Black Caucus were working hard in 1975 and 1976 to create the House Select Committee on Assassinations (HSCA), which was to conduct an investigation into Dr. King's death. At this time there was a tremendous clamor for the truth about these political assassinations. Harold Weisberg had written *Frame-Up*, about the murder of Dr. King, and Mark Lane had a best-seller with *Rush to Judgment*, a criticism of the Warren Commission Report on the murder of JFK.

At this time you would still frequently see deep political researchers on television, including Mark Lane; Mae Brussell, with her protégé, John Judge; and Robert Groden, Dick Gregory, and Harold Weisberg. It would take ten or fifteen years before the dominant media would begin to cast them as "nuts" or "conspiracy buffs."

On September 17, 1976, the House of Representatives passed House Resolution 1540, to conduct a full investigation into the murders of President

Kennedy and Dr. King. At first, the Robert Kennedy assassination was to be part of their investigation as well, but Sirhan's mother was reportedly fearful of that. In August, the mutilated body of ultrapatriotic CIA-associated mobster Johnny Rosselli had been found in Biscayne Bay in Florida. Rosselli was trying to sell the story of these CIA-Mafia plots to Hollywood. Though it was meant to look like a Mob hit, Rosselli had been drugged prior to his mutilation, which leads me to think it was a government operation. Was this hit timed to make certain Rosselli never testified before the HSCA? The HSCA bill was treated with enthusiasm by Congress in 1976; the House voted 280–65 to pass the resolution submitted by Rep. Henry Gonzalez.

Within months of the HSCA's creation, carefully written critical articles were placed in the *New York Times* and other mainstream periodicals. Behind-the-scenes shenanigans had already removed the original HSCA members, Rep. Henry Gonzalez and Richard Sprague, who were clearly eager to play hardball with the intelligence community. The new leadership preferred to play hardball with anyone who believed in the possibility of government-sponsored political assassination in the United States of America.

Consequently, from September of 1976, until their final report was announced in July 1979, the HSCA wound up spending just under 6 million taxpayer dollars to reinforce the official government line. Mark Lane, who helped craft the committee, was soon commenting negatively about the monster that he had helped to create. "I know how Dr. Frankenstein felt," he said. The FBI was at it again, mostly through their counterintelligence arm, Division Five, known for its use of sexual blackmail in silencing people. Lane was a victim of their blackmail in their plot to change the committee from its roots as an honest investigative force.

The feds started leaking that Mark Lane was either gay or bisexual. Whether or not he cared, I can't say, but he became James's lawyer nonetheless. My lawyer for my HSCA testimony was DC-based Jim Lesar. Our brother Jerry's lawyers at the time were Flo Kennedy, one of the founders of the National Organization for Women, and Dr. William Pepper. Mark Lane and Bill Pepper were marked men for the FBI/Justice Department's fabricated sex scandals. Miraculously timed, Pepper was charged on July 6, 1978, with four felony counts of transporting teen boys for sexual activities.

A family man, he adamantly denied the charges. Pepper was never convicted, but he had been thoroughly shamed. He moved to the UK in 1980.

Any hopes in my mind that the HSCA would be honest went by the board when they hired Vietnam War–era Army Security Agency (ASA) intelligence operative Pete Baetz to serve as their investigator within the St. Louis area. Baetz had been working in the mid-1970s in law enforcement in Madison County, in lower Illinois. It was Pete Baetz who set up polygraph tests for all the Rays. The House members wouldn't approve it, so they dropped the idea of giving us lie detector tests. Later, Baetz's polygraph expert was accused of improper conduct on other cases, specifically of rigging the results to favor the prosecutors.

One of Baetz's activities for the HSCA was to renew the undercover activities of former FBI mole Oliver Patterson. In the 1960s, Patterson had reported to the St. Louis FBI office, and his case officer was Stanley F. Jacobson. Patterson used to spy on ultra–right-wing organizations, from the Minutemen to J. B. Stoner's National States Rights Party. In the early 1970s, when my brother Jerry accepted employment with Stoner, Oliver Patterson became acquainted with Jerry.

Patterson was contacted by the FBI in St. Louis before Pete Baetz and another HSCA operative showed up at his back door. The HSCA wanted to have another spy on my brother Jerry. So they put Patterson in place to bug Jerry's hotel room, and also to travel with him and report back to the committee. Patterson would copy letters from James that were found in Jerry's hotel room and then give them to the HSCA. He would also tape-record conversations for possible later use. The public has never seen these letters, which indicates that they don't help to make the government's case credible. Patterson's activities were so obvious that he was offered a place in the witness protection program. However, Patterson switched sides before it was over, and the feds dumped any protection for him.

Almost simultaneous with the creation of the committee was my brother James's October 1976 request for the U.S. Supreme Court to review his case. Jim Lesar, who would represent me before the HSCA, represented James in this Supreme Court request. Lesar, whose father was an associate of William Webster's, had no sex scandals, but no hearing was granted, either.

It was at this time, a couple of weeks before the resolution passed, that I went before the U.S. Parole Commission for the first time, after having served six years, a third of my sentence. I was resigned to serving the entire eighteen years. As expected, the U.S. Parole Commission denied me, saying that I was going to have to do my "entire sentence." To make it simple for those who have not been in the federal penal system, what the board meant was that I must serve two-thirds—twelve years—of the eighteen-year sentence.

Since the King case was in the news again, James was hoping that he could manipulate the situation to force the feds and the State of Tennessee to give him a real trial. By this point it was becoming clear that the HSCA was not going to be the salvation he had initially hoped for. This left James so depressed that he came up with another plan: He would escape, and only give himself up if he could get the real trial that he never got in 1969, when he was forced to plea-bargain.

Jerry received an encoded letter from James, telling him that the escape was indeed going to transpire, so he left food and clothes at a particular tree near the prison. Jerry had been flown to Tennessee by a reporter who was interested in a story on the Ray family's reaction to the conduct of the HSCA.

Unfortunately, James foolishly shared his escape plan with another inmate, Doug Shelton. After that, there was either a leak, or the code he used in his letters was broken. Just after 7:00 P.M. on June 10, 1977, James, Doug, and three other convicts who independently decided to join the action, escaped from the Tennessee State Prison at Brushy Mountain. The last three had noticed the ladder after they had been let out into the yard at 6:00 P.M. for exercise. There must have been an informant in their midst, because somehow, the escape turned into a plot to have James killed as an escaped prisoner. At around 7:00 P.M., a fight among the inmates was coordinated to distract the guards. Simultaneously, a jogging prisoner faked an ankle injury to complete the distraction scenario.

James and his escape partner had placed a makeshift ladder against the outside wall of the prison compound. The ladder was made from pipes that James had stored in the back of a washing machine. It was assembled on the scene, including its curved ends for hooking over the stone wall. All their advance planning did not protect them, however; when they went over the wall, one man was shot by the guards and was hauled back into Brushy Mountain.

Historians who have studied the assassination of President Kennedy know that most of the telephones in DC went dead for an hour after the murder. This was surely done to control the story. When James escaped, his success was also ensured when all of the Brushy Mountain telephones went dead for one hour; and, of course, there were no cell phones yet.

Waiting for James were nearly fifty flack-jacketed FBI sharpshooters, maneuvered into position all too soon after the escape. And oddly, the feds were responding to the escape of a Tennessee state prisoner. Reporter J. J. Maloney, who was sent out from the *Kansas City Star*, described them in a series of articles. It baffled the late Maloney that these men were placed into position so quickly. The feds were fearful that James would not stick to his safe 1969 story in his open testimony before the HSCA. According to Maloney, who had been an inmate with James at Jefferson City, James would have been shot if then governor Ray Blanton hadn't shown up and ordered the FBI sharpshooters out. Only threat of imprisonment caused the FBI to leave the state.

The FBI guarded Coretta Scott King until James was captured, in a phony show that was designed to convince the public that the "legend" created for James was actually true.

On June 13, just after 2:00 in the morning, James was apprehended; he had only made it eleven miles in three days. Although he was initially charged with the escape, he was never tried for it. James's lawyer, Mark Lane, was contacted multiple times by prosecutor Arzo Carson, trying to get a guilty plea out of James. When he didn't get James's guilty plea, the charges were dropped. The prosecutor and the judge were seemingly afraid that James and Mark Lane would raise questions about the King murder before reporters. The judge allegedly threatened to charge Mark if they brought up the case in public.

Again the media pumped out their propaganda to control the story and reinforce the yet-to-be-published conclusions of the HSCA. James was on the cover of *Time* on June 20, 1977. The cover story was "Ray's Breakout." It called James a "scruffy born loser from the underworld." Before his army years, he was nothing of the kind.

Early the next year, in 1978, I was called back in front of the U.S. Parole Commission. This was only about eighteen months after they had told me that I would have to serve six more years. Something was amiss. This early parole board hearing was spurred on by the creation of the HSCA. They were hoping I'd cooperate. The parole board was trying to tell me that they were going to parole me to a halfway house in St. Louis—meaning they were trying to make a deal for me to testify on behalf of the government. Anyone who knows the system knows that a deal was meant to be made.

Word came down to me from someone in the Congressional Black Caucus that it wouldn't be a good idea for me to be in this halfway house, so close to the street. I was further informed that the feds were going to put me in a very rough, all-black Washington, DC, jail and then let it be known that I was the brother of James Earl Ray. They were playing games, telling me that if I cooperated, I could have it good; if I didn't cooperate, I would have it much worse. There were stories of guys getting raped multiple times if they got placed in those rough jails. The Watergate gang had been fearful of getting thrown in the DC jails for the same reason I was.

I cleared out my cell and got rid of anything I didn't need, hoping that I was going to the halfway house. But on the day I was to be transferred, nothing happened. It wasn't until the next day that I was transferred to the halfway house, known as Dismas House. Its name came from Father Charles Dismas Clark, the priest immortalized in the 1961 Don Murray film, *Hoodlum Priest*. Following my transfer, I was ordered to the first of three sessions before the HSCA. I believe it was April of 1978 when I received a letter at Dismas House from the HSCA, ordering me to the field office of the Federal Bureau of Prisons (BOP) by way of the marshals' office, which was being used by the BOP. I was told that I was to get money to pay for my trip to DC to testify. I was called to the office of a guy nicknamed "Buster" (not to be confused with Buster Wortman) of the BOP, by way of the marshals' office, because what they hoped was about to transpire was to be a secret deal between the feds and me. Before the meeting, the marshals told me what they thought the FBI and the Justice Department were trying to do to me. The marshals were mad because the BOP was using the U.S. Marshal's office for their dirty work. The culture of the marshals, especially at that time, was reasonably decent.

Buster was a little man who talked like a big tough guy. The gist of what Buster told me was that if I gave the testimony the feds wanted to hear regarding the King murder, I would be released from custody. I would be a free man. Buster told me that the HSCA was especially concerned with covering up where James's money came from in the 1967–68 era. The government had no plausible explanation that didn't lead directly (or indirectly) back to them. Buster told me that I was to plead guilty to an unsolved bank robbery, and that this was going to be the explanation for James's rolls of twenties. I responded to Buster: "If I give testimony, I am going to tell the truth." This made him mad.

"Well, you were in that Commie group. I'm going to make sure that you get sent to New Alcatraz, and that they bury you so deep inside the prison, they have to pipe sunlight to you." This was unusual, to be called a "Commie," as I was usually called a redneck or a Nazi. No matter which one of these slurs is applied, if they can label you with one of them, they can degrade you and discredit your word. I walked out of his office.

The problem the HSCA had in explaining where my brother James had gotten all of his money during the 1967–68 period was evident throughout my first testimony. During my first trip to Washington to testify before the HSCA, they asked me about the robbery of a supermarket and a heist at the Bank of Alton. Ultimately, the HSCA settled on the 1967 robbery of the Bank of Alton in our hometown as the "official" explanation of how James was bankrolled. They were trying to blame this heist, which took place before the King assassination, on Jerry, James, and me. The fact that for ten years, the local police had never considered us suspects in the robbery didn't stop the feds from trying to make a connection. The committee did everything it could to pin the robbery of the Bank of Alton on the Ray boys without even attempting to answer the obvious question: Why would we rob a bank in a town where everyone knows us?

Throughout my adult life, I have traveled numerous times across the country for work, but the committee was trying to paint my trip to California in the fall of 1967 as a quick getaway from Illinois because of the Bank of Alton heist. The HSCA, the FBI, and the media had access to my social security records, which showed that I had worked at honest jobs from the time I was released from Menard Prison in Illinois on February 1, 1960, until I was arrested for the St. Peters bank robbery ten years later on October 26, 1970. I had worked as a union bartender all over the country, from Flamingo City in the Florida Everglades to the Concord Hotel in the Catskill Mountains of New York, and a number of country clubs in the Chicago area.

When I arrived back at Dismas House, I received word from Buster that if I continued with this type of testimony, I could expect incarceration. The HSCA's game was to make everybody first testify in closed executive session to assess the way they could manipulate the situation, before holding a public session on the record. The first two times I testified in executive session behind closed doors, my message was the same: "I didn't rob the Bank of Alton. And if I did, why would I give the money to James?"

I told the committee that I wasn't going to cooperate in the sham. So they had a problem with the issue of James throwing several thousand dollars around that couldn't be traced to any source other than Raul or the Mob. In the year 2029, when my executive session testimony is released from congressional seal, those who are still among the living will be able to read what I said.

During that testimony, I mentioned Ernest Turley's situation. Take my word for it: As soon as I mentioned his name, they called the governor of Missouri and had sixty-five-year-old Ernest Turley turned out—released from prison.

To the best of my knowledge, my second testimony was in June of 1978. Afterward, when I got back to the halfway house in St. Louis, I received a call from Buster of the BOP. Buster told me that I had given perjured testimony and that the HSCA could prove it, because of a witness named Oliver Patterson. At this time I hadn't yet heard of Oliver Patterson, so I had no idea what he was getting at.

During this same month, I fulfilled the feds' parole plan, something you have to do before you are released from the halfway house. I had been working for several weeks driving a truck, and I'd spent the money renting an apartment and installing a phone. I was to be released from Dismas House on parole the next day, and was at my new apartment preparing things when I received a message from a federal counselor to report back to Dismas House to pick up my parole plans. I tried to beg off, claiming that I was tired from driving the truck all day, and asked if I could pick them up the next day.

"You must pick up the plans within the hour," he responded.

So I climbed on the city bus and headed to the halfway house. When I got there, some guys were waiting for me. Buster was there with a handful of cops, sitting in a side room. With him was Father Zimmerman of Dismas

House. Before I knew it, Buster, totally unprovoked, hit me in the head with a marshal's chain. I was paying the price for not cooperating with the feds. They charged me with assaulting a federal employee. I was arrested and moved to solitary confinement at Marion, called New Alcatraz by the inmates. They kept me in solitary until I went to testify before the committee, my third appearance.

I got dizzy spells in Marion from being hit with the marshal's chain. I later complained about this to a well-known doctor in Marion. I went into the clinic and this MD gave me some pills, which I took. By the time I left the hospital and returned to my cell, my head was swelling dramatically. It scared me. I looked deformed. So I headed back to the hospital, but by the time I got there, the doctor had supposedly left. I raised a little hell, scared of what was happening to me, which got the prison "goon squad" brought down to me. Just then I saw the doctor was peeping at me through the white curtains.

I said, "There's the son-of-a-bitch now!" I could barely see him since my eyes were nearly swelled shut. The doctor said, "I gave you Green Carter aspirins that I give patients for imaginary illness." The prison goon squad didn't know what to do. So the doctor said, "I can give you something which will bring down the swelling." I drank some liquid, had a seat, and within minutes, the change was miraculous. To this day I don't know if they were experimenting on me, but it was all over the news that I was complaining about my dizzy spells.

Just before I was to testify for the third time, they shipped me back to the halfway house. I have Oliver Patterson to thank for the transfer. On August 7, 1978, Oliver Patterson was supposed to give a press conference for the HSCA, revealing his activities for the HSCA and to barbecue the Rays. However, feeling guilty about his activities for Pete Baetz and the committee, Patterson flipped sides. He threw away the notes prepared for him by Baetz and met secretly with Mark Lane. Patterson still conducted the press conference but spoke honestly. One of Patterson's revelations was about how they had framed me for my supposed parole violations. At this time I hadn't met Oliver Patterson, but I wish I had. He admitted that in the HSCA's executive sessions, he just simply read answers given to him by HSCA staffers.

After getting out of Marion, I got a job driving a shuttle bus to the St. Louis airport. The HSCA was nearing an end and they were going to have to justify their budget. Shortly before my final testimony, my supposed fellow bank robber, James "Foolbird" Rogers, who was on parole in California, came through St. Louis and called me up. I met him out by the airport. He was probably in his early fifties by this time, and had had a heart attack behind bars sometime earlier. He had a relative in the hotel business and had inherited a hotel of his own. Foolbird told me what the HSCA was up to: The parole board had told him that if he didn't implicate me and give the testimony they wanted, they were going to revoke his parole and put him behind bars. He didn't want to be an informant, or worse, make up a story. Rogers would probably die behind bars if he didn't cooperate. The judges would convict him and essentially sentence him to death, since the poor health care behind bars would quickly kill him.

I told him, "I'll tell you what I want you to do: When you go in there, just say 'yes' or 'no' the way they want, but don't add or make up anything." He agreed. Foolbird would pay dearly if he didn't go along with the feds. He was a family man, and nothing he could say in my favor would change anything. Why should he go back to prison when the feds were going to keep me behind bars one way or another?

Prior to my third, televised public appearance before the HSCA, I was arrested on the false charge of burglarizing someone's house. The prosecuting attorney in St. Louis was put up to filing false charges against me in order to discredit me before my public HSCA appearance. The U.S. Department of Justice released this burglary information in order to seal the deal.

I testified on December 1, 1978. When I arrived for my public testimony, the committee had huge charts trying to tie the 1967 Bank of Alton robbery to the Ray brothers, as well as the other bank robberies after the murder of Dr. King. I wasn't going to budge; I wasn't going to make their work any easier. It was all a scam to cover up the real sources of James's money in the 1967–68 period, and to keep me behind bars. Even the written interviews the committee produced were signed by ASA intelligence operative Pete Baetz, who was employed by the HSCA as an investigator, which was actually against committee rules. This third appearance before the committee was the one that was put on the record and published by the House. They had studied the case and developed their strategy before my questioning went on the public record.

By this time the formerly idealistic staff at the HSCA were wearing shirts imprinted with the saying REALITY IS IRRELEVANT. The researchers donned these shirts after being told by Chief Counsel Blakey to limit their investigations due to financial and time constraints. The HSCA presumed they were going to get my confession if they put enough heat on me. They didn't know that they were dealing with the Old Missouri Mule. The federal government had me held in solitary confinement at New Alcatraz; I was nearly burned alive in my cell in Leavenworth. Did they think I was going to be their patsy for them? I told what I believe to be the truth about Webster and his cohort, J. Wallace LaPrade.

Here's an example of my testimony:

> So, Mr. Goldenstein told me, as I have stated—he stated his trial was fixed, and that he posed as the principal; he was held in a trap while they legalized his search under the Hot Pursuit Doctrine. The case was reversed by the U.S. Court of Appeals, which subsequently stated it was going to release him to the streets, which they did. That the person involved in fixing this trial was, like I mentioned, was a federal district judge, William H. Webster. Subsequently, he was promoted to the director of the FBI for fixing this trial. J. Wallace LaPrade, he was also involved with Judge William H. Webster, and subsequently was made head of the FBI in New York City. And while both these conspirators were engaged themselves, engaged in committing felonies, J. Wallace LaPrade was committing burglaries around the St. Louis area and got charged while he was head of the New York FBI office. Judge William H. Webster, he was engaged in a felony . . .

At that point, Walter Fauntroy cut me off. When I was done with my third and final testimony, I was brought down to the basement of the building. It reminded me of the place where Jack Ruby had shot Lee Harvey Oswald. I got in the car and drove out of the District of Columbia to Maryland. When I looked back, there must have been twenty cars following me; it looked like a funeral procession. I had spoken honestly about Webster fixing my trial—at least, until they had cut me off. I believe PBS carried my testimony, and the feds didn't want me to be killed right after I had accused the new FBI chief, Webster, of fixing my trial as part of a cover-up of the assassination of Martin Luther King. They would have had a very difficult time explaining another Oswald-type shooting after the accusations I had made.

Back in St. Louis, I still had to deal with prosecuting attorney's charges against me. I made St. Louis reporter John Auble aware of what was going on. John Auble, who still works at a FOX station in St. Louis, contacted the prosecuting attorney, scaring him so bad that he turned me out with no shoes, barefoot in the winter. He was later charged and convicted of using office funds for the patronizing of prostitutes.

One of the things that would influence members of the committee was the publication of various books and magazine articles. The extremely convenient release of George McMillan's book, *The Making of an Assassin*, was well timed for influencing the HSCA, and not just the Sixth Circuit Court. By the way, the job of reviewing McMillan's book for the *New York Times* was given to former FBI assistant to the director Cartha DeLoach's good friend, Jeremiah O'Leary. O'Leary's own article about the case for *Reader's Digest* had been reviewed before publication by the FBI's Crime Records Division. What did O'Leary have to say about *The Making of an Assassin?*

> McMillan has done a good deal of the committee's work already when it comes to deciding whether the world knows all there is to know about Ray and why he set out to kill Dr. King, and did so with as much skill as the fictional "Jackal" of screen and novel. This is a most important book and extremely timely, since the King assas-

```
sination will soon be probed by a committee
which does not have six years in which to
reach a conclusion.
```

Just months later, McMillan was rebutted by Mark Lane and Dick Greg-ory and their look at Dr. King's murder in the book *Code Name "Zorro."* By the 1970s, people were regularly saying that the FBI was involved in the conspiracy to kill Dr. King. Perhaps the HSCA was allowed to exist because the powers that be thought they could use the committee to take the heat off of the feds.

Even though James was still very much alive, and I didn't want to cross him or put him in danger, I did try early on to give important information, including information about the shooting of Washington, to one of the com-mittee members who I felt was an honest man. His name was Michael Eber-hardt. He was talking to me about something relating to the committee, so I gave information to him, once we were away from the government line Chief Counsel Blakey. I passed on the information related to James's army record and to his having joined the CIA in Germany. I don't recall saying anything about the shooting of the soldier, Washington; I believe what I said was, "Are you going to bring out James's army record?" I heard later, the second time I testified, that Blakey knew about James's army record, but that he planned to withhold it from the public.

The third time that I testified, the very two-faced Indiana congressman, and committee member Floyd Fithian approached me in the hallway, acting like he was going to hit me because I didn't give "the right testimony." He told me that he "knew" I had served time in Indiana, and that it was con-nected with the Ku Klux Klan. He then tried to act like he was a Klansman, apparently trying to get on my good side. Now, I don't have any connection to the Klan, but he certainly seemed to believe the government's propaganda. I made the same revelation to Fithian about James's army record and about the abrupt changing of his U.S. Army serial number to the CIA (or intelli-gence-related) one. At this time, I didn't know that they had hushed it up, or even why they would do so. I just wondered why the shooting of Washington wasn't brought out. It could have strengthened their case by framing James as a bigot.

At first, James said he wasn't going to testify, so I was surprised when he was on national television. It actually made me a little mad. When he did testify, he spoke about my fixed trial, but he should have demanded that both of us get turned out from prison if he was going to cooperate at all. And essentially, he did cooperate by telling the same limited Raul story he had been telling for years, because he was so afraid of the Mob and the government, certain that they would kill him. I personally believe that they killed James anyway by denying him proper health care for his hepatitis C, in spite of his clinging to this watered-down version of the story.

Prior to giving testimony, Mark Lane and James announced that James had been beaten up the night before. He was afraid for Carol, Jerry, and the rest of his family. For the life of me, I don't know why people like Coretta Scott King and Mark Lane would stand for seeing the CIA and FBI take over an investigation without making the strongest of statements in public, but this is what they chose to do.

Jerry spent quite a bit of time with Mark Lane, who is known to have been with army intelligence in his youth. My brother Jerry always seems to get involved with people like George McMillan and his CIA-associated wife, Priscilla Johnson, who became the constant companion of Marina Oswald (Mrs. Lee Harvey Oswald) after JFK was shot by the same federal-Mafi network that killed Dr. King.

Jerry at this time was often seen with an East Coast reporter who claimed to be twenty-two but looked about forty. This reporter was always full of fed-style information on Mark Lane's sex life, claiming Mark was gay and the like. I don't like to talk about someone's sex life, and I wouldn't even bring it up here, except that it shows the modus operandi of these FBI assets. They discredit people with false talk, and if there's nothing real to get them on, they can always make up things about their supposedly scandalous sex life. Unless this guy followed Mark Lane around and peeped in his windows, how would he know who or what Mark Lane was involved with? They did the same thing to King when they sent doctored tapes to his wife in 1965, "exposing" King's supposed extramarital sex life.

The results of the HSCA hearing revealed that James had indeed shot King. Their "lone nut" conclusion to the murder of Dr. King didn't change anybody's mind, among those who knew better. Oliver Patterson's activities are all included in the public record, and speak very loudly. Walter Fauntroy said to me many times that he knew the FBI and the CIA were behind the murder of Dr. King. He was afraid to say it publicly, but Fauntroy, like most black people, instinctively knew the truth. My own question for him would be: Why didn't you say it to the press? Why did you keep James and me behind bars?

The HSCA also harassed my sister, Carol Ray-Pepper. Carol is an honest, hardworking, middle-class woman. She worked as a teacher in the Head Start program. The HSCA tried to make her look like a bag woman for the Mob, collecting thousands in dope money. They tried to do anything to degrade the Rays. Carol and her husband Albert worked every day, sometimes two jobs, to build a future for themselves and their children. When I visited Carol at their home, she would show me her bank books to prove how hard she had been working, and how they had been getting by without, in order to show their children a better life. And these deadbeats in DC, who only got ahead because they went along with the Justice Department–CIA program, made her their victim. Carol was deeply frightened by their actions. Ten years before, the FBI had illegally bugged her house, and even against the wishes of attorney general Ramsey Clark, they had dummied up a case against me. So at the time of the HSCA, they went after Carol.

The final report of the HSCA put a different spin on the murder of Martin Luther King Jr. Their investigator, Pete Baetz, was known to say that the 1968 story about the killing being racially motivated was not believable, in light of the fact that James hung out at integrated clubs and lived in very integrated buildings in Los Angeles. The committee members had to come up with something new to justify their $6 million budget, a tremendous amount of money at that time. So they concocted this story about these two dead guys, John Kauffmann and John Sutherland, who had nothing to do with anything, but supposedly put out a bounty to kill Dr. King.

In 1978, Sonny Spica's brother-in-law Russell George Byers publicly testified that twelve years before he was approached by John Kauffmann. Byers had been a friend of Kauffmann's deceased brother. Byers testified that Kauffmann introduced him to John Sutherland, a racist who made a contract offer to kill King, the amount of which has varied.

The feds got it wrong about how these contracts are executed. But above all, they made certain that the plot to kill King stayed in St. Louis with these two dead guys, and that it didn't cross the river to East St. Louis, with its ties to Chicago. By the way, it was Kauffmann who owned the drug company, Fix-A-Co, whose amphetamines flooded into the prison at Jefferson City. I think they just took people from the real story and twisted them around.

After my brother James died of liver failure in 1998, Pete Baetz was quoted in the press as saying, "John Larry Ray is the only living person who knows the truth about the King case." This could mean two or three things. This could mean that I'm the only one who knows the truth about the shooting of the soldier Washington, or the murder of King twenty years later to the month. Maybe he only meant that I knew about a stupid bounty from two racists that nobody ever heard of, Kauffmann and Sutherland. But for once, whether deliberately or not, Baetz spoke the truth: I am the only one left who knows the truth about the shooting of two black men, one around April of 1948, the other twenty years later in April of 1968.

Interestingly, the one question that the committee never asked me was whether I had any connection to the murder of Martin Luther King Jr. That's probably because they already knew the answer.

eleven

Federal Vendetta

However, if the conspirators included family members—a charge that all Ray's relatives have persistently denied—then he would have an incentive to remain silent. The special bond among the Rays would prevent James from turning in the only people he ever trusted.

—*Killing the Dream,* Gerald Posner

February of 1980, the month of my forty-seventh birthday, I decided that I had enough of playing these games with the feds. Weeks from parole, I walked out of the medical center at Springfield and caught a Greyhound bus and got a job.

On May 29, 1980, National Urban League director Vernon Jordan was shot in the back and wounded outside a motel in Fort Wayne, Indiana, while in the company of a white woman named Martha Coleman. Ms. Coleman was on the local board of the Urban League and had invited director Jordan, with seeming innocence, back to her home for a meal. Coleman drove Jordan back to his motel at two o'clock in the morning, and dropped him at the side entrance, near his room. He was climbing up to his room when a bullet from a .30-06 rifle tore into his back. The .30-06 bullet, designed to kill deer at a distance, left a wound the size of a man's fist. Another one like it had done the same thing to his friend Martin's jaw, twelve years earlier. He lay there bleeding while guests peered out from between the drapes on the upper floors, afraid to leave their rooms.

Over the next three weeks, Vernon Jordan would have five operations to save his life. One of the first telegrams Jordan received was from former governor George Wallace, who was shot in 1972 and wound up in a wheelchair. Wallace ran for president in 1968, and in 1972, as well. During the '68 election, the local police allowed me to keep my tavern open late, in return for keeping pro-Wallace literature on display.

Rather than have the local cops investigate Jordan's shooting, it became a federal matter. The supposed reason was because Jordan was a black man and the shooting had happened at a motel. If there was more to the shooting, perhaps the feds just wanted the local cops out of there. William Webster was still the FBI director at this time. While Jordan recuperated, the FBI came around requesting Jordan's permission to give him a lie detector test. He was still hooked up to IVs on their first visit. When he realized that they wanted to give the test to him, the victim, Jordan told the feds, "You need to go talk to somebody else."

After he was transferred to a New York hospital, agents came around and wanted to hypnotize him. Wisely, Jordan told the FBI agents that he didn't yet have control of his body and that he wasn't about to "lease my mind to the FBI." Startled by the agents showing up and wanting to hypnotize him, Jordan called up FBI director, Willie the Bender, who knew all about the hypnosis. Webster told him it was "part of the investigation."

At the same time a single lone bank robber held up the Farmer's Bank of Liberty, in Liberty, Illinois. I had nothing to do with either of these crimes, but a warrant was issued for my arrest for the bank robbery. Not long after, the FBI issued a statement that they wanted to question me in the shooting of Vernon Jordan. The statement was made by FBI Director William Webster. This statement was issued even though I wasn't within 400 miles of Fort Wayne at the time of the shooting

I was arrested on June 23 in Alton, Illinois. My arresting officer was Conrad "Pete" Baetz. Small world. This is the same former ASA intel officer Pete Baetz who worked as an investigator for the HSCA. Baetz claimed that I had a gun, I had no gun.

I feared I was going to be tried as an ex-felon in possession of a weapon. I knew that if found guilty the feds would have the judge impose the Special Dangerous Offender Act, which would get me thirty years.

The U.S. attorney in East St. Louis explained to my lawyer that "Washington wants something on Ray's record." He went on to say, "It's coming down from Washington; I'm getting heat from FBI Headquarters and the Justice Department. I've got nothing against Ray." I was, however, to threaten to go public with my certainty about my brother's CIA involvement and the King assassination hoax.

So word of my threats must have gotten to DC, because shortly afterward, an FBI special agent came down from the Springfield field office to tell me that Washington was getting sick and tired of dealing with me, and that the feds wanted to make a deal. They wanted me to testify against Joseph Paul Franklin, who was on trial for the shooting of Vernon Jordan. If I testified for them, they would drop all charges against me and make me a free man. Franklin, by the way, is the man who shot Larry Flint and put him in a wheelchair. Franklin's real name is James Clayton Vaughn. He renamed himself after the very odd combination of Joseph Paul Goebbels, minister of propaganda and enlightenment in Nazi Germany, and Benjamin Franklin. The special agent told me that if I didn't cooperate with them, they'd put me away under the provisions of the Dangerous Special Offender Act. I rejected the deal.

A lot of big city jails and larger prisons have secret super-solitary cells, which hold special cases. The feds have quite a few of them scattered throughout the world. The one they put Joseph Paul Franklin in was underneath the hospital at Marion federal prison. John Gotti was down there, too. They keep you down there until you die or they kill you or you make a deal. Franklin made a deal and admitted to some racially motivated shootings, which helped the Department of Justice and FBI. He was tried and found innocent of the Jordan shooting. But it's common for guys to admit to crimes they didn't do, to lighten up their own situations. That is the nature of these fed deals.

The FBI likes to throw dirt in the faces of the juries, especially with someone like Franklin. He pleaded guilty to shooting a Jewish man in Missouri to get out of super-solitary, even if it meant putting him on death row. A lot of prisoners prefer to be put on death row rather than spend their life in super-solitary.

Through 1981 and 1982 the authorities pulled unsuccessful legal tactics to keep me behind bars mostly dealing with the Farmers Bank of Liberty.

Early the next year, 1983, a deal was made about "my gun." My attorney swung a deal with the U.S. attorney Frederick J. Hess in federal court in Illinois. The whole thing was a farce. Just in the state of Missouri alone there were twenty-three hundred ex-felons who were licensed to carry shotguns and rifles. Hess, who wasn't a bad guy, was getting heat from Washington to put me away. He told my lawyer, "I've got nothing against John; it's coming down from above." So he did what he could for me. This was the deal: If I would plead guilty to possession, they'd drop the Dangerous Special Offender Act. I was exhausted from the constant battle and accepted the deal. They had been trying to put forty to fifty years on me. By the time my deal was struck, they had transferred my money to the prison at Springfield.

I was shipped to Leavenworth, where I was held in solitary confinement. From Leavenworth, I was shipped west and locked in solitary confinement in Lompoc, California. Lompoc Prison is located 175 miles northwest of Los Angeles, next to Vandenberg Air Force Base. I know very little of what the prison looks like, because all of my time was served in solitary.

Next I was shipped to the Community Treatment Center in Chicago for about three months in solitary. Here I had to watch it, because these Mafia boys will cut your throat or get somebody else to do it for them. In Chicago the guards are scared of the prisoners. The Chicago outfit was powerful, anyway. From here, I was put on a bus and shipped to Sandstone, Minnesota, but then, as if somebody had changed his mind, I was immediately rerouted to the federal prison in Oxford, Wisconsin. I spent the next five years there.

In September of 1984, I had served my fifty-one months and was called back in front of the U.S. Parole Commission to be released. There are two types of guidelines these parole boards use: One is for new inmates coming into the system after their conviction; and the other is an institutional guideline that they can use to add to your time if you have violated the prison rules while serving your sentence. These are seldom used because all inmates break institutional guidelines, being late to work and the like. Even if they choose to add more time, they have to stay within the institutional guidelines, which can only add thirty to ninety days.

When I appeared in front of the parole examiners, I had been written up once for heating up coffee in my cell with burning paper towels, which is common. Sometimes they bring you cold coffee, sometimes you just want to drink it later. Sometimes you set a small fire in your concrete cell, because you just want to keep warm and it's freezing cold. It's standard practice. The cells are always steel and concrete, after all, and not much of a fire hazard. However, when I appeared in front of the parole board, they accused me of an "act of arson" and claimed that I could have burned down the whole prison, causing "dozens or hundreds of deaths." They then illegally used the felony guideline rather than the institutional guideline, and ordered me to serve thirty-six more months, which I did.

In April of 1985 I was called into the office of my caseworker and told, "You're not going to the funeral."

"I don't know what you're talking about," I said.

"Your father has died, and the word has come down from DC that you won't be allowed to attend the funeral, because a detainer has been filed against you by the State of Washington." I would never find out what this was about. That night I thought about it all, wondering about this detainer. I had never even been to the State of Washington; I didn't know anybody there. I had, as of this time, been under the feds' custody for fifteen years, so I was pretty sure that the statute of limitations would have run out on anything but murder.

The next day, I asked my caseworker for a copy of the warrant. He said there was no detainer because the warrant had been withdrawn. The caseworker was playing mind games with me. I didn't know if my father was alive or dead (although I found out later that he had died). My feelings about not being allowed to attend my father's funeral were the same as when my brother James got stabbed, and I wasn't allowed any info about his condition. You bury your feelings deep behind bars for many reasons. It doesn't do you any good to dwell on things you have no control over.

In September of 1987, they booted me out the front door of the joint with mandatory-release parole papers. At that point, the feds had found ways to hold me from just after the Jordan shooting in June of 1980, until September of 1987, seven years and three months. Incidentally, they piled on three years because I was late submitting a copy of my handwriting to the FBI lab. I served another three years for the incident where I was heating up coffee in my cell. Prior to this, I had served eleven years for not picking up someone on the highway who was found not guilty of robbing a bank. And, of course, after my release, I still had time to serve on parole.

When I was released I immediately went to see my brother Jerry at the golf course where he was employed. I stayed there in Medina, a suburb of Chicago, working with Jerry from September to January of 1988.

In 1988, I didn't know anything about diabetes, and to the best of my knowledge, nobody in my family had it. I discovered that I had the disease, even though I had been completely unaware of it for ten years. Every time a new prison accepted me, I was given a full physical, but no word was ever said about my diabetes. The prison doctors stamped all of my documents "Healthy Male." One of the few clues I got about my condition was ten years earlier, when I was given a full physical at the time of the HSCA and their doctor whispered his hint to me that I might have diabetes.

When I got out to the country club, they had me working outside in the cold and I literally froze my feet. Since I didn't have a medical plan, I had to make a choice between asking the Federal Bureau of Prisons for medical care or do without care. If you climb on the bus to go to a federal prison, even for medical attention, it could be two or three years before you get out. This is especially true if your last name is Ray. Soon I had gangrene and needed an amputation. I had heard lots of stories about what they did to other inmates while they were under the knife, and those other inmates didn't know the secrets of the murder of Martin Luther King. So I violated my parole and went down to the City Hospital in St. Louis. They operated on me and made me an amputee, minus most of both feet. I checked into the hospital on my fifty-fifth birthday—the same hospital my mother and grandmother had checked into, but never checked out of.

I was now a fugitive from justice, missing parts of both feet. What was I going to do? I had no money. I couldn't walk without the aid of a brace. I couldn't work. I had hit rock bottom and had no place to go. The only thing I thought I could do was turn myself in to the feds and let them take charge of my life. But they were the ones who had caused these problems in the first place. I decided that I would rather climb up to the roof of the hospital and go over the side.

Shortly after my surgery, I had a vision of a visitor during the night. He was draped all in white, and I couldn't see his face. He spoke softly to me:

"Don't worry—we'll take care of you." I did worry, but I started to think about the vision my father had had in the Iowa prison as he hung by his thumbs. After he'd seen his vision, the next thing he knew, he was a free man, and remained so for sixty years.

If I had known about the unemployment compensation law, I could have stayed in Chicago and gotten immediate care. I was sadly ignorant. If you're doing a job and you have a foot removed, you are entitled to medical care. It was sometime later that someone came around from the Social Security office, wanting me to sign some papers saying that they were going to get me some money since I was unable to work. A bit later they came around with a $1,200 check and told me that I was going to get this $400 every month. I had been out of circulation for so long, I didn't know that this was standard in cases like mine.

Today, when I get dressed and put my shoes on, I must apply a brace that balances out the place where the amputated portion of my foot used to be. The conspiracy to deprive me of medical care for my diabetes would be very similar to the jailhouse medical conspiracy against my brother James when he developed hepatitis C in later years. It was this infection with the hepatitis C virus and his being fed the greasiest food by the prison which would destroy his liver and take his life, ten years after my avoidable amputation.

Some people would say that James and John Larry Ray fought the law, and the law won. Well, I'm perfectly all right with taking the lumps in life that I have deserved, but my belief is that if this long-overdue book can prevent the James Earl Ray conspiracy from successfully completing its last phase, which is to fade into history with the safety of unchallenged silence, then a lot of that "win" will be taken away from those who never deserved it, and who played a series of games they never should have played in the first place. Now that the book is done, I wish I had told this story earlier. I am grateful to have had the opportunity to do so now; better late than never.

Truth at last.

Epilogue

I have been trying to reveal what I know about the murder of Martin Luther King Jr., for a long time. In 1993, while Jimmy was still alive, I told the truth on a local Christian television show in St. Louis about the source of James's 1967 funds: Obie O'Brien, Buster Wortman, and the Mob.

In one way or another I've been trying to bring out the truth about the shooting of the black soldier, Washington, ever since James told me about the conspiracy in 1974 while we were cellmates in the Shelby County Jail in Memphis, Tennessee. But, over the years I found out there was a "no-truth-wanted wall" that I constantly ran up against. I felt I was the only one who was trying to get to the truth. I took the case to the far right and to the far left, and not only got the silent treatment, but also had false words put in my mouth. It was always the same: My words were twisted by the FBI, CIA, and the rest of these supposed law-and-order groups.

Once my brother James died in 1998, I could see no reason to keep searching for the truth about the shooting of the soldier, Washington. I had always been the man in the middle, with James on one side and the feds on the other. I had always believed there was much more to the story of Washington then just a soldier getting shot. Why would all the CIA directors since 1968 cover up the truth about the Washington shooting? Why all the FBI directors since

1968? Why the attorneys general? Why so many members of Congress? Why the mainstream media?

There were several reasons why I did not want to go on searching for Washington; among them, the feds had made me disabled for life by withholding the truth from me about my diabetes—I couldn't have asked for insulin for a disease I didn't know I had. I simply did not have the energy to keep searching for this unknown soldier. There were some other unanswered questions that made me feel uneasy, such as: Was Washington working for the CIA, too? If not, why didn't he come forward in 1968 when the feds said James had shot Martin Luther King Jr.? Was he dead by then?

James made information available to me while we were cellmates in Shelby County Jail, which I will make available to the Washington family if and when I locate them. This information will prove that the feds fixed Washington's army trial, too, and his family will have a powerful case against the feds. I put the search for Washington out of my life because I wanted some peace. But before I did so, I recorded a video of myself explaining what I knew about the shooting of the young black soldier. As fate would have it, my revelations in the video sparked the interest of Lyndon Barsten, a man James and Jerry had known who had long admired Dr. King. Somebody sent it to Lyndon and he did the same for others.

Lyndon suggested that I mail copies of this video to several people, including Jim Lesar's Assassination Archive and Research Center and an academic, professor Gerald McKnight, who wanted to know the truth. The documentation discussed within this book was found after that, with Lyndon's help. Additionally, it was revealed that Jimmy's VA number had begun with a 7 in 1968, which is code for a "sensitive" file. Strangely, the VA still has James under both army serial numbers. All of this documentation verifies my story, as it was found after I recorded the video. Since we found the documentation after the video was taped, and not vice versa, it backs up the story, proving it wasn't simply a case of incorrect entry of serial numbers and the like.

Most criminals I have known maintain a certain modus operandi. Obie was so skilled at cracking vaults that the FBI knew it was him immediately, just from the evidence alone. The U.S. government is no different; it has its own MO. Look at the murders of JFK and MLK. The similarities raised eyebrows in 1968. Lee Harvey Oswald was a "Communist." James Earl Ray was a "racist." Their individual personas are so simple, they can be summed up in these one-word labels. Both men had been in the armed forces—James in the army, Oswald in the marines. Both men appear to have been used by Intel in a different capacity after the military, before the assassinations. Both of their military histories are rather obviously tainted with intelligence work. Both Oswald and Jimmy were known to the Mob since childhood. In both the JFK case and the MLK case, the murder victims threatened the agendas of the power elite, the director of the Central Intelligence Agency, and the Joint Chiefs of Staff at the Pentagon.

In both cases the gigantic brainwashing programs the CIA and army were running at the time seemed to have had an impact on the patsy's psyche, and there are stories of odd shootings that are part of both cases. In both cases a rather lax attitude was taken in making the alleged murder weapon match the actual death slugs. James and Oswald did not smoke or drink or have legal troubles prior to entering the military. Both of them served honorably, but somehow did not receive an honorable discharge, and both of them had a problem with their discharges. Both of them wanted to leave the country after leaving the military. Both of them had unusual contact with federal agents after leaving the military. Both men made mysterious trips to Mexico. Neither of them received a fair trial.

It is my belief that the government agent in Jimmy's rooming house in 1959 was there to make sure he was arrested, convicted, and sentenced to the Missouri prison system, where the feds appeared to have operations. I believe he was likely warehoused there until needed. I believe that Warden E. V. Nash was murdered because he found out about federal operations there, or else, began to object to them. While James was incarcerated in the Missouri prison, James Cooper Green—a two-time loser who would later work for the FBI and who claimed to be a victim of mind control—supposedly dealt drugs with him. Benny Edmondson, who escaped from Jeff City just like James and trotted up to Chicago and Montreal just like James, was also imprisoned there. Is this coincidence? One might say these are conspiracy theories. But all detective work involves theories, as well as the process of attempting to put a crime back together in order to discover the missing pieces, the clues, and the answers. And although allegations of mind control might sound like something out of a science fiction novel, the CIA tried at one point to destroy all evidence of its program. Thirty thousand pages of mind control documents still remained after the attempted destruction, and they were released under the Carter administration.

In writing this book, by revealing what I know to be the truth, I am trying to do my part to fix the system. Why would I want to do this, when everyone from Jim Garrison in New Orleans to James's lawyer Bill Pepper has been discredited—really attacked by the mainstream press? The reason is that the people involved deserve their history even if it means trouble for me. Political conspiracies are as old as the murder of Julius Caesar. The King murder conspiracy lies with a hundred others: Pat Tillman's apparent murder and the destruction of his effects after he turned against the war; the caging of black voters; the oddities relating to the September 11 attacks and other terrorist connections; the crash of Senator Paul Wellstone's plane; the suspicious deaths of Ron Brown and companions; Vince Foster's "suicide"; war for oil and profits; the Bush administration's covering up global warming; Iran-Contra; the twin shootings of Reagan and John Lennon; the attempted shooting of Bob Marley, and later, his cancer; a deeper story to Watergate; propaganda assets in the press; the development of HIV/AIDS; the CIA dealing drugs; the inconsistencies in the Murrah Building bombing in Oklahoma City; the deliberate murder of children at Waco . . . The list goes on and on.

The truth cannot be held back forever. The majority of the population is well aware that something is corrupt in America . . . that something is very wrong. A recent poll revealed that only one in five people believe the mainstream media. We must fix this land. If my words do nothing else, may they help Americans reach critical mass in our demand for democracy and the truth—the truth at last.   B. S.

Acknowledgments

Special thanks to: Sharlene Martin of Martin Literary Management in Los Angeles and to Anthony Flacco, for working miracles and having the vision to understand the importance of this story to our historical record.

Thanks also to Cheryl Carlotta Barsten for patience. Thanks to C. D. Stelzer who sacrificed professionally for truth in this case. Thanks to John Judge and Tamara Carter of the Coalition on Political Assassinations for intellect and support, and Ed for information.

Thanks to Suzanne for early help and Mary McDunn for her intellect. Thanks to James Casey (author of *The Sturgis Experience*) and Cindy Wadsworth for belief and assistance. Thanks to the Freedom of Information Act team: Jimmy Montan and Marty Bragg.

Special thanks to Marty McGann at the National Archives in College Park for doing a great job at what he does. Special thanks to Charles Miller and Whitney Paige Shelton at FBI Freedom of Information; if only all public servants were of their fine quality.

Good karma to Michael Gabriel for taking such good care of James Earl at the end of his life when he really needed help. Thanks to Tupper Saussy, Ed "tree frog" for information, Pat Shannan, and Dr. Gerald McKnight, eloquent speakers of the truth. For moral support, thanks to Keith and Teri, Terry and Verne.

ACKNOWLEDGMENTS

Thanks to Mark Schreiber for his knowledge of the Jeff City Prison. Thanks to reporter John Auble for forty years of being a supporter of the truth in this case. A very special thanks to Ronnie Gramazio at The Lyons Press. It took an Australian-born man to understand the importance of this story to America; may the horrible truth he helped reveal aid the resurrection of Jeffersonian democracy in America. Thanks also to Jenn Taber at The Lyons Press for her brilliant help crafting this important story. Thanks to Invaders Dr. Coby Smith (and Constance) and to Charles Cabbage.

To the late Dr. Harold Weisberg—may these revelations help you rest in peace.

Bibliography

Freedom of Information Act Releases

Federal Bureau of Investigation

MURKIN FILES

HQ	44-38861	
Field Offices:		
Memphis	44-1987 (Office of Origin)	
Los Angeles	44-1574	
Chicago	44-1114	
HQ	62-28270	Roy Wilkins
St. Louis	92-538 S	teamfitters Local 562
Portland	91-3157, Serial 76	Benney/Goldenstein
Knoxville	88-7223	James Earl Ray Prison Break

Articles

Auble, John. "Brother of Ray Found Hiding Himself Here," *St. Louis Globe-Democrat,* May 22, 1968.

Bryans, Raleigh. "Grieving Jackson Appeals for Strength in Mourning," *Atlanta Constitution,* July 1, 1974.

"Eagleton's Niece Will Talk to Jury," *Quincy Herald Whig,* August 27, 1980.

"Foreman Concerned of Brand as Traitor," *Commercial Appeal,* November 14, 1968.

Green, Cliff, and Ed Jahn, "Suspect in King Case Is 'Not Sure' He Killed," *Atlanta Constitution,* July 1, 1974.

Huie, William Bradford. "The Story of James Earl Ray and the Plot to Assassinate Martin Luther King," *LOOK,* November 22, 1968.

—."I Got Involved Gradually and I Didn't Know Anybody Was Going to Get Murdered," *LOOK,* November 26, 1968.

—."Conspiracy or Not? Why James Earl Ray Murdered Martin Luther King," *LOOK,* April 15, 1969.

"The King Assassination Revisited," *Time,* January 26, 1976.

Leeming, Frank. "James Ray's Bitter Youth," *St. Louis Post-Dispatch,* May 13, 1968.

Maloney, J. J. "Who Shot Martin Luther King?", http://crimemagazine. com/Assassinations/who.htm, September 7, 1997, accessed by the authors December 4, 2006.

"Mystery about Ray Is Cleared Up: He Was a Dishwasher in Illinois in '67," *New York Times,* October 25, 1968.

O'Brien, Edward D. "Steamfitter Gift 'Loophole' is Denounced," *St. Louis Globe-Democrat,* June 9, 1967.

"Officials Mystified on Way Ray Left Lounge Sanctuary," Associated Press, June 10, 1968.

"Ray Appeals Conviction in King Murder," Associated Press, October 9, 1976.

"Ray Attorney: Bullets Fired From Ray's Gun Don't Match Fatal Bullet— FBI tests from 1968 sought in King slaying," July 11, 1997, www.cnn. com/US/9707/11/ray.rifle/index.html, accessed by the authors January 12. 2007.

"Ray's Breakout," *Time,* June 20, 1977.

"Ray, Sirhan—What Possessed Them?", *LIFE,* June 21, 1968.

"The Revealing Story of a Mean Kid," *LIFE,* May 3, 1968.

"300,000 Passport Pictures Examined in Search for Ray," UPI, June 9, 1968.

Walsh, Denny. "6 in Prison Experiment Tell of Pain Reaction," *St. Louis Globe-Democrat,* January 24, 1964.

Books

Ayton, Mel. *A Racial Crime.* Las Vegas: ArcheBooks, 2005.

Blair, Clay, Jr. *The Strange Case of James Earl Ray.* New York: Bantam Books, 1969.

Frank, Gerold. *An American Death: The True Story of the Assassination of Dr. Martin Luther King.* Garden City, NY: Doubleday, 1972.

Garrison, Jim. *On The Trail of the Assassins.* Lebanon, IN: Grand Central Publishing, 1991.

Groden, Robert J. *The Search for Lee Harvey Oswald.* New York: Penguin, 1995.

Huie, William Bradford. *He Slew the Dreamer.* Montgomery, AL: Black Belt Press, 1997.

Jordan, Vernon. *Vernon Can Read.* New York: Public Affairs Publishers, 2001.

Lane, Mark, and Dick Gregory. *Code Name "Zorro."* Englewood Cliffs, NJ: Prentice-Hall, 1977.

Lomax, Louis. *To Kill a Black Man.* Los Angeles: Holloway House, 1968.

Melanson, Philip H. *The Murkin Conspiracy.* New York: Praeger, 1989.

Posner, Gerald. *Killing the Dream.* New York: Random House, 1998.

Ray, James Earl. *Tennessee Waltz.* St. Andrews, TN: St. Andrews Press, 1987.

Russo, Gus. *The Outfit.* New York: Bloomsbury, 2002.

Weisberg, Harold. Martin Luther King: *The Assassination* (originally published as *Frame-Up*). New York: Carroll and Graf, 1993.

—.Whoring with History: How Gerald Posner Protects King's Assassins. Unpublished manuscript 1999.

U.S. Army Records and Publications Records of the 7892nd Infantry Regiment, April–June 1948.

National Archives and Records Administration (Archives II), College Park, MD.

State Agencies

Missouri State Hospital #1 File of James Earl Ray.

Missouri State Prison File of James Earl Ray.

Shelby County Archives: The District Attorney General's file on James Earl Ray and the murder of Martin Luther King.

State of Louisiana Department of Public Safety, Bureau of Identification, No. 224 971 6.

Legal/Court Documents

Brief for James Earl Ray for Ray vs. Rose, 1974 Evidentiary Hearing, prepared by James Lesar, Bud Fensterwald, and Robert Livingston, October 1974.

Transcript Eighth Circuit Court, Eastern District of Missouri U.S.C. 456F2D555, 1972.

Transcript of James Earl Ray plea bargain, March 10, 1969.

Trial transcripts, Missouri Supreme Court # 48583, James Earl Ray, filed May 5, 1983.

U.S. Congressional Publications

Report of the Select Committee on Assassinations of the U.S. House of
Representatives, Washington, DC: 1979, Ninety-fifth Congress.

U.S. Army Morning reports (1948)

7892nd Infantry Regiment

7838 Reserve Vehicle Detachment

16th Infantry Regiment

U.S. Army Publication

Parr, Frank and Ralph J. Crawford and William R. Lembeck. *Redesignation
Day.* Frankfurt am Main, Germany, 1948.

Non–U.S. Government Documents

New Scotland Yard Document, "Schedule of Movements of James Earl
Ray," 1968.

New Scotland Yard Document, 10 June, 1968, Statement of A. E. Thomas.

RCMP Document 68GIS 790-170 (Montreal) Division C, (also released as
FBI HQ 62-109060 Serial 6518).

Archived Collection of Papers

McMillan, George, University of North Carolina at Chapel Hill, Wilson
Library.

Television

Guilt or Innocence: The Trial of James Earl Ray, Home Box Office, April 4,
1993.

Who Shot Martin Luther King?, ABC News, Turning Point, June 19, 1997.

Lecture

Judge Joe Brown. "Ballistics in the Martin Luther King Murder." Lecture, Coalition on Political Assassinations Conference, November 21–24, 2002.

INDEX

About the Author

JOHN LARRY RAY is the eldest brother of James Earl Ray and was witness to much of his brother's covert life. John has spent 25 years in federal prison falsely imprisoned by the federal government for knowing too much about the murder of Martin Luther King Jr. He lives in Illinois.

LYNDON BARSTEN is a lay historian who lectures frequently about the murder of Martin Luther King Jr. and has done so for the US Congressional Black Caucus. Barsten's activism has freed up tens of thousands of new pages of materials on the MLK assassination. He lives with his family in Minnesota.